# CHOOSE this Day

366 Devotions

RAY McCAULEY

CHOOSE THIS DAY

Published in 2011 by Struik Christian Books
An imprint of Struik Christian Media
A division of New Holland Publishing (South Africa) (Pty) Ltd
(New Holland Publishing is a member of Avusa Ltd)
Wembley Two, Solan Street, Gardens
Cape Town 8001

Reg. No. 1971/009721/07



Project management by Reinata Thirion
DTP by De Wet van Deventer
Cover design by De Wet van Deventer
Cover image from Shutterstock
Printed and bound by Paarl Media,
Jan van Riebeeck Drive, Paarl, South Africa

ISBN 978-1-4153-1494-4 (Print)
ISBN 978-1-4153-1605-4 (ePub)
ISBN 978-1-4153-1604-7 (PDF)

**www.struikchristianmedia.co.za**

# Contents

# Introduction

*Choose This Day* is a series of devotions by one of South Africa's outstanding preachers, Pastor Ray McCauley of Rhema Bible Church (North). These easy-to-read devotions give you a fresh word for each day, helping you to deepen your relationship with God through prayer and further study of the Word of God.

Broken down into daily chapters that you can read and pray about, *Choose This Day* is premised on Deuteronomy 30:19:

> I call heaven and earth to record this day against you, that I have set before you life and death, blessing and cursing: therefore choose life, that both you and your seed may live.

One of the most amazing faculties God has given us is the power of choice. In the above Scripture, God is challenging us to exercise this faculty, and to do so wisely. He knows what a hard choice it can be between choosing life and death. And so He tells us what He desires us to choose – life.

# January

## CHOOSE TO BE REDEEMED

*Jesus Christ is the beginning, the middle, and the end of all. In the Gospels He walks in human form upon the earth, and accomplishes the work of redemption.*

– Philip Schaff

## CHOOSE TO BE STRENGTHENED

*Strength – … that quality which tends to secure results; effective power in an institution or enactment; security; validity; legal or moral force; logical conclusiveness.*

## CHOOSE COURAGE

*God places the heaviest burden on those who can carry its weight.*

– Reggie White

## CHOOSE RIGHTEOUSNESS

*A chameleon has the ability to change its colour to blend into its environment. We must not be 'chameleon Christians', trying to blend in wherever we are, instead, we must be strikingly different.*

# A New Year, a New Beginning

*Therefore, if anyone is in Christ, he is a new creation,*
*the old has gone, and the new has come.*
– 2 Corinthians 5:17

It is a New Year and a new beginning and you need to choose today to live the life God wants you to and be where He wants you to be. It is a choice that you, and no one else, have to make.

Sometimes we live our lives based on the past and focus on what we could have done or should have done. When we do that, we lose perspective of the present and the future. There is very little you can do about the past year other than to learn from the mistakes you might have made.

Yes, there are areas where you might have missed God last year. The enemy could be reminding you of the sins you committed during the previous year. Rejoice on this first day of the New Year because those sins were forgiven when you confessed them. God does not remember them anymore. You have been redeemed as He promised and you need to see yourself that way – the redeemed of the Lord.

This is a new day that the Lord has made and in you He has created a new person. You need to stand up and get excited about the New Year and the tasks that lie ahead. There are new projects to be executed, new mountain peaks to be reached, new goals to be achieved and new dimensions to be discovered in your walk with God.

God's timing is always perfect. He knows why you made it into this New Year. You are not here merely to take up space while drifting along in life. God has kept, and indeed, redeemed you for a purpose. That which God begins, He always completes, and He wants to do exactly that in your life – whether it is personal, financial, emotional or physical. You can enable Him to do that by leaving behind your past and embracing the newness of life He has given you. Get up and do what needs to be done.

# You've Been Redeemed by the Blood

*In Him we have redemption through His blood, the forgiveness for our sins, in accordance with the riches of God.*
– Ephesians 1:7

Sometimes we become victims of our fear. We think of what could happen, instead of what we can make happen, and it stops us from doing the things we should. We allow ourselves to hold on to our past mistakes, regrets and failures.

But Jesus has redeemed us from our past sins and He has picked us up from the deep pits we were in and given us new life in Him. The surety of our redemption lies in Him through his blood. Isn't that wonderful? That is what the above verse says. Jesus has, through his blood, not only redeemed us but provided collateral (security) for the same redemption. Nobody (Satan and his demons included) can challenge our redemption. There is no better indemnity or guarantee beyond the blood of Jesus.

In the Old Testament, the word redemption generally means a 'ransom price' and in the New Testament it means the 'great price' which Jesus, the Redeemer, paid for our liberation from sin. Whichever way one looks at it, the concept denotes buying or purchasing. When man fell in the Garden of Eden, that produced humanity's servitude under Satan. The Redeemer, Jesus Christ, has 'purchased' you from the power of darkness into the Kingdom of Light. And this has been done according to his riches – riches not defined by the streets of gold in heaven but the ones found in the blood of Jesus. No wonder it is called the 'precious' blood of the Lamb.

Be careful how you value yourself and how you allow other people to value you. The accuser of the brethren (Satan) and others might have told you that you are worthless and will never amount to anything. God thought you were worth the blood of his Son. Therefore, walk, talk and act like one who is worth the blood. Recognize God's redemption and go into the New Year excited about what He did for you at the cross. Yes, you can say today, like that most prolific hymnist in all of history, Fanny Crosby, once wrote: Redeemed, how I love to proclaim it!

CHOOSE TO BE REDEEMED: 3 JANUARY

# We've Been Made Perfect

*Because by one sacrifice He has made perfect forever,*
*those who are being made holy.*
– HEBREWS 10:14

By giving his life for us, Jesus has made us whole. He became our Substitute and took our punishment. Salvation is a legal matter and, lawfully, no punishment can be meted on us because Jesus has already served the sentence for us. In 2 Corinthians 5:21, the Bible says Jesus (He who knew no sin) was made sin for us that we might be made the righteousness of God in Him. We have been made perfect, not temporarily but for ever.

When man sinned, Jesus offered to take our penalty and die in our place. Revelation 13:8 says that He was the Lamb slain from the foundation of the world. His mission in relation to us was well captured by John the Baptist when, upon seeing Jesus, he said: 'Behold the Lamb of God, which taketh away the sin of the world' (John 1:29). How profound that the sinless One was willing to become a sacrifice for a sinful race.

No angel could die in our place. Only Jesus and his sinless nature could match the law of God. He had the nature and the character that could ransom for our fallen race. The sacrifice was offered and when we accept Christ as our Lord and Saviour, his blood is applied on the doorposts of our personal lives and we get exempted from the wages of sin, which is death.

We need to recognize the value of our worth in the eyes of Him who redeemed us and handpicked us for his Kingdom.

Jesus knew the pain which lay before Him when He would be crucified. Yet He did not turn back. Instead, He chose to follow through because God's love for us is greater than anything we can ever imagine. We are special creatures in his eyes. We were worth the life and sacrifice of his only Son. So how can we not choose today to be revitalized in the Word, in his glory, and in our lives? Choose to recognize and accept the sacrifice He was for you.

# We're Dead to Sin

*In the same way count yourselves*
*dead to sin and alive to Christ Jesus.*
– Romans 6:11

We should never have an excuse not to eagerly pursue the life God has promised us. We have nothing to fear in moving forward, for Jesus promises to be with us and encompasses the characteristics we need to have.

We are dead to sin and our past. We are redeemed through his blood and we are alive in his Name. Our fallen nature was not changed or modified at conversion but was rendered inactive, made of no effect. Whereas we were controlled by sin before we believed in Christ and received salvation, we are now dead to sin.

This dying to sin did not happen by our own strength but through Jesus Christ. The old nature was crucified with Him so that the old life is rendered inoperative. This is a truth that as believers we can rely upon to confront sin. Having died with Christ, the controlling power of sin in our lives is broken and is rendered powerless or ineffective. Being dead to sin means a change in relationship to sin. Sin is no longer our master but Christ is. It means we no longer want to continue in sin but in obedience to our new Master.

Before we were saved we had a cordial relationship with sin – it was our way of life. Indeed, we were fully yielded to our sinful nature. However, through Jesus' death and resurrection, we also died to sin and now walk in the power of his resurrection. The issue is the believer is no longer under the power of sin. That is what the death of Jesus accomplished for us – it did not only pay for our sins but caused us to die to sin.

As believers, we are under no compulsion to live our lives under the control of sin. This does not mean we shall not be tempted. What it does mean is that we do not have to yield to the temptation because sin does no longer have a hold on us.

# Justified Freely by Grace

*Being justified freely by His grace through the redemption that is in Christ Jesus, whom God set forth as a propitiation by His blood, through faith, to demonstrate His righteousness.*
– ROMANS 3:24–25

Paul here speaks about us being justified freely by God's grace. But what does justification mean? When Adam and Eve committed sin in the Garden of Eden, we inherited that original sin which in turn destroyed the righteousness man originally had.

But because of the love and mercy of God, Jesus Christ willingly paid for our sins through his crucifixion and resurrection, thus meriting the redemption of humanity. Whoever believes in and confesses the crucifixion and resurrection of Jesus can have their sins forgiven and become children of God. From this perspective, justification means being transformed from a state of unrighteousness to divine sonship through Jesus Christ.

The justification takes place through grace. But what is grace? Grace is the free and undeserved favour that God gives us to respond to his call. Man cannot be justified or acceptable in God's sight except through his grace. However much people may believe that a good man can earn favour and acceptance with God, humanity cannot of itself meet God's standard of righteousness. Whatever we do, we cannot win God's favour except through Christ.

Through our redemption, God has made us righteous. God promised to bless us, provide for us, give us peace and protect us. He has a plan and purpose for each of our lives. As his children, He wants only the best for us. He promised to complete the good work that He has started in us. But unless we choose to allow Him to complete the good work in our lives, we will not experience the joy of his power and love. He wants us to rise to every challenge and grab hold of every opportunity that He presents us. He wants us to shine in his Name. Jesus has taken care of the worst part when He was nailed to the cross. All we need to do is be faithful to God and his purpose in us. Choose today to embrace his grace and the free justification He has given you.

CHOOSE TO BE REDEEMED: 6 JANUARY

# The Firstborn Has Made You King and Priest

*To Him who loved us and washed us from our sins in His own blood, and has made us kings and priests to His God and Father, to Him be glory and dominion forever and ever. Amen.*
– Revelation 1:5–6

This passage speaks about Jesus Christ as the Firstborn from the dead. If there is a firstborn, then there must be other siblings in the family. You and I are those siblings.

Jesus had his own natural family when He physically lived here on earth. But when He died and rose from the dead, He brought about another family, which includes you and me. His resurrection was not like the previous raisings of the dead. His was the dawn of the new creation, a decisive transition to the new family of God. Those of us who identify with his death and resurrection and accept Him as our Lord and Saviour are the 'many brethren' the Bible refers to in Romans 8:29.

However, Him being the Firstborn is not only confined to chronological order (first to be resurrected) or the importance of rank or place He occupies among his brethren, but points to Him as the Pioneer and Inaugurator who opened the way for mankind to have access to God. No one can come to the Father except through Him.

The Firstborn, this passage tells us, has so much loved his brethren (us) that He has washed us from our sins in his own blood. See who did the washing – the Firstborn Himself, and not using the blood of rams and goats but his own blood. He took an active interest in our redemption.

He did not stop there. He then made us kings and priests to his God and Father. Because He is our High Priest, He could make us priests. Priests in the Old Testament could approach God without any earthly mediator. This should tell you that, by making us priests, Christ has authorized us to worship God without any earthly mediator.

CHOOSE TO BE REDEEMED: 7 JANUARY

# Hard-Pressed But Not Crushed

*We are hard-pressed on every side but not crushed; perplexed, but not in despair; persecuted, but not abandoned; struck down, but not destroyed.*
– 2 CORINTHIANS 4:8, 9

We know that no matter how dark the clouds, high the waves or strong the winds are, the sun always shines in the end. If you fly under a storm, all you will see is darkness, clouds and lightning. But if you fly above the clouds, you will also see the sunshine. That does not mean the sun was not shining, it was just obscured by the clouds.

In the same way the sun always shines, Jesus always shines upon us. Yes, dark clouds will sometimes hover around us and we will face the storms of life. Some of the storms will come upon us suddenly and some will come slowly and envelope us gradually. Whichever way the storms come, one thing is certain: They will not destroy you. That is the promise we have in the above passage.

It is in the storms of life that our God shows Himself strong and mighty on our behalf. It is through the storms of life that our character is refined. No one who wishes to be of value in this world will escape the storms that shape and mould us. An oak tree becomes great and celebrated in the forest because of surviving the storms and the rains that beat down upon it. The same applies to the palm tree that gets beaten by heavy winds and all it does is to bend and not break. These types of trees are said to have roots that sink deep into the soil.

That is how we are in Christ, especially when we are rooted in his Word. We may be beaten from all directions but because we are firmly rooted in Him, we remain standing even after the winds and the storms have passed. There is always hope and victory at the end of a storm. All we need to do is to choose to rise up and believe his Word. No storm is greater than the Word of God.

CHOOSE TO BE STRENGTHENED: 8 JANUARY

# Be Strong and Courageous

*Be strong and courageous. Do not be terrified or discouraged; for the Lord your God will be with you wherever you may go.*
– JOSHUA 1:9

In this chapter, we see God repeatedly telling Joshua to be strong and courageous. Joshua was just about to lead the children of Israel on a journey from the wilderness to their Promised Land. They had been in the wilderness for 40 years. I don't know how long you have been in your own wilderness. But what I do know is that God is about to take you from that wilderness to your Promised Land. But it is going to require something from you – strength and courage. The Israelites were going to face a lot of obstacles on their journey to the Promised Land. It was not going to be easy and that is why God said they must be strong and courageous.

The wilderness was their place of transition. They were between the slavery of Egypt and the Promised Land. You may be in a similar transition in your life. You may have just come out of an abusive relationship. Be strong and courageous. You may have just come out of a long sickness. Be strong and courageous. You may just be coming out of a difficult financial situation. Be strong and courageous. You may be in the middle of changing careers. Be strong and courageous. You may have just graduated and are about to start a new job. Be strong and courageous.

But how do I become strong and courageous, you ask. By knowing and obeying the Word of God. God instructed Joshua to talk about the Word, meditate on the Word, and do the Word. There is no source of strength and courage outside the Word of God. Also, we remain strong and courageous because of God's abiding presence. God promised Joshua that He was going to be with him wherever he went.

God did not promise him that it was going to be easy. He told him He was going to be with him and therefore there was no need for Joshua to be terrified. The same applies to you. God is with you and therefore do not be terrified or discouraged. Whatever situation or obstacle you may face, He is right there with you.

# Strength to Do the Impossible

*I can do all things through Christ who strengthens me.*
– PHILIPPIANS 4:13

One of the biggest mistakes we often make as children of God is to doubt the ability we have through Christ. Yet the Bible tells us we can do 'all things' and not just some things. Now, if you just read the first part of this verse, it could come across as arrogance: 'I can do all things.'

But the next two words in the verse place this ability or seeming boastfulness in its proper perspective: 'through Christ'. Paul is not boasting of self here but of Christ: 'I can do all things through Christ.' Humanism can say 'I can do all things' but Christianity can only say 'I can do all things through Christ.' There is a world of difference between the two.

Paul had had abundant experience of this ability through Christ and it had enabled him to survive storms, preach the Gospel with power, meet persecutions and run his race with success. When we wake up to what we can do through the strength we derive from our Redeemer, we can change the course of history. Our human limitations do not limit God.

God used Moses, who stuttered, to liberate the children of Israel from slavery. He used a shepherd boy called David to defeat the Philistines. Paul was a persecutor of the Christians but went on to achieve mighty exploits for the Kingdom of God. Timothy had ulcers but God used him. Hosea's wife was a prostitute but God still used Hosea as his vessel. Amos' only training was in the school of fig-tree pruning. Jacob was a liar. Abraham was too old. Peter was afraid of death. Lazarus was dead. John was self-righteous. Naomi was a widow. Jonah ran away from God's will. Gideon lacked confidence. Thomas was a doubter. Jeremiah was depressed and suicidal. Elijah was burnt out. Martha was a worrywart. Noah got drunk and Peter had a short fuse.

All these characters are celebrated in Judeo-Christian tradition not because they were perfect. I believe God wants us to see that He can use anyone who will believe in his strength.

CHOOSE TO BE STRENGTHENED: 10 JANUARY

# Joy: the Best Source of Your Strength

*'... For the joy of the Lord is your strength.'*
– NEHEMIAH 8:10

In our pursuit of what we consider to be greater spiritual strength for ourselves and others, it is very easy to miss the basics. The Bible is very clear on what the source of strength is. However, many of us have not sufficiently considered the relationship between joy and strength.

Jesus used joy to strengthen Himself for the suffering He had to undergo in order to procure our salvation. Hebrews 12:2 tells us that Jesus '... who for the joy that was set before Him endured the cross, despising the shame, and has sat down at the right hand of the throne of God.' Jesus needed a lot of strength to go through the suffering of the cross. How did He cope? He focused on the joy He would receive when He ultimately sat down at the right hand of the throne of God. The joy that was to come strengthened Him.

It is a principle that looks simple yet is so profound and applies to many facets of our lives. An athlete endures a lot of hard training and deprives himself/herself of certain pleasures and indulgences because of the joy that will come with winning the medal. A student does the same because of the joy that will come with passing the exams. Joy, whether present or future, is an important form of sustenance.

There is no motivation more powerful, no inspiration more potent, than the prospect of the joy of the Lord that Jesus spoke about in Matthew 25:21: 'Well done, good and faithful servant; you were faithful over a few things, I will make you ruler over many things. Enter into the joy of your lord.' When you feel drained and somewhat worn down in your walk with God, consider for a moment the joy that is set before you when Jesus shall say to you: 'Enter into the joy of your Lord.' That should give you the strength not to lose heart but to continue in your labour for Christ.

# Finding Strength When You Are Weary

*He gives strength to the weary and increases the power of the weak.*
– Isaiah 40:29

Isaiah pronounced these words over Israel at a time when things were not going well with the nation. He was speaking these words of comfort to a nation held captive in Babylon. It was a time when the children of Israel felt faint-hearted, weak, weary and exhausted.

Maybe you are in that situation today. You are feeling the debilitating effects of a severe turbulence you have been through. It could be through a loss of a loved one, a limitation that prevented you from achieving a goal, or a disappointment because of a relationship or business deal that did not work out. Indeed, the result can be a sense of hopelessness. But God promises you strength and power during this difficult time. We can trade our weakness and powerlessness for his strength and power.

Many of us have experienced great losses, tragedies and other undesirable events, which make us weary and look to our future with pessimism rather than hope. Sometimes we just get weary of it all. This is not a strange thing. All human beings, even the redeemed, get exhausted and their strength runs out once in a while. The difference with us, though, is that there is hope in that we can tap into the inexhaustible strength of God. This text reveals that although we all get weary and fed up with life, there is an unlimited reserve of strength and power for us.

Do you need strength and power to get you through the difficult times? Have you had it with life? That is precisely the point to which the text speaks. You can draw from the One whose strength and power are inexhaustible. He gives strength to the weary. The present tense 'gives' means He gives strength again and again. Therefore, if you are weary and weak, look to your God – the omnipotent, omniscient and sovereign God. He will enable you to move from strength to strength until you fulfil your purpose in life.

# Strength to Endure Temptation

*My flesh and my heart may fail, but God is the strength of my heart and my portion forever.*
– Psalm 73:26

In your Christian journey, you can be assured that you will be tempted. Indeed your heart and your flesh may at times fail. But there is an even greater assurance. No temptation or trial beyond human resistance will come to you. In 1 Corinthians 10:13 the Bible says no temptation that is unusual for human beings will come to you and that God will not allow you to be tempted beyond your strength.

The same passage tells us that when we are tempted God always provides a way out for us. Here Paul gives us a promise from the faithful God. We do not walk this journey of faith without a God-given ability to do so. We are well equipped for the journey. Therefore, stop doubting whether you can live the Christian life. The fact that others fold under temptation does not mean you have to follow suit.

God is faithful to his Word. You can trust Him not to allow you to be tempted and tried beyond your ability and strength. He will always give you the power to endure. Many of us think we can get to our destinations without temptations and tests. The truth, however, is that we will face obstacles, trials and temptations. Jesus was tempted in the wilderness (Matt 4:3–10) but there was a way of escape for Him – and that was the Word of God. His answer to Satan was, 'It is written.' Here we have a model of how to deal with temptation – confront it with the Word.

God does not want us to be spoilt brats but wants us to grow up like Jesus – through the tests we encounter. He wants us to go through the storm and not around it. He will, however, get us out of what we are in because He is faithful. Whatever temptation you may face, know that God has set boundaries both in the spirit and physical world. Demons cannot control you and Satan cannot make you do anything. The Word of God is your strength.

CHOOSE TO BE STRENGTHENED: 13 JANUARY

# Standing Firm in Faith

*Be on your guard; stand firm in faith; be men of courage, be strong.*
– 1 CORINTHIANS 16:13

Paul is encouraging the Corinthians to be strong and stand firm in faith. But how does one stand firm in faith? How does a young person faced with peer pressure stand strong? How does a teenager with raging hormones within, crying out for sexual fulfilment, stand firm against sexual temptations? How does a Christian in business resist unethical and corrupt practices when everyone is doing it?

How does one stand firm in the faith? We do it by following the example of the saints who have gone before us. Their stories are in the Bible to teach us lessons of how to stand strong in our faith. To follow their example and that pattern is to follow the Word of God. There is a verse from the Old Testament that asks the same question we are asking today. How does one stand firm? Or as Psalm 119 expressed it, 'How can a young man keep his way pure?' And the answer the psalmist gives is, 'By living according to your Word.' And so, looking to the Word is the first thing we must do in order to stand firm.

A second thing we need to do is to focus on the eternal prize. Paul says, 'For, as I have often told you before and now say again even with tears, many live as enemies of the cross of Christ. Their destiny is destruction, their god is their stomach, and their glory is in their shame. Their mind is on earthly things. But our citizenship is in heaven' (Phil 3:20). Remembering that we are just passing through this earth can help us stand firm in our faith in spite of what the world can throw at us. If we keep our minds focused on the fact that we don't belong on earth, but that we belong in heaven, we will stand firm in our faith.

Paul wrote, 'Therefore we do not lose heart. Though outwardly we are wasting away, yet inwardly we are being renewed day by day … So we fix our eyes not on what is seen, but on what is unseen. For what is seen is temporary, but what is unseen is eternal' (2 Cor 4:16–18). If we want to stand firm, we need to keep our eyes fixed on our heavenly citizenship.

# Staying Connected to Him

*Have you not known? Have you not heard? The Lord is the everlasting God … He does not faint or grow weary; His understanding is unsearchable … Even youths shall faint and be weary, and young men shall fall exhausted; but they who wait for the Lord shall renew their strength; they shall mount up with wings like eagles; they shall run and not be weary; they shall walk and not faint.*
– Isaiah 40:28–31

Sometimes we forget who gave us breath. Indeed we sometimes believe that we do not need God in our lives – that we can do it all by ourselves. Yet the truth is that we can do nothing without Him. We can do nothing in the spiritual sense and in the life of God without Christ being the centre. God says that if we abide in Him, He will abide in us and if we ask anything in his Name, He will give it to us.

In life, there are times when we need to be still and know that He is God. In an age where too much trust has been placed in what man can achieve, remembering who gives us the power to do the things we do can be difficult. However, the truth is that we are nothing if we do not have the Lord in our lives. Naturally, man cannot do anything creative outside of God.

We can do nothing in spiritual strength, without Christ being the centre of our lives. If you abide in Him and if He abides in you, you can ask what you will and He will give you the desires of your heart.

We can all serve God and we are all worthy of his love and power. If we want to bless, promote and fulfil what He has called us to do, then we need to know that there is amazing power in serving God. We need to stay connected to God and to the plan and purpose that He has for us. Nobody stands alone – God prepares us by never allowing us to be alone. If we choose to stand alone and be absent from God, the Bible says that we will lack all wisdom and sound judgement in our lives and with the people in it.

Wherever we are and in whatever we are, we need to stay connected to God and allow Christ to be formed in us. That is God's desire for us – to grow in the likeness of his Son.

CHOOSE COURAGE: 15 JANUARY

# You Are Never Forsaken

*'The Lord himself goes before you and will be with you; He will never leave you nor forsake you. Do not be afraid; do not be discouraged.'*
– Deuteronomy 31:8

We are never alone – even though it may seem like we are. Before Jesus ascended to heaven, He made a promise to his disciples and the rest of the world that He would not leave us 'orphaned'. Jesus said He will be with us and that He and the Father will make their home among us.

Even in the middle of your worst storms in life, God is always with you. The story of Jesus in the boat with the disciples when a storm arose at sea is particularly instructive for our lives. The disciples thought they were about to perish because of the severity of the storm but Jesus woke up to calm the storm. There are situations in life that sometimes threaten to overwhelm us. Take heart, don't panic, Jesus is with you in the boat. Though the disciples panicked, there is one thing you cannot fault them for – they ran to Jesus for refuge. Because you are human, you may also panic when faced with a crisis. But what is important is knowing who to run to.

When Jesus left the earth, God gave us the Holy Spirit so we will always be surrounded by his profound power and love. How then can we not rejoice and enthuse at the plan He has for us when He promises to lead us to it and take us through it as our Guide, Comforter, Protector, Provider and Father? We know that, regardless of how dark things appear, the sun is always shining above. No matter what we are going through with circumstances, people, relationships or business, remember God will never leave us. God is always with us, in us, and for us. If He is for us who can be against us? They will come against us, but they will flee because our God will always be with us. We can always trust in Him to be there for us, no matter how hard and how far we fall.

CHOOSE COURAGE: 16 JANUARY

# Fear No Man But God

*Fear of man will prove to be a snare,*
*but whoever trusts in the Lord is kept safe.*
– PROVERBS 29:25

The ministry of Jesus and how the Pharisees always tried to set up a trap for Him demonstrates to us how man 'will always prove to be a snare'. People, generally, will always try to put one another down. This is because of man's sinful nature. Without wanting you always to be suspicious of even the well-meaning, it is important to keep a balance and take heed of the above verse.

The Pharisees tried to put guilt on Jesus by accusing Him of all manner of things. He refused to cave in under the burden of guilt they wanted to impose on Him. Equally, we need to refuse to live under the burden of guilt, shame and condemnation (as a result of the pressure society puts on us). Once we allow ourselves to become victims, we will always be trapped in the past and fail to move forward in God's Name.

Your past may not be impressive and people (even Christians!) are likely to remind you of it. Don't fall for their snare. You must forget about what you did in the past because you are a brand-new creature. You should not allow people to keep you down but should rise up and stand tall. Remember how David refused to be put down by his elder brother when he (David) was about to confront Goliath? Have the same attitude.

Stop making excuses because with Christ all things are possible and whatever God has decided for your life, the devil cannot stop it. The Bible tells us God will finish in us what He has started. Who is man, then, to put you down and stop midstream what God has already started in your life?

Everyone of us, regardless of our past, is welcome to do what God wants us to do. We need to fear God more than we fear man, stigmatization and society. Once we are able to overcome the fear of man and defy the limitations people put on us, we will be able to achieve anything in God's Name.

CHOOSE COURAGE: 17 JANUARY

# The Courage to Defy Man-made Limitations

*The Lord is my light and my salvation – whom shall I fear?*
– PSALM 27:1

If you're like most human beings, you'll probably get more advice than you want – and often from sources you haven't pursued. Although advice is generally helpful, don't always assume that everyone who gives you advice means well. People can kill your dream or vision. Just because someone questions whether you can persevere in a certain direction, or predicts you will never achieve your goals, don't abandon your plan and become sidetracked. Ultimately, it is the Lord who is your Light and Salvation.

The story is told of a young Japanese woman, Naoko Takahashi, who loved to run but was not winning any big races. After college she wanted to join her employer's running team, but company officials told her she wasn't good enough for the company to pay her way to its running camp. Determined to pursue her passion for running, she paid her own way to the camp.

In 1997 she switched from 5 000- and 10 000-metre races to marathon training. In 1998 she set a new national record, and also won the Olympic marathon in Sydney, Australia, to become the first Japanese woman to win a gold medal in the marathon. The lesson? We must not allow people to tell us what we can and cannot do, nor allow ourselves to be dictated to.

We must also be careful not to allow people to make us believe that because of what we are, we cannot be anything other than that. Other people's opinions will keep us bound. It is only God's opinion that counts. We need to move forward and fly like eagles and be in the light – because God has removed us from all darkness. We need to rise above, since the Lord is our salvation and our *El Elyon* – our Most High.

Thank God that Jesus is our Lord. We should not let darkness, people and past mistakes keep us bound. We need to forget because the blood has cleansed us. Do not live in denial but live in his freedom in Jesus' Name.

CHOOSE COURAGE: 18 JANUARY

# A Letter of Encouragement from Heaven

*For God has not given us a spirit of fear,*
*but of power, of love and a sound mind.*
– 2 Timothy 1:7

'My child, you have allowed fear to overcome you and failure to stalk you, concerns to overwhelm us. Yes, this is how the enemy works. In the fertile soil of anxiety and fear he will develop those things and cause you to fail, but know this, I am your God. I am greater than those things that you face. I want you to look beyond, and where you are, because that is where victory lies.

'I do not want you to become caught up in those circumstances, to fail, to let your heart fail you, to cause you to tremble and to fear. Look beyond where you are, because I am your God. Understand that there is a victory to be won, but how shall this battle be taken with those who are lame in their knees, those who cannot move, those who are caused to fear by the enemy?

'Have I not said that I will take you through? Have I not said that I will take you over? Am I not the One who leads the way before you? So look to Me and not to the problem – look to Me. You look to the challenge and you say "How can this be?" and "How can this happen?" You dwell on the negative things that cause you to fail, but I say unto you, lift up your eyes to where I am and look beyond your need. Look beyond your problems and look beyond the challenge for I am calling you to rise up. This is the time that I will do and accomplish great things in the earth for you, to those who trust, to those who have the courage to stand firm and rise up beyond their circumstances.

'I have not placed those circumstances there. They are there to foil you, to put you off-side, but look to Me and let all those rejoice who put their trust in Me. Let them ever shout for joy, for I defend them and let all those who love my Name call out and be joyful in Me for I defend the righteous, I bless the righteous and with favour I will surround them like a shield.'

# Courage to Cross Your Jordan

*When you pass through the waters, I will be with you and when you pass through the rivers, they will not sweep over you. When you walk through the fire, you will not be burned; the flames will not set you ablaze. For I am the Lord, your God, the Holy One of Israel.*
– Isaiah 43:2–3

In Joshua 1:9 God tells Joshua that as a leader of the children of Israel, he will lead them to the Promised Land. God says: 'Have I not commanded you to be strong and of good courage?' He never *said* it would be a good idea for Joshua to be strong and of good courage. On the contrary, He *commanded* it.

But it is important to note that Joshua's encouragement to his commission proceeded straight from God's revelation to Joshua. First, God speaks and commissions Joshua and then calls him to be strong and courageous in light of God's promises. Because of the Word from God, Joshua speaks to the people and gives them instructions for preparing to cross the Jordan in three days. This is followed by the response of the people to these instructions which, of course, had its source in the Word of God (Josh 1:16–18). Thus, God's revelation, which is equivalent to our possession of the Bible today, became the source of courage for both Joshua and the people.

If we want to cross the Jordan and enter our Promised Land, we have to make that definite choice in our lives. God says we should be courageous and not afraid. We can only be courageous because of his Word. Fear will blind us to our future. Fear will neutralize us today so that we do not walk into our Promised Land tomorrow. Fear will tell us what we can do and what we cannot do. Fear will focus on what we cannot do.

God said: 'Do not be afraid for the Lord your God is with you wherever you will go.' So we need to be courageous in all things we do and encounter in life. If we do not have courage, our lives will not reach the full potential they are meant to. We will not see the true promises God has made and the gifts He has entrusted to us. We have to place ourselves responsibly and we have to have the spiritual guts to see God do what He said He will do through us.

CHOOSE COURAGE: 20 JANUARY

# The Kingdom of God Has Come

'... *and say unto them the "Kingdom of God has come near you."*'
– LUKE 10:9

The Kingdom of God has come and is now within us. No other kingdom can stop it. No other nation can destroy it, for it is in the hands of God's children. If we abide in his Name and in his Kingdom, we can rule in life.

Some Pharisees once asked Jesus when the Kingdom would come (Luke 17:20). You can't see it, replied Jesus. But Jesus also said, 'The Kingdom of God is within you' (v 21). Jesus was the King, and because He was teaching and performing miracles among them, the Kingdom was among the Pharisees. Jesus Christ is in us today, too, and just as the Kingdom was present in the ministry of Jesus, it is present in the ministry of his church. The King is among us; his spiritual power is in us, even though the Kingdom is not yet operating in its full power.

We have already been brought into God's Kingdom (Col 1:13). We are already receiving a Kingdom, and our proper response is reverence and awe (Heb 12:28). Christ 'has made us to be a Kingdom' (Rev 1:6). We are a holy nation (1 Pet 2:9) – already and currently a holy Kingdom – but it does not yet appear what we shall be. God has rescued us from the dominion of sin and transferred us into his Kingdom, under his ruling authority.

An essential element that is needed to have a kingdom is a citizenry. Citizens of any kingdom have rules by which they live and are entitled to certain rights and benefits. The same applies to us as children of God. We are citizens of his Kingdom, with certain duties, rights and benefits. We have a duty to serve God and the King that He has appointed to rule the earth, Jesus Christ.

The Kingdom of God is here, Jesus said. His audience did not need to wait for a conquering Messiah – God is already ruling, and we should be living his way now. We don't yet possess a territory in the natural realm, but we do come under the reign of God. We do reign with Him in heavenly places, the Bible tells us.

CHOOSE COURAGE: 21 JANUARY

# The Courage Not to Compromise

*'And if you be unwilling to serve the LORD, choose this day whom you will serve, whether the gods your fathers served in the region beyond the River, or the gods of the Amorites in whose land you dwell; but as for me and my house, we will serve the LORD.'*

– JOSHUA 24:15

We do not have to conform to the norms of this world because we are not of this world. When the world cheats and defrauds, we do not have to join in. When the world compromises truth, as Christians we have to distinguish ourselves from those among us who compromise truth.

Practising one's faith in an uncompromising manner can sometimes invite disdain from some. But let us look at Joshua for inspiration. When the children of Israel had compromised truth and started worshipping gods, Joshua took a bold stand to serve the Lord regardless of its popularity. In Joshua 24:15 he told the Israelites, 'And if you be unwilling to serve the LORD, choose this day whom you will serve, whether the gods your fathers served in the region beyond the River, or the gods of the Amorites in whose land you dwell; but as for me and my house, we will serve the LORD.'

By faith we must take a stand even when the spiritual course is unpopular. We do not have to be mean-spirited about our stance but a stance we must take. There are instances when we should not care what people think or say but serve the Lord. Choose to serve Him and only Him. Walk in God's way. We need to choose to be committed – regardless of how old-fashioned and outdated commitment may seem to be.

Someone said that if people think something is right then it is okay for them to do it. Yet, what if that person thinks it is right to molest a child? Is it still okay? The world tells us that everything is relative and whatever we think or do is okay. However, what we may be thinking or doing could have negative consequences for ourselves and our children. Relative morality is not the way we can serve God and raise our children. So we need to move away from trying to fit in and doing what is 'socially acceptable'. Instead, we need to set ourselves apart from the rest and do what is right in the eyes of God.

# Shine Like the Brightness of Heaven

*'Those who are wise will shine like the brightness of the heavens, and those who lead many to righteousness like the stars for ever and ever.'*
– Daniel 12:3

David is a prime example of character and integrity. God said: 'If you look at David, he is a man after My own heart.' And God said that because when David sinned, he went transparently, authentically and truthfully before God and said: 'God I have sinned – my sin is before you. I am not in a place where I should be, but I thank you for your mercy.' The Bible is very clear on what we need to do when we have sinned. We need to go before God, confess our sins and repent. God is faithful and just to forgive us and cleanse us from all inequity, provided we confess and repent.

However, many people are not truthful before God and although it does not mean we should, by our own efforts, be perfect in the eyes of the Lord, we should have character and integrity. We should not tell other people that God told us to do something when it is wrong. When God commands us, we just need to do it. We are the salt of the earth – if salt loses its flavour, then it is good for nothing and it is thrown out and stamped on by men. We should not allow ourselves to become useless. We need to remember that we are the light of the world. A city that is set on a hill cannot be hidden. Nor is a lamp lit and put under a basket, but it is put on a lamp-stand to provide light to all in the house.

Likewise, we need to let our light shine. It means that we can then walk through darkness. Our light needs to shine before men so that they may see our good works and glorify our Father in heaven. This can be done through strong character, communicated credibility and consistency. When, through our lifestyle and character, people can see God in us and be led to righteousness, the Bible says we are like stars for ever and ever.

CHOOSE RIGHTEOUSNESS: 23 JANUARY

# The True Measure of Giving

*Sow for yourselves righteousness, reap the fruit of unfailing love and break up your unploughed ground; for it is time to seek the LORD.*
– HOSEA 10:12

God wants us to become people with something to give. He wants us to become generous beings, so much so that our generosity will shine through us and people around us will immediately recognize the generosity operating in our lives, which is unique and different to anything else.

It is therefore important to understand that the measure of our worth is not how much money we make, where we live and what we drive, but how much we give of ourselves. We will never be poor if we live to give. It is not just about the lives we bless, but also about the lives we neglect to bless.

It is important to remember that God will not judge us on the material gifts that He has given us, but on what we accomplished with what He has given us and how much we give from it. We will be held accountable to Him for that. For the true measure of good stewardship is not how much one has made and kept, but how much one has made and distributed.

God will never instruct us to do something He Himself is not prepared to do. He was the first one to sow for Himself righteousness. Jesus is the righteousness God sowed in the world and look at the fruit He has reaped for Himself. He has one Son who was righteous and now He has multitudes of righteous children.

# Staying Focused

*Looking unto Jesus the author and finisher of our faith; who for the joy that was set before him endured the cross, despising the shame, and is set down at the right hand of the throne of God.*
– Hebrews 12:2

We serve a God of fire and the fire was borne out of an act of obedience of the prophet to obey the Word of God and to say to the whole nation: 'How long will we be double-minded?' God wants us to focus on Jesus.

Being lukewarm is worse than being either hot or cold. If we are cold, we know we are cold. If we are hot, we know we are hot, but being lukewarm is like tiptoeing and not knowing whether we are in or out. We have to make a decision whether we are going to believe and follow God or not. If we decide not to, then we should not play church, because God wants to work and He cannot work if we are not sure whether we want to follow Him or not.

God is ready to confirm his Word in a powerful manifestation, bearing absolute fire in a young generation, but we have to make the choice and we have to make it now. Isaac Burrows said: 'Nothing of worth or weight can be achieved with half a mind or with a faint heart or with a lame endeavour.' Jesus understood this principle. He was focused on the cross. He chose the cross knowing full well where his actions and words would lead Him. When Jesus asks us to 'take up our cross', He is asking us to do the same thing: to make a choice to take the stony path of discipleship that requires choosing God above all else – family, possessions, wealth, comfort, safety and security.

That is what single-mindedness means. And this is not something that happens to a person but a way of life we choose. We need to be sure of who we are and the direction we want to take if we are going to achieve anything significant in life. We need to settle moral issues before we are confronted with them.

# Living Worthy of the Gospel

*Whatever happens, conduct yourselves in a manner worthy of the gospel of Christ. Then, whether I come and see you or only hear about you in My absence, I will know that you stand firm in one spirit, contending as one man for the faith of the gospel.*
– Philippians 1:27

The most effective way of making an impact on other people is for them to see Jesus in us – less of us but more of Him. By doing that, God will allow for a seed to be planted in that person and it will grow.

We have to create a culture of accepting people for what they are and still love them. God accepted us for what we were – sinners – and drew us to Himself by his love. It was his act of love, demonstrated by the giving of his Son, that we were drawn to Him. Similarly, we have to demonstrate love and allow God to reflect through us for us to be witnesses to so worthy a gospel. Then people will want to embrace the same light and love that God has in us. God will bring the increase in our and their lives and we will see God create a work and a change in them.

There are times when we will try to tell people what the will of God is and they will simply not understand it. They do not comprehend because we are trying to make the increase in their lives instead of allowing God to be in control and to make the increase. What will take us five years to do God will do in a second.

The devil will try to disconnect us from God but we need to hold on to Him. We need to get to know God in an authentic way. In spite of all our trials, tribulations, defeats, hurts and pain, we must believe that God will carry us through and never let go of his promise. Therefore, we must give of ourselves and present our bodies as a reasonable sacrifice.

Pray that you will grow spiritually this year and that you will become more Christ-like. Pray that not your will but his will be done.

# Watch What You Say

*'Your words now reflect your fate then: either you will be justified by them or you will be condemned.'*
– Matthew 12:37

It does not require an outright lie or slander to harm another person. A little insinuation is often enough. The Bible has a lot to say about our use or abuse of the tongue. We regard what we say as insignificant, but the Word of God tells us otherwise – what we say can determine our faith, so said Jesus in the above verse.

There are many verses in the Bible that tell us the significance of what we say and why we therefore need to watch our tongues. 'Does any of you want to live a life that is long and good? Then watch your tongue! Keep your lips from telling lies! Turn away from evil and do good. Work hard at living in peace with others' (Ps 34:12–15). 'Some people make cutting remarks, but the words of the wise bring healing' (Prov 12:18). 'I will not tolerate people who slander their neighbours. I will not endure conceit and pride' (Ps 101:5). 'As surely as a wind from the north brings rain, so a gossiping tongue causes anger!' (Prov 25:23). 'Fire goes out for lack of fuel, and quarrels disappear when gossip stops. A quarrelsome person starts fights as easily as hot embers light charcoal or fire lights wood' (Prov 26:20). All these verses warn us about the potential destructive power of words.

As seen in Matthew 12:37, Jesus Himself had a lot to say about the tongue. In fact, in the verses that precede verse 37, Jesus said, 'A good person produces good words from a good heart, and an evil person produces evil words from an evil heart. And I tell you this, that you must give an account on judgment day of every idle word you speak.'

But perhaps the most hard-hitting lesson about the tongue is James' letter (Jas 3:1–18). James shows the power of the tongue by comparing it to a horse's bridle and a ship's rudder. It is a little part of the body but can change the course of a person's life. Indeed, when the tongue is set on fire by hell (used in a sinful way), it can defile the entire body and cause great harm. Make a commitment to watch what you say.

CHOOSE RIGHTEOUSNESS: 27 JANUARY

# Allow God to Forgive You

*Remember, too, that knowing what is right to do and then not doing it is sin.*
– JAMES 4:17

God means that if we are not in his light and if we are doing things or are involved in things that are outside of his Word, then we must confess and own up to our sins, instead of denying it. If we deny the wrong we are doing and believe that what we are doing is not us doing it, then we are liars. Then we will remain in a place where God cannot wash us or cleanse us.

We need to stop justifying our wrongdoings by blaming other people or circumstances for why we choose to do wrong.

For example, if someone upsets us and we start shouting and swearing, and someone comes and says our behaviour is not Christian, but we respond by saying that we are being provoked – then we are lying and deceiving ourselves. This will only keep us in the darkness.

What God wants us to do is to come to Him in truthfulness. He wants to be the first to deal with our hearts. If we do not judge ourselves, then God will have to judge us. Nonetheless, there is power in confession and through the blood of Jesus we will be washed and made whole. We will walk in the light and have fellowship with Him.

Reinhardt Bonnke once said that you can work in a soap factory and still stink. Many of us believe that coming to church will immediately make us forgiven. Yet we are only forgiven after we own up our wrong actions and confess.

There is power in the blood through confession. God is not asking us to be perfect but to be honest and authentic in all we do and to have especially clean hearts. In this way, He can look at our hearts and be faithful to forgive. The great heroes of faith – Abraham, Moses, David and many others – all missed it at some point in time. But the difference is that they repented. If you have missed it, don't run away from God, run to Him.

# Dealing with Bitterness and Unforgiveness

*Stop being mean, bad-tempered, and angry. Quarrelling, harsh words, and dislike of others should have no place in your lives. Instead, be kind to each other, tender-hearted, forgiving one another because you belong to Christ.*

– EPHESIANS 4:31–32

We cannot get ahead this year if we are trying to get even. If we are living in bitterness, it is like drinking poison and expecting the other person to die. Being bitter, resentful and offended, angry and unforgiving are some of the things we need to deal with. It does not matter who is right or wrong.

Mother Theresa once said: 'If people are unreasonable, illogical and self-centred, love them anyway. If you do well, people will accuse you of selfish and ulterior motives. Do well anyway. If you are successful, you win false friends and true enemies. Succeed anyway. The good you will do today will be forgotten tomorrow. Do good anyway. Honesty and frankness make you vulnerable. Be honest and frank anyway. What you spend years building may be destroyed overnight. Build anyway. People really need help but may attack you if you help them. Help people anyway. Give the world the best you have and you will get kicked in the teeth. Give the world the best you have anyway.'

God wants us to love everyone as He has loved us – regardless of what that person has done to hurt or harm us. We do not have the right to be bitter – even if we are right. We are not victims and we must be careful not to place ourselves in a state of self-pity. God is on our side and in his Word He says that greater is He that is in us than he who is in the world.

Jesus gave us very important commandments to follow; one of them was to love one another, as He has loved us (John 15:12). Love is the exact opposite of unforgiveness, envy, jealousy, hate, pride and bitterness. You can't truly love somebody and hold bitterness or unforgiveness against him. We need to deal with bitterness and unforgiveness. Yes, you can deal with them because you are God's righteousness.

# Choose to Forgive

*'Your heavenly Father will forgive you*
*if you forgive those who sin against you.'*
– MATTHEW 6:14

Forgiveness is such a vital part to our growth and renewed spirit in the New Year. Joseph's life gives us remarkable examples of forgiveness, persistence, and unshakable faith in God's care for his children in all circumstances.

Remember that Joseph's brothers had done terrible things to him. They wanted to kill him, but they then sold him as a slave (sometimes you will be hurt by people who are closest to you). They lied to his father, saying that he was killed by a wild beast. They did not care what happened to Joseph. Therefore, he had every right to be bitter. It was more than 20 years after the offence when he first saw his brothers, and the first time he saw them (Gen 42) he pretended to be a stranger and spoke harshly to them. By the time they came the second time, he was ready to begin to deal with forgiveness. In being sold, God cleaned him, prepared him and put him in the place that God wanted him to be.

We must create a culture of authenticity like Joseph did. We should not pretend to love and forgive when we are still bitter inside. We need to reflect forgiveness both inwardly and outwardly. If we do that, we will allow God to go through his planned process in our lives. Process comes before promotion. If we do not get our act together, we will remain in the same place. Forgiveness will empower and build your character and in turn this will allow you to achieve heights far greater than you can imagine. It happened to Joseph. He would not have risen to be what God intended him to be had he harboured bitterness and unforgiveness in his heart.

Jesus taught us that when we pray, we must ask God to forgive us as we forgive others. Following that prayer in Matthew 6, Jesus said that if we forgive people who sin against us, He will forgive us. However, if we do not forgive others, He will not forgive us. He illustrated this in Matthew 18 with the parable of the unforgiving servant when Peter asked about how often to forgive. The one not forgiven was the one who did not forgive.

# Following in Jesus' Footsteps

*Follow God's example in everything you do just as a much loved child imitates his father. Be full of love for others, following the example of Christ who loved you and gave Himself to God as a sacrifice to take away your sins.*
– Ephesians 5:1–2

Jesus said: 'Love the Lord thy God with all thy heart.' If we love God with all our heart, we will love everything about his Kingdom the same way.

Paul encourages us in the above passage to imitate God like a child imitates his father and to follow the example of Christ. What does this mean? Our attitude should be like Christ's, who, although deserving worship and exaltation as God, emptied Himself and took the form of a servant. Our attitude should be like his: After humbling Himself, He became obedient even to death.

When we are weary and discouraged, his example of endurance in suffering should help us. When He was discouraged just before He faced the cross, He prayed and said, 'Not my will but your will be done.' His suffering and response to discouragement is an example of how we are to live.

He commanded that we love one another as He has loved us and laid down his life for us. Laying down his life for us is an example of how we should follow his example of service. Those who follow his example of serving will be great in his Kingdom. He overcame and sat with God in glory. If we overcome in this life, we will join Him in his glory.

Christ remained faithful to his calling and even suffered in his faithfulness. Like Him, we should stick to the purpose God has given us in this life. Also, like Christ, we should not seek our own glory but seek the glory of God. Study the life of Jesus and see how his footsteps can be our pathway. We should be merciful, just as God is merciful.

We should be holy, just as He is holy. We should be imitators of God and walk in love as He did.

CHOOSE RIGHTEOUSNESS: 31 JANUARY

# Jesus, Our Passover Lamb

*For you know that it was not with perishable things such as silver or gold that you were redeemed from the empty way of life handed down to you from your forefathers, but with the precious blood of Christ, a lamb without blemish or defect.*
– 1 PETER 1:18–19

During the Passover, God asked for the firstborn lamb (that is one without a spot or blemish) to be sacrificed. When we think about it, we realize that lamb was Jesus. He entered into the earth as the Lamb of God and was sacrificed. Pilate saw no fault in Him so He was without a spot or blemish. Jesus shed his blood for us and God made the ultimate sacrifice and that will establish how great God's love for us is and how great his desire is to see us saved. Passover pronounces redemption. To us believers, the Passover Lamb feast has a special meaning. Though we are not slaves, as God's people in Egypt, we were slaves to our sin, our own wants and desires. Sin was our master until Jesus, the Passover Lamb, delivered us from our Egypt.

Whenever God executes judgement, it is accompanied by grace and whenever God passes judgement, grace and mercy accompany it. God says: 'I am judging but giving you a way out.' Today, whatever the devil points a finger at in your past life, whatever is in your past life, God looks down and sees the blood which has cleansed and justified us – as if we have never before sinned.

We need to stop being self-righteous but instead we should embrace the gift of righteousness that God has given us. Then we will be delivered to progress and grow.

Remember that Jesus is our High Priest and we need to fix our eyes firmly on Him. He has made the ultimate sacrifice for us to have more purposeful and productive lives and whatever He promises, He delivers on.

God did not give ten per cent of Himself but everything He had. Therefore, when Jesus asks us to take up the cross and follow Him, we need to obey Him. God wants us all to take up that cross and follow Him. If we do, He promises to make us fishers of men.

# February

## CHOOSE WISDOM

*Intelligence is like underwear. We should all have it,*
*but we should not show it off.*

## CHOOSE PURPOSE

*The purpose of life is a life of purpose.*

– Robert Byrne

## CHOOSE CHANGE

*He who rejects change is the architect of decay.*
*The only human institution which rejects progress is the cemetery.*

– Harold Wilson

## CHOOSE YOUR ATTITUDE

*There is a world of difference between a person who has*
*a big problem and a person who makes a problem big.*

– John Maxwell

# God Will Finish What He Has Started

*Being confident of this very thing, that He who has begun a good work in you will complete it until the day of Jesus Christ.*
– Philippians 1:6

Do you ever feel like giving up? Do you sometimes wonder if you will be able to complete the purpose for which God has placed you on earth? Don't give in to hopelessness, no matter how bleak things look. You are on a journey that God wants to help you complete. You have a promise from God that should spur you on. He will complete the good work He has started in you.

Remember the story of Moses after he had killed the Egyptian and fled to the desert? Moses was born for a purpose – to liberate the children of Israel from the bondage of Egypt. But he must have wondered sitting in the middle of a desert in exile whether he was still going to be able to fulfil his purpose in life. But God finished in Moses what He had started. Moses liberated the children of Israel from Egypt.

Sometimes there are circumstances that will arise in your life which, if perceived with the natural eye, could suggest it is all over. Don't give in and don't give up. It is not over until God says so. Yes, it is easy to get discouraged as we go through life. The human tendency is to complain and grumble when things don't turn out the way we had expected. Our society encourages such behaviour as well. As a South African, I hear a lot of moaning and complaining in the new democratic dispensation.

But we need to look at biblical examples for us to understand how to handle disappointment and delay. The best example is the children of Israel. God had promised them Canaan. He delivered them from Egypt, miraculously provided them with manna and quail on a daily basis and divided the Red Sea to give them safe passage. But what was their response when they encountered the first difficulty? They doubted God and some even wanted to go back to Egypt. Their problem is that they thought it was within them to finish what God had started. We need to let God be God instead of trying to finish what He has started. God will do it.

# Your Source of Wisdom

*The fear of the* L*ORD is the beginning of wisdom;*
*all who follow His precepts have good understanding.*
*To Him belongs eternal praise.*
– PSALM 111:10

There was a kid in school called Johnny. The teacher said: 'Johnny, if you do not sit down, you are going to get a hiding.' So Johnny sat down. But Johnny thought: 'Outside I am sitting down, but on the inside I am still standing up.'

Some of us are like little Johnny. We do not fear (revere) God. We want to do his will not because we love Him and are willing to obey but because we are afraid of the consequences. Of course, we should be afraid of the consequences of sin and disobedience but that should not be the primary motive for our obedience. We should obey God because we love Him and desire to please Him.

Now, I know that most of us associate the word fear with terror. For many, this would describe the feeling you get when you see a snake or are faced with extreme danger. It is dread of the unknown. But this is not the sensation the author of this psalm is referring to. In our context as Christians, 'the fear of the Lord' refers to reverence, awe, great respect. When we truly fear the Lord, we will have a deep reverence and respect for the Lord. We will literally be awed and humbled by his presence and recognize that He is the Creator and we are the creatures.

Fearing God – holding Him in awe and worshipping Him – has its benefits. The psalmist says that revering God is the beginning of wisdom. Do you want to be wise? Revere God. If you want to have good understanding, then follow God's instructions.

The best place to begin the search for true wisdom is not in philosophy and academic pursuit (important as these are) but in the fear of the Lord. True fear of the Lord is born out of a knowledge of how infinitely powerful and majestic God is. Oswald Chambers once said: 'The remarkable thing about fearing God is that, when you fear God, you fear nothing else; whereas, if you do not fear God, you fear everything else.'

CHOOSE WISDOM: 3 FEBRUARY

# God Wants the Best for You

*I will instruct you and teach you in the way you should go;*
*I will counsel you and watch over you.*
– Psalm 32:8

Many times when a father wants what is best for his child, at that moment, the child may not agree that it is the best. But it ultimately turns out to be the best. Fathers, by virtue of their age, wisdom and experience, are there to teach the child in the way they should go. They are there to provide counsel and watch over their children.

A child who grows up without the benefit of parental/guardian teaching, guidance and counsel, faces a high risk of being a problem child and never fulfilling his or her potential. Such is our relationship with God. Those who go through life without our Heavenly Father's instructions, guidance and counsel are likely to be problem children in the spirit realm and never turning out to be what God had intended them to be.

The reason God says He will instruct and teach us in the way we should go is because He is looking out for our interests. All He wants is the best for us. He is not giving us instructions because of any reason other than that He is on our side. He knows best which way we should go. Sometimes the way we or others want us to go is not the best. In fact, it could be a pretty dangerous route. God created you and me. He has been there from the eternal past and will be there in the eternal future. Surely, He knows better than anyone else which way we should go?

God always wants what is best for us, and has made us for greater things than we often experience as life bumps and bruises us. In order for us to realize those greater things, He gives us instructions and counsel on the way we should go. The one way to become the best you, is by following His way, and refusing to live by your own way or by other people's ways. God alone knows what is the very best for you, and God alone has the power to make that potential He built into you a reality in your life.

CHOOSE WISDOM: 4 FEBRUARY

# The Value of Wisdom

*Surely you desire truth in the inner parts;*
*you teach me wisdom in the inmost place.*
– PSALM 51:6

Let us begin by asking ourselves why God wants to teach us wisdom in our innermost parts. The first reason is because wisdom enables us to gain true and lasting happiness. Proverbs 3:13 says, 'Happy is the man who finds wisdom and the man who gets understanding.' Your happiness does not lie in the pleasures of this world. It certainly does not lie in what displeases God but in you getting wisdom.

Secondly, God teaches us wisdom because it gives us a hope-filled future. Proverbs 24:14 says, 'Know that wisdom is such to your soul; if you find it, there will be a future, and your hope will not be cut off.' In other words, by means of wisdom you can build yourself a future that is full of hope.

Thirdly, God wants to teach us wisdom because getting it is proof that we love ourselves. Proverbs 19:8 says, 'He who gets wisdom loves himself.' In other words, do yourself a favour and show that you love yourself: Get wisdom! The command, 'Get wisdom; get insight,' is very important to us as believers. Proverbs 16:16 says, 'To get wisdom is better than gold; to get understanding is to be chosen rather than silver.' That is how important wisdom is.

But then what is wisdom and where can one get it? Is it, for the athlete, the breaking of new records? Is it, for the preacher, the preaching of a great sermon? Is it, for the executive, the climbing of the corporate ladder and the wheeling and dealing in the stock market? While all these things can be achieved through the practical application of wisdom, they are not of themselves wisdom.

True wisdom begins with knowing and fearing God. Wisdom is found in the Word of God. Therefore, if you want to be wise, you must apply yourself to studying, meditating and doing the Word of God. And I also commend not only studying the Bible, but regularly reading Christian books and literature books that distil the wisdom of the greatest students of the Word, both past and contemporary.

# God Gives You Wisdom and Understanding

*To God belong wisdom and power; counsel and understanding are His.*
– Job 12:13

If wisdom, power, counsel and understanding are His, and I am His, then all of these can be mine too. But I would like to focus on wisdom and understanding.

The Bible says, 'If any of you lacks wisdom, he should ask God, who gives generously to all without finding fault, and it will be given to him' (Jas 1:5). Whenever we need answers in life's day to day decisions, when we need to know what to do, we should not be afraid to ask God for wisdom. His Word declares that when we ask Him for wisdom, He gives us generously. When God says He gives He means He gives. Wisdom in response to our asking is a gift. We do not earn it. It is given freely from God without even a second thought.

In giving us the wisdom to know what to do in response to our asking, God does not scold us. He never puts us down. God does not rebuke us for asking Him what to do. He never says, 'How could you ask me that!' or 'How could you be so stupid!' He just gives the wisdom freely, 'for the Lord gives wisdom, and from his mouth come knowledge and understanding' (Prov 2:6).

In addition to wisdom, God gives us understanding because He wants us to know his will even more than we want to know it. If we are going to know the will of God concerning our lives, then we need his understanding. You see, God does not want you to be an unthinking robot that is programmed to do his bidding. He wants you to be a mature child who shares his concern and love for the world. He wants you to reflect and think through facts and feel his compassion.

As you prayerfully evaluate your calling, opportunities, gifts and circumstances, you need the kind of understanding that will help you develop a conviction about the course you should take – an assurance difficult to acquire in any other way except through the understanding God gives you.

CHOOSE WISDOM: 6 FEBRUARY

# Operating in the Wisdom of God

*To the man who pleases him, God gives wisdom, knowledge and happiness, but to the sinner He gives the task of gathering and storing up wealth to hand it over to the one who pleases God. This too is meaningless, a chasing after the wind.*
– ECCLESIASTES 2:26

If we look at the life of Joseph again, we can clearly see that God gave him wisdom, knowledge and later in his life happiness. Joseph received all of this because his heart was set on pleasing God. Remember how he ran away from sin after Potiphar's wife tried to seduce him? That is just one example of how he desired to please God.

He was thrown into a pit for having a godly vision. Having a godly vision requires wisdom and knowledge. We again saw his wisdom and knowledge in operation when he was managing Pharaoh's house in Egypt. The Bible tells us he ran Pharaoh's house so well that Pharaoh left everything to Joseph's care, concerning himself with nothing except the food he had to eat. Now, a ruler will not leave his household's responsibilities to anyone but a wise and knowledgeable servant.

But even before then, Joseph had shown great wisdom and knowledge while he was in prison. When Pharaoh had had two dreams, it was Joseph who interpreted the dream. That was God-inspired wisdom in operation.

Joseph did not give Pharaoh just the interpretation of his dreams but also proposed a plan for dealing with the famine that was predicted. Joseph suggested that they hold back a fifth of the harvest. That was an economic solution for Egypt. That is what happens when God gives wisdom and knowledge to those who please Him – they can solve national problems! But even for our own personal finances, Joseph's suggestion is a wise one – we should never spend every rand we have just because we happen to have the money in our hands! Egypt stored up for the famine and Joseph and his father's household benefited from that. Indeed, they may gather and store up the wealth but if you please God that wealth will be handed over to you.

# Wisdom to Save Your Household

*When the Son of Man returns, the world will be like the people were in Noah's day. In those days before the Flood, the people enjoyed banquets and parties and weddings right up to the time Noah entered his boat, and the flood came to destroy them all.*
– Luke 17:26–27

When you look at the specifications God gave to Noah for the building of the Ark, they were very detailed and complicated. The Ark was a very large vessel that could only be built through God-inspired wisdom. But Noah's wisdom was not just mechanical – it was also spiritual. When humanity had completely forgotten about God, Noah has the spiritual perception to hear God and foresee the destruction that was to come. Wisdom is not just confined to the intellect but is a matter of spiritual perception.

A hundred years went by from the time Noah began to build the Ark until the time the flood came. One hundred years! And yet some of us cannot wait 100 minutes. Noah had never seen a flood because at that time it had never rained before. What he was doing had never before been done in history. That is what happens when you are full of divine wisdom – you don't need historical precedents. And because of that, some might think you have lost your mind. Great things are achieved and great projects accomplished when you tap into divine wisdom.

When was the last time you did something for the first time? We tend to get so comfortable with life that we do not realize how neutral we have become. It was the eternal wisdom of God that wrote humanity's redemption story. God had never given his Son before. It was the first and the last time with us. There are times when things have to be done for the first time.

Also, Noah obeyed God even when nobody else would. It was going to be one thing if he had had a million people helping him to build the Ark and a church with 50 000 members coming for a prayer meeting inside the Ark, but *nobody* stood by him. While they continued ridiculing him, laughing and mocking him, he just kept building. Noah was obedient and wise and that saved him and his entire household.

CHOOSE PURPOSE: 8 FEBRUARY

# Chosen for a Purpose

*'You didn't choose me, remember; I chose you, and put you in the world to bear fruit, fruit that won't spoil. As fruit bearers, whatever you ask the Father in relation to Me, He gives you.'*
– JOHN 15:16

God is the one who chose us first. He has put you and me in the world for a purpose – a purpose that will be fruit that won't spoil. He wants us to live productive lives that will leave a legacy that will not ruin. But for all of this to happen, we need to get into agreement with Him. We need to choose to commit and work through and act on what God chooses for our lives. We need to make it an adventure, make it exciting and something we are passionate about.

You see, God has already told us what his intention is for us – to bear fruit that will not spoil. He wants us to be fruit bearers now and in the future. That is his purpose for our present and future. Therefore, we do not have to be pessimistic about life. A pessimist is a person who, regardless of the present, is disappointed with the future.

We need to be positive about the future, find out what God's life is for us, wrap ourselves around it, and get busy with it, so we can lead a fulfilled, satisfied and blessed life. It is important for us to choose to make a difference.

Next we need to make the decision to let God make our lives different. When we keep doing the same thing that we should not be doing, we should not expect a different result. How many of us want a closer relationship with God than we have ever had? Are we making the adjustments or doing something differently to get a different result? We all want God to do great things in our lives. Yet, we do not realize that we will not change if we do not change ourselves.

When the devil whispers to you that you are good for nothing, remind him that God has already chosen and put you in the world for a purpose. You are chosen.

# Don't Lose Your Saltiness

*'Let me tell you why you are here. You're here to be salt-seasoning that brings out the God-flavours of this earth. If you lose your saltiness, how will people taste godliness? You've lost your usefulness and will end up in the garbage.'*
– Matthew 5:13

If we do not embrace what God has invested in us and are not committed to doing what He wants for us, we become good for nothing. Consequently, we will be trampled under foot by people around us. We will not make a difference, stand out, make an impact, or reach our potential.

All we will do is take our gift and bury it, making sure everyone else buries their gifts as well. After all, birds of a feather flock together. We will find ourselves around people who make excuses for everything in their lives. But we need to break loose from this negative cycle. We need to overcome the situation that we find ourselves in, by managing our daily decisions by doing what God wants us to do. Only then can we be what God intends for us to be.

For example, if we want to run the Comrades Marathon but do not train for it, no amount of faith in God, prayer, confession, believing that we will win, or even using Scripture (e.g. 'Every place my foot shall tread God has given it to me' in Joshua 1:3) will enable us to complete the race. Instead, we might faint after 3 km. So when it comes to God, we believe we can do all things. However, we are too tired to do the work or to train.

Where does God make the difference? God calls us and gives us the ability. Yet we have to cooperate and do the right thing. God cannot do it for us. If we want God to do great things, we will have to do our part so that He can do his. And He will give us the favour and honour to achieve it. Nevertheless, we have to make the right decisions. We have to cut ties with whatever stops us from going to where we need to go.

CHOOSE PURPOSE: 10 FEBRUARY

# Being Generous for a Purpose

*'Listen carefully to what I am saying and be wary of the shrewd advice that tells you how to get ahead in the world on your own. Giving, not getting is the way. Generosity begets generosity. Stinginess impoverishes.'*

– Mark 4:24–25

If we do not engage the Word of God and apply it, we will be totally neutral and become like salt that has lost its flavour. There are many kinds of advice we get in life – from books, friends, parents, etc. All of these sources can be good. But don't be naïve, some can be bad. Jesus says we need to be careful of people who offer us advice on how we can get ahead in life on our own. The truth is that without God, we cannot get ahead in life. Even those who deny Him, do so using the breadth of life He has given them. They do so using the body part – the tongue – He has given them.

God has very clear principles in his Word. He says giving is the way. The world says hoarding is the way. The advice the world gives us is that if you accumulate and hide away, you will be successful. But God says you will increase by giving away. Generosity begets generosity. If you are tight-fisted, you will be poor.

When we speak of generosity, we tend to limit it to monetary or material things. However, there are many other types or forms of giving – the gift of time, life, freedom, effort and so on. God gives us the perfect example of giving. Of all the different things He has given us – the earth, children, a spouse if you are married – He gave us eternal life through his Son. God has not limited his giving to one form. Because we live in an age that is obsessed with material things, our perception of giving is that it has to be tangible. But that would be a flawed understanding of giving as it would mean those who have nothing tangible cannot give.

But we know that God has made it possible for all of us to give – we can give love, comfort, a smile, time, and so much more. Remember, you are blessed for a purpose – to be a blessing.

CHOOSE PURPOSE: 11 FEBRUARY

# Living a Life of Purpose

*See then that you walk circumspectly, not as fools but as wise, redeeming the time, because the days are evil. Therefore do not be unwise, but understand what the will of the Lord is.*

– Ephesians 5:15–17

With so many programmes and institutes coaching people on how to discover and fulfil their purpose, the term 'purpose' has become somewhat of a fad. Yet purpose is at the very core of why God put us on earth. Purpose is not just a buzzword but something connected to eternity. I'd go as far as to say that it's not only important but vital!

With this in mind, let us review the above passage. The Greek word used here for 'redeeming' means, 'to buy up; ransom: to rescue from loss (improve opportunity)'. God wants us to rescue our time from loss. He does not want us to lead purposeless lives that are just going to be a waste of time. How do we achieve this? By understanding his will.

When we understand what God wants from us, and do it, then we have found our purpose in life. The reason why we are here on earth and have been given our allotment of time is to fulfil our purpose. But when we do not understand our purpose, then we will not walk circumspectly. The above passage says when we do not understand the will of God – his purpose for our lives – then we are unwise.

Paul is warning us that if we do not know our purpose or live intentionally, our lives can be wasted. Because we do not know how much time we have on earth, it is important that we live every day of our lives purposefully. That is what redeeming the time means. More tragic than a shortened life, is a life lessened in meaningful impact because of lack of purpose. Graveyards are full of people who exhausted their days on things other than the purposes of God. Don't add to that statistic. Live a purposeful life.

CHOOSE PURPOSE: 12 FEBRUARY

# Value Character More Than Talent

*For what shall it profit a man, if he shall gain the whole world, and lose his soul?*
– Mark 8:36

This is Jesus speaking and telling us to put first things first in life. God is more interested in what we are becoming than in what we are accomplishing. Achieving in this life but failing the test of eternal life does not please God. In fact, it pains Him to see even one soul go to hell. Yet so many of us place emphasis on what we achieve here on earth and forget to answer some tough questions about our souls and eternity.

You see, your talent must not take you where your character cannot keep you. We must strike a balance between honing our talents and developing our characters. Going back to the example of Joseph, it is clear that his talent elevated him to, amongst other achievements, running Potiphar's large estate and household. But it was Joseph's character that kept him when Potiphar's wife made some sexual advances to him. Joseph's talent had placed him in a situation where a rich woman tried to use her sexual and social power to dominate him.

Joseph found himself in a sticky situation. He had to either offend the wife or betray her husband. Character enabled him to conclude that the former was less dangerous, and rejected the woman. One day when they were alone in the house she again made sexual advances to Joseph. In the physical tussle that followed, she pulled off Joseph's clothing. Naked, Joseph ran out of the room and then out of the house altogether, leaving his clothing behind. In that situation, Joseph needed his character and not his talent.

We have to let God prune and mould us into what He wants us to be. He is at work in our lives. Like clay in the potter's hand, let us allow Him to bend and shape us into what He wants us to be. There are things He may have to flatten and cut out in the process. But then, that is how we develop character.

CHOOSE PURPOSE: 13 FEBRUARY

# Make Wise Choices

*'I call heaven and earth today to witness against you: I have set before you life and death, the blessing and the curse. Choose life, then, that you and your descendants may live.'*
– Deuteronomy 30:19

Life consists of daily choices. When God said He places before us life and death; it means the same as when we talk about sowing and reaping or the law of gravity. However, here we are talking about the law of life and death and blessing and cursing. It is a law set before us 24 hours a day, every day of the week and every month of the year. Wherever we turn, life confronts us with choices.

But two words in this Scripture reference take precedence over the others; it is the words 'choose life'. We do have a choice and it is important to know that God will not make the choice for us. He will motivate us to choose correctly, but He cannot choose for us. Remember when Joshua challenged the children of Israel to make a choice between the One True God and some gods to whom their hearts had turned. Joshua made his choice clear, 'As for me and my house we will serve the Lord' (Josh 24:15).

We have to make the choice – the choice of life. Then God can get committed to that choice we make and birth that which He says will come forth from that choice.

Everybody has the right to choose but once we have chosen we become a servant to that choice. You are today the sum total of the choices you made in the past. If you want to change the course of your future, it starts with the choice you make today.

God says in his Word that if we choose life, our children will live. There is an emphasis on children. Why? For the same reason Joshua made a choice for his household. The decisions we make today can affect our future generations. A teenager who decides to fall pregnant and drop out of school has already made a choice on the quality of the life of her child. Short of a miracle, it will be a life of struggle. The choices you make will affect your future generations.

CHOOSE PURPOSE: 14 FEBRUARY

# Your Future Is Secure

*'For I know the thoughts and plans that I have for you, says the Lord, thoughts and plans for welfare and peace and not for evil, to give you hope in your final outcome.'*
– JEREMIAH 29:11

Erwin Raphael Manus said: 'We see the past as the present and we see the present as the future but we see the future as the past. So we wait for the good old days to come again, but they won't come.'

A fear of the future causes blindness and anxiety but we do not have to fear the future. God says He has already given us hope in our final outcome. Our future is guaranteed. God is in control and although the world is going in another direction – which is so destructive – God has already spoken about it and settled it. Know one thing – God is an awesome God and He is in control. He will always extend and establish his Kingdom in this world. His Kingdom will just keep coming and keep growing. The former glory will not be as good as the glory that is about to come.

The only way to receive the greatest gift of the future is to unwrap the present. We must leave the past, engage in the present and create the future. We need no anxiety in our lives. If you were ever in doubt about what God thinks about you, be assured and comforted – He has thoughts of peace and welfare towards you.

The Church will go beyond where it has ever been before. We should be so excited and blessed, not threatened or insecure about it. We must engage in the change that is coming, we must encounter God and his plan for us and be regenerated in our lives.

God must be real to us – alive and living in our lives. We need to minister change in our lives and move away from our places of comfort and compromise, so that we will not miss what God has for our lives. This is the greatest gift we could ever have.

CHOOSE CHANGE: 15 FEBRUARY

# Be Willing to Grow

*We grow in the grace and the knowledge of our Lord Jesus Christ.*
– 2 PETER 3:18

Growth implies change. We cannot grow in our faith and walk with God without change taking place in our lives. In fact, it is the willingness to change from being sinners into being children of God that enables us to experience his grace. God's grace is there but those who are not willing to change might never experience it. In the story of the prodigal son, it was his willingness to change and grow up that saw him enjoy the grace of his father.

Without question the Church was established on the promise of change – that hearts will be changed, families changed, marriages changed, communities changed, and cities changed by those swept up in the movement of God.

Something is happening all over this earth that we need to be aware of. Generations of young people, especially, have experienced a transformation and regeneration in their lives. Therefore, it is vitally important for us to understand certain things about change.

Some people did not like the fact that we were embracing total change in our church. So when we changed the music, platform and lights, we started to experience resistance from people who were comfortable in what they were in. They did not welcome the changes because they did not want to change.

But change is necessary. In order for us to live our new life, we need to understand that our past and who we were and the life we led no longer exist. Instead, we have a new life in God and in Christ. Thus we need to choose to embrace change today. John Powell said this: 'We think we have to change, grow and be good in order to be loved. But rather we are loved and we receive his grace so we can change, grow and be good.' The only limit to growth in our lives is the degree to which we are willing to change.

CHOOSE CHANGE: 16 FEBRUARY

# God Will Give You a Spiritual Makeover

*'I will give you a new heart and I will put a new spirit within you.'*
– Ezekiel 36:26

We do not come to church to be entertained. Instead, we come to encounter God – that is our priority, what is real and life-changing. We need to come to church to encounter God in a real way because God wants us to have a metamorphosis and regeneration.

It is nothing new to God and nothing He has not done before. So He wants us to experience this now. God wants to put a new nature and a new life – a brand-new, vibrant, energetic and powerful life – into your heart and into your life. Once we allow ourselves to go through the metamorphosis, we will literally be renewed. We will begin to develop a different outlook on life and a closer relationship with God.

Just as a caterpillar transforms from an ugly state into a beautiful butterfly, we will be able to transform ourselves from the darkness of the past into a wondrous light in our future. But we can never experience that kind of metamorphosis if we do not take a conscious decision to embrace change. You see, we all long to serve God with grace and strength, to reflect Christ in every word and action. Yet we find ourselves struggling to make this a reality in our daily lives.

Our desire to do the will of God is challenged by our inclination towards rebellion – what Paul called the struggle between flesh and the spirit. But when we allow God to put a new heart and a new spirit in us, that directs our attention past our shortcoming to the God who is ready and willing to make a new person out of our selfish and sinful selves.

All God requires from us is to invite Him into the hidden places of our souls and be willing to give him full permission to redeem and make us new. Only then can we experience a complete makeover, from the inside out. This is the new heart and new spirit Ezekiel is talking about.

# Come Out into the Open for God

*Jesus answered and said unto him, 'Verily, verily, I say unto thee, except a man be born again, he cannot see the Kingdom of God.' Nicodemus saith unto him, how can a man be born when he is old? … Jesus answered, 'Verily, verily, I say unto thee, except a man be born of water and of the Spirit, he cannot enter into the Kingdom of God. That which is born of the flesh is flesh; and that which is born of the Spirit is spirit.'*
– John 3:5–6

There was a man named Nicodemus who came to Jesus by night and asked Him if He was a teacher come from God, to which Jesus replied: 'Unless one is born again, you cannot see the Kingdom of God.'

Jesus meant that unless one is born of the water and of the Spirit one cannot see the Kingdom of God. So Jesus is talking here about two births – one is of the flesh and the other is of the Holy Spirit. If man in Christ is a brand-new creature, then old things are passed away. We cannot live the life God asks us to live unless we have had regeneration. We cannot walk in the things of God unless we have the Spirit of God to give us the ability to do it. You can say you love church – but have you encountered God?

Nicodemus was a religious person. He was a spiritual leader who believed in Jesus but would not openly identify with Him and declare his allegiance to Him. The reason for all the secrecy is obvious. It would not have been good for his public image if he had openly identified with Jesus. In many respects, he was no different to Peter, another religious leader, who denied Jesus and would not openly side with Him at a crucial time.

There are still some religious people today who are exactly like Nicodemus and Peter. They want to identify with Jesus secretly and will not come out when it matters for fear of what others will say. These modern Nicodemuses want to approach God under cover of darkness and will not take an open stand for his Word for fear of consequences. Almost every church has its share of people like this who will hide in the crowd while the Word is denied and compromised. While they know the Word of God, they choose to remain secret agents. Come out into the open for God.

CHOOSE CHANGE: 18 FEBRUARY

# Leave behind Traditions, Grow in His Grace

*But grow in the grace and knowledge of*
*our Lord and Saviour Jesus Christ.*
– 2 PETER 3:18

There is a story about a leg of lamb which perfectly illustrates how we allow actions we perceive as traditions to continue in our lives.

There was a mother who was cooking Sunday lunch and her little daughter was watching. The mother took the leg of lamb and cut the corners, folded them over and then put it in the oven.

'Why do you do that?' the little girl asked her mother. To which her mom replied: 'I do not know. I guess it is because your granny always did and because she did it, I do it.'

When the grandmother arrived later that day the little girl ran to her and asked why she cut the corners of the lamb. And the granny replied: 'Because my oven was too small.' Some of us are still cutting our legs of lamb, even though our ovens are large enough to accommodate more than one leg of lamb.

Relating this to our spirituality, we have to realize that things are no longer the same. Ours is a better covenant with better promises than the old covenant. We have a better and larger oven! But because of our traditions (the way we have always done things), we have limited the capacity God has given us under the new covenant. In Jesus we have a better High Priest than the Levitical priesthood under the old covenant. Our High Priest does not just live with us, He lives in us. That is why we can say: 'Greater is He who is in us than he who is in the world.'

But if we are going to realize the better promises of the new covenant, we have to be prepared to grow in grace and in knowledge of our Lord and Saviour Jesus Christ. We have to be prepared to leave behind the old traditions of the old covenant, discover the new covenant promises and appropriate them for ourselves.

CHOOSE CHANGE: 19 FEBRUARY

# You Are Free in Christ

*You, my brothers, were called to be free.*
*But do not use your freedom to indulge the sinful nature.*
– Galatians 5:13

In this text, Paul calls our attention to the freedom we have in Christ. In fact, a good part of the book of Galatians deals with the subject of freedom in Christ because there were certain Jewish Christians who were teaching that all Christians needed to obey the Mosaic Law.

This is a tendency that exists in the church even today – where other Christians want to impose and prescribe for others how they must live, what they should wear, what they must eat, who they must marry, and so on. When people try to do that, you need to stand your ground. Paul said, 'Stand fast therefore in the liberty wherewith Christ hath made us free, and be not entangled again with the yoke of bondage.' Paul reminds us that we are free in Christ.

In verse 13, however, he reminds us that freedom is not anarchy or an occasion to the flesh. We have to use our freedom in order to serve, love, minister and walk in the life that God wants for us. But if we say we are free, we must understand free from what. We are free from sin and free from the Mosaic Law. Once we accept Him, we become free in Christ. He who sent his Son has set us free and so we have to be the best possible individuals we can be, and not allow anyone to impose their demands on us, or to be their clones.

However, having freedom does not mean that we are free from all things. Freedom from all things is lawlessness, and sin is lawlessness. Indeed, true freedom can only be obtained when we recognize that we have limitations on our actions. As Christians we are not free from Christ. Peter, Paul and James all considered themselves bond servants to God and Christ (Tit 1:1; Jas 1:1; 2 Pet 1:1).

# God's Righteous Jealousy

*'You shall have no other gods before Me. You shall not make for yourself an idol in the form of anything in heaven above or on the earth beneath or in the waters below. You shall not bow down to them or worship them; for I, the LORD your God, am a jealous God …'*

– EXODUS 20:3–6

God says He has a divine jealousy and does not want us to compromise our relationship with Him in any way. God is not a lucky-dip packet, or a get-rich-quick scheme, a take-away or a dial-a-prayer. He is not going to let you do whatever you like whenever you want, and then still bless you. He said we should not worship any other God or human being.

You may be surprised at the use of the word 'jealous' in relation to God. However, it is important to understand how the word is used. In this case it is used differently from how it is used to describe the sin of jealousy in Galatians 5:20. Normally, we use the word in the sense of one person being envious of another because they have some possession that makes them stand out.

But in the case of God, He is not jealous because someone has something He does not have. Here God is jealous when we worship idols and make them our gods. Worship is his and his alone. God is protective of the worship and service that belong to Him. It is a sin to worship or serve any other god other than Him. So, whereas it is a sin when we are envious or jealous of someone because they have something we don't have, what God is jealous for belongs to Him – worship and service belong to Him alone. A practical example here will help. When a husband sees another man flirting with his wife, he has the right to get jealous. There is nothing sinful about that for only he has the right to flirt with his wife. However, when you are envious or jealous of something that is not yours, then it is sinful.

We do not compromise and bow down to a person, because God says we will not worship any other images. Every time God judges and measures out justice, grace will be accompanied. Yet we cannot compromise our walk with God and we cannot sell out and worship other gods.

CHOOSE CHANGE: 21 FEBRUARY

# A New Creation Looks Like You

*Therefore, if any man is in Christ he is a new creation.*
*Old things have passed away and a new order has come.*
– 2 CORINTHIANS 5:17

The amazing feature of salvation is the extreme makeover we undergo when we accept Christ as our Lord and Saviour. A man in Christ is a new creation, not just improved or reformed but totally remade. God renews our spirits and we are able to rise above the things of yesterday and move into today and tomorrow.

If we look at the life of Paul who was persecuting Christians, we cannot believe that someone like him could ever be changed. During his Damascus encounter with Jesus, Paul was converted and made whole. As a new creation, he was transformed into an apostle of Christ and began to share the Gospel of Christ. Despite being mocked, whipped and stoned for his passion for Christ, he continued his work for God. Paul became one of the greatest apostles ever.

He was imprisoned numerous times because of his work for the Lord but still he continued, because when God touches our lives, we will be changed for ever. Indeed, we will experience light and love in our lives like no other time. It will carry us through the dark times, give us strength in the weak times and renew our spirits during depressing times. When you look at Paul's life before his encounter with God and the post-Damascus Paul, you begin to grasp what the Bible means when it says in Christ we are a new creation. But let us not go that far back in history. Look at yourself now and compare it with what and who you were before you got born again. You are a witness of how a new creation looks like!

When we allow ourselves to be transformed in the image of God, the love we experience will help us through – regardless of what trials and persecutions we experience. God promises to lift us up above it all. Old things will pass away and God will allow for a new order to come in.

# Have the Right Attitude and Be Blessed

*You were taught, with regard to your former way of life, to put off your old self, which is being corrupted by its deceitful desires; to be made new in the attitude of your minds; and to put on the new self, created to be like God in true righteousness and holiness.*
– Ephesians 4:22–24

Attitude is a choice and our attitude determines our altitude. It does not mean that we will not have days when we are down. Paul says we have to be made new in the attitude of our minds. Why? Because our attitude will determine how we respond to feelings of depression and discouragement.

A godly attitude is faithful, loving, positive and encouraged. It is not what happens *to* us but what happens *through* us. Victor Frankl, a psychiatrist, told the story about when he was in a concentration camp and they were beating him up and hitting him on his head with a stick until he was bleeding all over.

He turned to the guard and said: 'I love you,' and the guard hit him again. Every time he said those words, the guard got angrier and angrier and then screamed at him saying: 'How can you say you love me when I am beating you up with a stick?' To which Frankl said: 'Because if I don't tell you, I'll be just like you.'

The world wants us to row downstream but God wants us to row upstream. Although it is easier to become part of the negative cynical crowd, it is better to be someone who is different from the unbeliever. People must be able to see what distinguishes us as believers. Remember Caleb and Joshua in Numbers 33. They showed a different attitude when they came back from spying the land of Canaan. They had the courage to be different. They had the courage to have the right attitude even if it meant they were the only two in the entire nation of Israel to do so. As a result, Joshua and Caleb saw the Promised Land while the others died in the wilderness, never coming into their blessings – all because of their attitude. Joshua and Caleb had a different attitude and they were blessed for it.

# Learn to Put Up with Others

*Bear with each other and forgive whatever grievances you may have against one another. Forgive as the LORD forgave you.*
– COLOSSIANS 3:13

Among the greatest of New Testament appeals for unity is Paul's pleas to the believers in the church of Ephesus, 'As a prisoner for the Lord, then, I urge you to live a life worthy of the calling you have received. Be completely humble and gentle; be patient, bearing with one another in love. Make every effort to keep the unity of the Spirit through the bond of peace' (Eph 4:1–3).

Of special interest in this particular devotional is the phrase 'bearing with one another in love'. The same phrase appears in Colossians 3:13. Bible scholars say this phrase appears 15 times in the New Testament. 'Bearing with' means 'to hold oneself up against' or 'put up with'. In order to have unity with others in church or at home does require some 'putting up with in love'! Here, Paul is definitely not speaking about putting up with immoral behaviour and erroneous teaching. He denounced both of these.

He is actually talking about tolerating each other's inconsistencies, idiosyncrasies and oddities – we all have our own – for the sake of peace. The issue of living peacefully with other believers was very important to Paul and we should take it equally serious. He once wrote a letter to two women in Philippi, Euodia and Syntyche, who seemingly could not stand each other and were constantly fighting. Paul pleaded with them to 'agree with each other in the Lord' (Phil 4:2–3). As believers we are expected to live peaceably with all men. Jesus said, 'Blessed are the peacemakers for they shall be called the children of God' (Matt 5:9).

As said above, we all have our own idiosyncrasies and expect others to be tolerant. If we say we don't, we are lying and this could be a sign of pride on our part. Yet we are so quick to find fault in others and be less forgiving. Make allowances for people's mistakes and oddities. It's the right attitude and God does so in your case.

# Count Your Blessings

*Do not grieve God. Do not break His heart. His Holy Spirit, moving and breathing in you, is the most intimate part of your life, making you fit for Himself. Do not take such a gift for granted. Make a clean break with all cutting, backbiting, and profane talk. Be gentle with one another, sensitive.*

– Ephesians 4:30–32

Ungratefulness moves us towards bitterness. An ungrateful heart makes us bitter, cynical and pessimistic. We complain about everything – even though we should feel blessed for everything we have. We need to stop complaining, for we are blessed in all things we have.

A little boy was starting school but his mom had no money for shoes. So she walked him to school and left him at the gate. On her way home she prayed that he would not feel inferior or be teased. She asked God to help him go through his day with ease.

She went home and prayed the whole morning while school was on. In the afternoon she heard her son come home and prayed that he was okay and that school was not a disaster. When he came in, she asked: 'How was school?' He answered: 'It was great.' Confused, she looked at him and said: 'Are you sure? Did no one mock you for not having shoes?' And he replied: 'No mom, because the boy next to me had no feet.'

We can always look at somebody who is better off than us and make an excuse. We can be upset and bitter about someone who has hurt us. We can resent our circumstances in life. Or we can embrace God and know that God loves us unconditionally. Because He is a God of mercy and grace, He has a great present and future for us.

As the words of that great hymn say, 'When you look at others with their lands and gold; Think that Christ has promised you his wealth untold; Count your many blessings; Wealth can never buy your reward in heaven; Nor your home on high.' Blessings are gifts from God and we sometimes fail to see what the Lord has already done. As we give thanks to God for our many blessings, naming them one by one, we will be surprised by what the Lord has done.

# Encourage Yourself in the Lord

*Unrelenting disappointment leaves you heartsick,*
*but a sudden good break can turn life around.*
– Proverbs 13:12

Sometimes you go through one disappointment after another. We all know that some days are better than others. Sometimes we even feel like we should have stayed in bed.

But unrelenting disappointment – when you are never encouraged – makes people ill, defeated, negative and cynical. So you have to be careful and make sure that in the midst of a whole lot of disappointments, you will find something to focus on that is positive.

If we are negative, discouraged, depressed and cynical, it means we have taken this Scripture reading and thrown it out of our lives, because all we are doing is looking at the problem and not through it. Circumstances may not be of our choosing but attitude is. It is easier to maintain a godly attitude than to regain it. Our attitude determines our actions and that determines the ultimate outcome.

In 1 Samuel 30, King David and his men came to Ziklag and discovered that the Amalekites had invaded the city and destroyed it. The Amalekites had taken everyone who lived in the city captive – wives, sons and daughters.

Needless to say, David and all his men felt an 'unrelenting disappointment'. The Bible says in 1 Samuel 30:4 that they cried until they had no strength left to cry. But just when it looked like it couldn't get any worse, it did. The men became embittered with David and threatened to stone him to death. But then, David did something unthinkable. Verse 6 says he encouraged himself in the Lord. That was like the 'sudden good break that turned life around'.

When David encouraged himself in the Lord, he gained supernatural wisdom and strength. Verse 18 says, 'He recovered all that the Amalekites had carried away.' You may have to do the same in order to turn your situation around – encourage yourself in the Lord!

# Make an Attitude Adjustment

*Rejoice in the Lord always; again I will say, rejoice! Let your forbearing spirit be known to all men. The Lord is near. Be anxious for nothing, but in everything by prayer and supplication with thanksgiving let your requests be made known to God. And the peace of God, which surpasses all comprehension, shall guard your hearts and your minds in Christ Jesus.*
– PHILIPPIANS 4:4–7

There is a story of two buckets in a well and one bucket always came up crying while the other bucket always came up rejoicing. One day the crying bucket asked the rejoicing bucket: 'Why are you always so happy?'

To which the rejoicing bucket replied: 'Why are you so depressed and discouraged and always crying?' And the crying bucket said: 'Every time I go up full, I come down empty.' And the rejoicing bucket laughed and said: 'Well every time I go down empty, I come up full.' The moral of this story is that our attitude towards the various situations in our lives determines our path forward in life. The rewards we will receive are based on that attitude.

We all have the tendency to be unsettled and dissatisfied with life and the situations we often find ourselves in – whether we are the full bucket or the empty bucket. And we tend to have a poor attitude when a good attitude is all we needed in order to get out of a particular mood or situation.

In many instances, we do not have the kind of attitude God requires us to have – rejoicing always. Sometimes we do need a miracle or an intervention by God. All we need is an attitude adjustment. David, as pointed out in the previous devotional, adjusted his attitude and all else fell into place.

CHOOSE YOUR ATTITUDE: 27 FEBRUARY

# Meet the Need, Don't Over Analyze it

*Walking down the street, Jesus saw a man blind from birth. His disciples asked, 'Rabbi, who sinned: this man or his parents, causing him to be born blind?' Jesus said, 'You're asking the wrong question. You're looking for someone to blame. There is no such cause-effect here. Look instead for what God can do. We need to be energetically at work for the One who sent Me here, working while the sun shines.'*
– John 9:1–7, 39

Is it not interesting how the first question is to wonder why he is blind, instead of how he can be helped or loved? Whatever happened in our past cannot be changed, so we should work on our present and future.

Jesus said: 'You are asking the wrong question.' There is no one to blame. Look instead for what God can do. We are so caught up in why, how and what happened in the past, instead of looking to God to see what He can do here and now. We should get to the place where we know God can make a difference in our lives.

Then Jesus makes a very important point: 'We need to be energetically at work for the One who sent us here. Working while the sun shines, for when night falls the day will be over. For as long as I am in the world, there is plenty of light. I am the world's light.'

What God is really saying is that we need to seize the moment and take the opportunity. We have to stop getting caught up in things that will confuse, complicate and blur our vision. Many times our vision is like taking a picture out of focus. We need to put our vision back in focus and come to a point where we do not complicate our lives.

Here was a man who needed help. Instead of addressing his need, the disciples wanted to start a whole religious debate about the cause of his blindness. Sometimes Jesus' 21st century disciples are exactly like that. We are preoccupied with who has done what and why things happened. Jesus' attitude was not to get caught up in religious disputes but to meet people's needs. We should adopt the same attitude.

Be conscious of meeting the need instead of over analyzing how the need arose.

# Count It All Joy

*Consider it a sheer gift, friends, when tests and challenges come at you from all sides. You know that under pressure, your faith-life is forced into the open and shows its true colours. So do not try to get out of anything prematurely. Let it do its work so you become mature and well-developed, not deficient in any way.*
– JAMES 1:2–4

When Jesus was led into the wilderness, Satan tried to get Him to worship and submit to him and not go the way of the cross. Jesus refused to be distracted or to take the short cut.

So many Christians want to live the Christian life but do not want to take up the cross and follow Him. We may be confused as to how we need to follow Him, but we need to take up the cross and walk with Him.

When everything seems to be coming down on us and every situation seems to be attacking us, that is the time to say, 'I will obey Jesus. I will follow Him.' Jesus promises that if you lose your life, you will find it. James tells us to count it all joy in the midst of our trials. What he says should make us think about how we should react to the things that take away our joy. We have all faced hurts, disappointments and challenges that have caused our joy to fade. But James says we should do the opposite.

James was not a sadomasochist who took delight in being hurt, neither was he suggesting that we must enjoy trials, or that trials are there for the joy of it. He is therefore not talking about relishing pain, but looking to its end, just like Christ, who for the joy set before Him, endured the cross. Christ did not enjoy the cross but He looked to its end. That is the attitude we should have when we are faced with tests and challenges. Something good can come out of those experiences.

Sometimes, so many of us as Christians do not know what is going on because we are not losing our lives to find the higher life. We must have total confidence and trust in the total faithfulness of God and his plans and purposes for our lives.

CHOOSE YOUR ATTITUDE: 29 FEBRUARY

# Praise the Lord

*Make a joyful noise to the Lord, all you lands! Serve the Lord with gladness! Come before His presence with singing! Know that the Lord is God! It is He who has made us, not we ourselves! We are His people and the sheep of His pasture. Enter into His gates with thanksgiving and a thank offering and into His courts with praise! Be thankful and say so to Him, bless and affectionately praise His name! For the Lord is good; His mercy and loving-kindness are everlasting, His faithfulness and truth endure to all generations.*
– Psalm 100

Praise Him today and shout unto God with a voice of triumph.
Give thanks and raise your hands to Him – rejoicing in his Name.
Praise Him with a heart of grace, thanksgiving and mercy.
We are healed through his grace and we are made whole.
God will take our brokenness and heal it, He will give us strength
And turn defeat into victory.
Be still and know that He is God.
He will never leave us nor forsake us.
He will never turn his back on us; for his mercy endures for ever.
Thank you, Jesus!
The Lord is good and greatly to be praised!

# March

## CHOOSE ENCOURAGEMENT

*Those who are lifting the world upward and onward are those who encourage more than criticize.*

– Elizabeth Harrison

## CHOOSE GENEROSITY

*Think of giving not as a duty but as a privilege.*

– John D Rockefeller Jr

## CHOOSE HUMILITY

*Nobody has ever expected me to be president. In my poor, lean lank face nobody has ever seen that any cabbages were sprouting.*

– Abraham Lincoln

## CHOOSE TO LOVE AND BE LOVED

*If you have love, you do not need to have anything else, and if you do not have it, it does not matter much what else you have.*

– Sir James M Barrie

# God Is on Your Side

*If God is for us, who can be against us?*
– Romans 8:31

Encouragement is a daily choice and we can choose to live a life of discouragement or a life of encouragement. We must choose to see a situation in terms of the positive and not the negative. For example, David could have either said that Goliath is too big to fight or too big to miss; he chose the latter. The late Dana Reeve, wife of the late Superman hero Christopher Reeve, summed it up perfectly: 'Some choices in life choose you. How you respond to them will define the context of your life.'

In life, we choose to see the glass either half full or half empty, because everything is based on our response to different situations. Our view can greatly affect the outcome of our lives. George Adams said: 'Encouragement is oxygen to the soul.' When people are able to see encouragement in us and through us, they will see a power in us that is different from the norm. There is mighty power in being courageous and having a life filled with encouragement.

Read the whole of Romans 8 and see how Paul carefully lays out one of the greatest truths for the Christian – that God is for us. Often, we think God is against us. No, He is not. He is against sin. God is on our side and no one can change or ruin what God is doing in our lives. Five times in Romans 8 the apostle Paul asks questions to draw out the amazing truth that God is on our side. Verse 31: 'If God is for us, who can be against us?' Verse 32: 'How will he not also with him graciously give us all things?' Verse 33: 'Who shall bring any charge against God's elect?' Verse 34: 'Who is to condemn?' Verse 35: 'Who shall separate us from the love of Christ?' If you feel discouraged today, prayerfully reflect on the truth that God is on your side.

# Comforted to Comfort Others

*Blessed be the God and Father of our Lord Jesus Christ,*
*the Father of sympathy and the God of every comfort,*
*Who comforts us in every trouble, so that we may also be able*
*to comfort those who are in any kind of trouble or distress, with*
*the comfort with which we ourselves are comforted by God.*
– 2 Corinthians 1:3–4

We may question God and wonder why He encourages us in every trouble, calamity and affliction. It is because we are the apple of his eye. We are his children, the recipients of his love. He says in his Word that He will encourage us, comfort us, strengthen us and be there for us. He will pick us up when we fall and be there so that we can reach our potential.

But when God does something for us, He often has more than us in mind. He blesses us so that we can be a blessing to others. Again, He comforts and encourages us so that we may also be able to encourage and console anyone else who is in trouble or distress. But if we are discouraged and build monuments to our discouragement, we will breed discouragement and also infect others with discouragement. Yet, if we can decide to walk in God's Word and be a source of encouragement in our everyday lives, we will stand out in the world.

People will automatically be drawn to us and see that we have something which is different – something that they are also in need of. Unfortunately, the world today is filled with people who feed discouragement. It is true what they say: 'Misery loves company.' There are not many people we can talk to today who will encourage us when we need to be encouraged, support us when we need support and give us comfort when we search for it. Instead, they will help us remain discouraged.

But choosing to be a source of encouragement every day will allow us to comfort those who are in any kind of trouble or distress. We will help them with the same comfort and encouragement that we ourselves receive from God.

# Encouraging Others in the Lord

*So you should rather turn and forgive and comfort and encourage, keeping him from being overwhelmed by excessive sorrow and despair. I therefore beg you to reinstate him in your affections and assure him of your love for him.*
– 2 Corinthians 2:7–8

We must be sensitive at times, especially when people are feeling discouraged. We must encourage and comfort them through God. We must always have something positive to speak about to them. We must show them that their future is much bigger than their past and that failure is not fatal because we serve a God of second chances.

Encouragement motivates and we need to ensure that every word and action which comes out of our mouths will motivate others. It is so sad how good news stays at home but bad news travels. It is always amazing that while people do great exploits (positive and amazing things) you always hear very quickly when somebody has failed.

The command for us as Christians is to encourage one another. In his letter to the Thessalonians, Paul said, 'Therefore encourage one another and build each other up, just as in fact you are doing' (1 Thess 5:11). Paul knew that encouragement can drastically change a person's life. We all tend to get discouraged from time to time and need encouragement. We may get discouraged about our state of finances for example, or maybe we are feeling down about having lost a loved one. Maybe someone you know is lonely, depressed or bedridden. Go and give a word of encouragement to that person.

Build up the distressed and demoralized, for this is what God wants us to do. It is part of our mandate as Christians to encourage others, to sing the Word as our source. Show the discouraged how much God values them and it will make a world of difference to their attitude. When we build up those who are hurting, it ultimately makes us feel better and encouraged too.

We also have to encourage our children by constantly telling them that they can do it. We must have a daily word of encouragement for them. In addition, we have to also encourage ourselves in the Lord.

CHOOSE ENCOURAGEMENT: 4 MARCH

# The Choice Is Yours to Encourage Yourself

*... David encouraged himself in the Lord his God.'*
– 1 Samuel 30:6

Mark Twain once said, 'The best way to cheer you up is to cheer yourself up.' If we are walking in encouragement and decide to be encouraged, we choose to be a person with courage who encourages others. We will walk our talk and have victory through and in Christ.

We must never forget that God said that if He is for us no one can be against us. Not only do we need to tell people of God's glory, we also need to reflect it in our appearance, our walk, the way we talk and by our actions.

We cannot tell people to be encouraged when we ourselves look like we came from God's funeral. Instead, we have to be a model of encouragement and lead by example in God's plan for us. David encouraged himself in the Lord his God. He and his band of soldiers had just returned home to Ziklag, only to find that their city had been burned to the ground, and their wives and children taken into captivity by the Amalekites.

The morale plummeted and the Bible tells us they wept so bitterly until they simply had no more power to weep. For David, it was even worse, for he was their leader, and his men were so consumed by grief that they even threatened to stone him. He was in great distress and this could have destroyed him completely. But David cheered himself up.

This required a definite resolve on the part of David. To do otherwise would only have deepened his distress and worsened a situation that was already bleak. If you look at the source of discouragement, you will see that it arose out of what their enemies had done to them. That should tell you something about discouragement – it does not come from God but from the enemy, the devil.

When faced with a discouraging situation, the choice is yours, as it was for David. To be victorious, at times, you are going to have to do what David did – encourage yourself in the Lord.

# God, Where Are You?

*Therefore I will look to the LORD; I will wait for the God of my salvation; My God will hear me. Do not rejoice over me, my enemy; When I fall, I will arise; When I sit in darkness, The LORD will be a light to me.*
– MICAH 7:7–8

Sometimes you find yourself in situations where you can be described as 'fallen' or in 'darkness'. In such situations, you are tempted to cry out and say, 'God, where are you?'

More than once you experience that some days are better than others. But unrelenting disappointment – when you are never encouraged – makes people feel ill, defeated, negative and cynical. Thus you have to ensure that, in the midst of a whole lot of disappointments, you find something positive to focus on. Micah knew that however bad the situation was, he was going to arise and the Lord was going to be a light to him.

You know that God is a God of encouragement. A perfect example of how we should never allow ourselves to become discouraged is the story about the only survivor of a shipwreck who was washed up on a small, uninhabited island. He prayed feverishly for God to rescue him and every day he scanned the horizon for help but nothing seemed to happen. Exhausted, he eventually managed to build a little hut out of driftwood to protect him from the elements and to store his few possessions.

But then one day, after scavenging for food, he arrived home to find his little hut in flames, the smoke rolling up to the sky. The worst had happened. Everything was lost. He was stunned with grief and anger. 'God, how could you do this to me!' he cried.

Early the next day, however, he was awakened by the sound of a ship that was approaching the island. The ship had come to rescue him. 'How did you know I was here?' the weary man asked his rescuers. 'We saw your smoke signal,' they replied.

It is easy to get discouraged when things are going bad. But we should not lose heart because God is at work in our lives even in the midst of pain and suffering.

# Jesus Has Already Overcome

*'I have told you these things, so that in me you may have peace. In the world you will suffer trials and tribulations, but be encouraged, because I have overcome the world.'*
– John 16:33

God wants to encourage us so that we do not feel hopeless. Jesus encountered a lot of opposition. Many people did not like what He was saying. The Pharisees in particular liked the religious status quo and were against anyone who wanted to tamper with it. For what He stood for, Jesus suffered a lot of persecution from the religious establishment of that time, so much so that they finally had Him killed.

The apostle Paul also ran into a lot of opposition and adversity in his ministry. One time he had a shipwreck while on a mission to go and preach the Gospel. In Acts 22 we see him preaching the Gospel in Jerusalem and coming across opposition and causing a riot in the city. He escaped from the angry crowd through the intervention of the Roman army that came to rescue him.

So Jesus and Paul knew from their own experience that we face problems and challenges on earth. It did not start with you. The Master Himself and the great apostle also went through trials and tribulations. One day when Jesus was talking to his disciples, they were so discouraged that they wanted to quit and return to their former lives. It did not start with them either. It happened to the children when they were going through the wilderness. They were so discouraged that they wanted to go back to Egypt.

Just like the disciples and the children of Israel, we often want to give up and quit because of the problems and challenges we face in life. But God encourages us to press on because we are not of those who draw back. Jesus, the Firstborn in the family, did not draw back when He was facing the cross. He knew that the enemy was already defeated. The redemption plan had been there before the foundation of the world.

When we get discouraged in the same way, remember what Jesus said, '… be encouraged, because I have overcome the world.'

CHOOSE ENCOURAGEMENT: 7 MARCH

# We Are Struck Down But Not Destroyed

*The crowd joined in the attack upon them, and the rulers tore the clothes off of them and commanded that they be beaten with rods.*
– Acts 16:22

This passage relates to the persecution the apostles faced when they preached the Gospel. Ninety-nine per cent of people at that moment would have had an attitude of defeat, anger, discouragement, resentment and rebellion. Christians think that if we do what God wants us to do then we will never be persecuted.

Forget it; it is the outcome we need to look at. Paul and Silas were thrown in jail with chains for delivering a slave girl who was possessed by a demon. Then, sitting there in prison with the highest show of courage, determination and positive attitude, they chose to pray and praise God. When God is with us, the darkest prison becomes a place of worship.

That is why Paul could write in Romans 5:3, 'We rejoice in our sufferings.' In 2 Corinthians 4:8–9 Paul said, 'We are hard-pressed on every side, but not crushed; perplexed, but not in despair; persecuted, but not abandoned; struck down, but not destroyed.' Paul and Silas knew God was with them and would show Himself strong and mighty on their behalf.

Not only that, as Paul and Silas sang and prayed, the rest of the prisoners were listening to them with great delight. In their suffering the apostles were nevertheless witnessing to God and his salvation by their praise and prayers. You see, it is only when grapes are crushed that the refreshing juice comes out. The suffering of Christians will produce the life of God which then can benefit others.

As they were praising God, there was a sudden great earthquake and they were set free. The prison guard stood trembling before them and asked what he should do to be saved. Paul, in the midst of one of the greatest manifestations of God, took this opportunity to bring God into the guard's life. He asked him to receive the Name of the Lord so that he and his family would be saved.

CHOOSE GENEROSITY: 8 MARCH

# You Are Blessed

*Blessed is the man who fears the LORD, who finds great delight in His commands. His children will be mighty in the land; the generation of the upright will be blessed. Wealth and riches are in his house, and his righteousness endures forever … Surely he will never be shaken; a righteous man will be remembered forever. He will have no fear of bad news; his heart is steadfast, trusting in the LORD. His heart is secure, he will have no fear; in the end he will look in triumph on his foes.*

– PSALM 112:1–3, 6–8

One of the traps that is easy for us to fall into is taking God's blessings for granted. The total world population today is said to be more than 6.4 billion. Out of this figure, many don't have enough food, clothing and other basic necessities. To put it in context, Rick Warren says, if you have food in your refrigerator, clothes on your back, a roof overhead and a bed to sleep in you are richer than 4 769 442 362 people in the world. You are in the top 25 per cent. You are blessed.

But being blessed is not an end in itself. You are blessed to be a blessing – to be generous. Generosity comes by having faith and disregarding any form of fear – for the reason that the very essence of being generous is to be able to give of ourselves without fear.

Greedy people are convinced that for them to have, someone else must have less, but generous people invest in the life, gifts and prosperity of others without thought of rewards for themselves. Someone once said: 'Successful people are always looking for opportunities to help others, but unsuccessful people are always asking, "What is in it for me?"'

Always remember that people will forget what we said, and they will forget what we did, but they will never forget how we made them feel in blessing them. They will cherish that good memory of our generosity for ever.

God empowers us through the gifts of generosity. The power God places in our lives is an empowerment to invest in others. When we obey God's plan and his Word, He will empower us to prosper, so we can become a greater blessing to others than we ever were before.

CHOOSE GENEROSITY: 9 MARCH

# You're God's Conduit for Blessing Others

*And you say in your heart, 'My power and the might of my hand has gotten me this wealth.' But you shall remember the Lord your God: for it is He that gives you power to get wealth, that he may establish his covenant which he swore to your fathers, as it is this day.*
– DEUTERONOMY 8:17–18

God wants us to be blessed because we cannot be a blessing until we are blessed ourselves. However, we should remember who blessed us and what for – so that He may establish his covenant as it is today through us.

The above verse suggests that how we handle money is really a test of our character. Our attitude to money and wealth is very important to God. That is why the Bible warns us against entertaining the thought that it is our power – ability – that gets us wealth. It is God who gives us the power to produce wealth so that He may establish his covenant here on earth.

Now, there is nothing wrong with enjoying any wealth God has given you as long as you know (and act accordingly) that God has not given you the wealth so that you can misuse it, but rather to confirm his covenant which He swore with our fathers.

Here it does not talk about our natural fathers but our fathers in the faith. The covenant God cut with our father of faith, Abraham, in Genesis 12:2–3 reads as follows: 'I will bless you and make your name great; and you shall be a blessing. I will bless those who bless you, and I will bless him who curses you; and in you, all the families of the earth shall be blessed.' That is the covenant – in us shall all the nations of the earth be blessed. As Christians we are heirs to the promises that God gave to our father in the faith, Abraham. Abraham was a very wealthy man.

Now I know that tradition has taught us to have feelings of guilt about prosperity and wealth. Many of us have grown up in churches where poverty is somehow identified with holiness and wealth is seen as worldly. Yet the preponderance of Scriptures suggests the contrary. We are blessed so that we can be God's conduit for blessing others.

# Lay Up Treasures in Heaven

*For where your treasure is, there will your heart be also.*
– Matthew 6:21

The mistake most often made by our generation is the belief that money can meet our needs for satisfaction, significance and security. Well, it can't. Only God can meet those needs.

This verse is often misunderstood and used against wealthy people. But whether you have a lot of money or very little money, what you do with it is indicative of what is important to you. Jesus, in verse 19 of the same chapter, warned not to lay up treasures on earth. Have you noticed what we in our materialistic society tend to do with our treasures? We invest it in things – a car, nice house, clothes and so on.

We as a society invest our treasures in things.

Is it wrong to own things? Certainly not. After all, Matthew 6:33 says it is God who adds things for us when we seek his Kingdom first. What is wrong is when things begin to possess us. That happens when our treasure is laid up on things alone and we forget about God in our lives. At the end of our lives all we have are things which wear away and disappear. These things mean nothing for eternity. When we are faced with eternity, we need something more powerful than earthly treasure in order to make it – we need eternal life. We can invest in eternal life while we are still on earth.

That is what verse 20 of the same chapter means – laying up treasure in heaven. That treasure is incorruptible. It will never wear away. And how do we lay up riches in heaven? Through our faith in Christ we enter heaven (our wealth cannot buy a spot in heaven) but through our faithfulness to God and our good works, we earn ourselves rewards in heaven.

In the context of money, we lay up treasures in heaven by using our money in ways that please God. We invest our money in what is important to God. One such way is giving to those who are less fortunate than we are (Prov 19:17).

Laying up treasure in heaven also means giving to God's work. The ministry of the local church and of reaching the world for Christ requires money. God has ordained that this money should come from his children.

CHOOSE GENEROSITY: 11 MARCH

# God Looks at the Heart of the Giver

*And He called His disciples and said to them: 'Truly and surely I tell you, this widow, she who is poverty-stricken, has put in more than all those contributing to the treasury. For they all threw in out of their abundance; but she, out of her deep poverty, has put in everything that she had on which to live.'*

– MARK 12:43–44

There are also various dimensions to giving. For instance, while the Bible is very clear about giving to the poor, it does not mean we must only give to them when we are moved by the Holy Spirit, anointed by God, or knocked down in the spirit to do it. We should give of ourselves always and without thinking about it or the emotional attachments we have to what we are giving.

Then there is also the giving of our lives and giving of our substance, which relate to responsibility, for instance the giving of tithes and offerings. Another type of giving is sacrificial giving – where we give up certain things we are emotionally attached to. For example, when Abraham had to give up Isaac, he had to make a sacrificial giving. There are times when God will move us to do that.

But when we are free in God and at a place where we are not fearful of what He asks us, we will discover how immense God's grace and love really are. Remember, whenever God asks us to do something it is because He can see further down the road than we can. If we could see what He sees, we would then freely do what He tells us to do. But we cannot and therefore we need to trust Him. That is why the Bible says the just shall live by faith.

When He tells us to do something it is because He has something for us down the road that is way beyond what we can even think or comprehend in the present. This is because we only see what is before us. Let us consider the biggest sacrificial giving ever made: Jesus gave his life for us and the Father gave his Son so that we may have life.

The widow in the above passage gave out of her poverty and Jesus considered her to have given much. Giving is therefore relative and is a matter of the heart.

CHOOSE GENEROSITY: 12 MARCH

# Love Gives

*'For God so greatly loved and dearly prized the world that He [even] gave up His only begotten Son, so that whoever believes in Him shall not perish but have everlasting life.'*
– John 3:16

The true measure of love is not in words but in the extent to which one is willing to give. If we say we love but are not willing to give, we are lying.

The triumphant message of the Gospel is that God loves us. But his love for us is not just a message in words. He demonstrated his love for us at great personal cost to Himself. He gave his Son for us. He didn't want eternal death to claim us, so He gave us the power of his love. Jesus sacrificed so we could have life.

There are many debates in the Church today about whether people should tithe or not. There's even debate about whether a tithe should constitute ten per cent of gross or net income. That is all legalism. If we are motivated by love in our giving, we would not be caught up in these debates. God did not give ten per cent of Himself, but everything He had. Therefore, when Jesus asks us to take up the cross and follow Him, we need to obey Him. God wants us all to take up that cross and follow Him and if we do that, He promises to make us fishers of men.

So, if generosity is about being free, then we have been made free by Christ and we shall be free indeed – free to give our possessions, free to release them and free to be in a position where we are not attached to them. We need to make the choice to be God's investors and not consumers. We should never leave a place without giving more than what we have taken.

CHOOSE GENEROSITY: 13 MARCH

# Being God's Distributor

*Remember this: he who sows sparingly and grudgingly will also reap sparingly and grudgingly, and he who sows generously will also reap generously and with blessings.*
– 2 Corinthians 9:6

Generosity is about giving because we want to give. Generosity is not giving as a grudging obligation, where we give because we feel we are forced to or we are worried that people are watching and we try to stand out and be popular.

We need to give with a pure and joyful heart. God loves a cheerful giver. In the above Scripture, the Bible talks about generosity three times in two verses. It emphasizes the importance of supplying in order to multiply. We need to keep sowing and being seed-conscious. We need to keep planting seeds. This is not only about financial giving but about giving in everything we do.

If we want to have friends we need to be friendly, smile, walk tall and encourage others. We must reach out and be known as a person who is generous in words and in actions, in our attitude, in the manner that we receive and embrace others. This kind of generosity will require from us to do the best, be the best and have the best attitude.

God's goal for our lives is to be generous because it is our generosity which reflects the God who created us. In gratitude we are human; in generosity we are divine: 'You received without pay, give without pay' (Matt 10:8).

The story is told of an admirer of the great German composer, Johannes Brahms, who left him 1 000 pounds in his will. Upon learning about the inheritance, Brahms was deeply moved. He wrote to a friend, 'It touches me most deeply and intimately. All exterior honours are nothing in comparison.' Then, in the very next sentence, he informed his friend that since he did not need the money, he was 'enjoying it in the most agreeable manner, by taking pleasure in its distribution'. This is the kind of life God wants us to live – taking pleasure in distributing whatever He has given us.

# You Are God's Steward

*For who separates you from the others? What have you that was not given to you? If then you received it, why do you boast as if you had not received?*
– 1 Corinthians 4:7

As stewards in God's Kingdom, we will recognize that what we have belongs to God and that we are just entrusted with it. God has given us the very breath we have and everything that pertains to godliness in life. When we have that revelation, it is so much easier to be a giver. A generous person is always open-handed, yet never empty-handed. There is no better joy or better feeling than to give to someone and know we have truly blessed that person and made a difference in their life. It leaves us feeling more blessed, more fulfilled in our hearts and more satisfied in our lives.

God promises us that as our Shepherd we shall not want. So we need to be generous people when it comes to the things of God. We must choose generosity and reject greed. No matter how little we have, or no matter how much we have, it is not an excuse not to be generous, because the God in us is a generous God. He will provide all our needs.

But more than that, we need to be generous because there is nothing that we have which we have created for or provided for ourselves. Everything we have has been given or entrusted to us by God. That includes our very own lives. We are merely God's stewards.

Now, stewards are at some stage expected to account to their master about how they have worked with that which was entrusted to them. Even in our case, the day to account will come – the Judgement Day. We have the choice to be good or bad stewards. We are bad stewards when we think and deal with our lives, our time and our possessions as though they are ours. We are good stewards when we deal with our lives, time and possessions in the manner God expects us to.

Good stewards can look forward to the Master saying, 'Well, done, thou good and faithful servant,' instead of being called a 'wicked and shameful' steward. Which one will you be?

# Walking in Humility

*Let no one cheat you of your reward,*
*taking delight in false humility.*
– Colossians 2:18

Humility is being Christ-like – becoming servants to others using our abilities, not denying our abilities. The latter (denying one's abilities) is false humility. Humility is giving honour to others rather than drawing attention to oneself. John the Baptist showed humility when he said, 'After me comes the one more powerful than I, the thongs of whose sandals I am not worthy to stoop down and untie'(Luke 3:16). This is an attitude we must all seek and sustain, though in today's advertisement-oriented society this can be quite a challenge.

But humility is not to be confused with stupidity or dressed-up arrogance. Humility is a willingness to see ourselves as we are – imperfect individuals who must trust in the only perfect One. That is what Paul displayed when he said of himself, 'For I am the least of the apostles and not even fit to be called an apostle because I persecuted God's church' (1 Cor 15:9). At some stage Paul referred to himself as the chief of sinners, 'This is a faithful saying, and worthy of all acceptation, that Christ Jesus came into the world to save sinners; of whom I am chief' (1 Tim 1:15). He also called himself the least of the saints, 'To me, the very least of all the saints, this grace was given so that I might proclaim to the gentiles the immeasurable wealth of the Messiah' (Eph 3:8).

That was not false humility on the part of Paul but good and noble humility – the kind that acknowledges that without God we are nothing. Dr Carmen DiCello makes the following prayer about humility: 'Lord, enable us to walk humbly with you and one another, but keep us from the politically correct and cowardly attitude of false humility. Keep us, in other words, from the pride that masquerades as humility.'

# Humility Is Not Cowardice

*'Now it came to pass when Jesus had finished these parables that He departed from there. And when He had come to His country He taught them in the synagogue and they were astonished and they said: 'Where did this man get this wisdom, these mighty works. Is this not the carpenter's son? Is not His mother called Mary and His brother James, Joseph, Simon and Joseph and His sisters are all with us? Where did this man get all these things?'*
– MATTHEW 13:53–57

The people of Jesus' town were offended by his wisdom and the mighty works He performed there. But Jesus said to them, 'A prophet is not without honour, except in his own country, and in his own house' (Matt 13:57).

Many who are nice in front of us actually despise us behind our back. They are jealous and they say nice things to us but nasty things on the side. But we need not worship at the altar of other people's approval. That is not humility. Jesus is portrayed at times as a weak guy who walked around bare feet with two lambs under his arms, patting kids on the head all the time. That is how many people perceive Jesus.

Jesus tells us to take up our cross, but what about taking up your whip? Do you know there were times when Jesus went into a place of worship and turned the tables over? The Bible says that He had a 'whip'. This does not mean that He was physically violent. Instead, it sends us a message saying that there are times when being nice and going to pray about it will not work.

We should not go and pray about it, listen to it, or be interested in it, but we should tell the truth for once. You see, we can be humble and assertive at the same time. Jesus had great passion, great purpose and great focus in his life and ministry. Indeed, He was the epitome of humility but certainly not of cowardice. There is a world of difference between humility and cowardice. We have not been called to be cowards but to be humble.

# Have the Humility of a Child

*At the same time the disciples came unto Jesus asking: 'Who is the greatest in the Kingdom of heaven? And Jesus called a little child unto him and set him in the midst of them. And He said: "Verily, I say unto you, except you be converted and become as little children, you shall not enter into the Kingdom of heaven. Whosoever therefore shall humble himself as this little child, the same is greatest in the Kingdom of heaven."'*

– Matthew 18:1–4

The greatest people under God's people are those who are as humble as children. Children are able to love and forgive unconditionally. They neglect to see the flaws in others. Instead, they are able to accept all types of people with arms open wide. Children are also fully dependent on their parents. Humility allows us to become totally dependent on God. Humility allows us to admit our needs and problems to God so that He may provide us with the tools to take care of them.

Humility also allows us to see our faults and failures and confront them just like children are able to openly tell you their needs, wants and concerns. Children are also forgiving and not ashamed of what their weaknesses and strengths are. They are open and honest about who they are and where they are going. God wants us to be the same as children. When we have that kind of humility in us, we will be able to appreciate Him, trust Him and give Him the glory.

In the above passage, the disciples had been arguing about who was the greatest amongst them in the Kingdom. Jesus told them, unless they turned and became like little children, they would never enter the Kingdom of heaven. In addition, Jesus essentially told them that they had not seen any greatness until they tried on the humility of a child.

Young children are content with being dependent on their parents. They do not doubt their parents' love and care. We need to do the same and have trust in the One who loves and cares for us – our Heavenly Father. Children are dependent upon and have trust in their parents. God desires for us to have the same attitude towards Him.

# Assertive Humility

*He stood before Pilate and He said: 'You say rightly that I am King. For this cause I was born and for this cause have I come into the world that I may bear witness to the truth. Everyone who is of the truth hears my voice.'*
– John 18:37

Jesus' admonishment to turn the other cheek does not mean to accept abuse. It means not to return evil for evil. Yet, if a man hits a woman in the face, she does not turn the other cheek – she comes to the pastor and we will deal with the man.

If it is for Jesus, we better suffer the persecution and take it. But if we are standing in a line to buy a ticket for a movie and someone pushes in before us, we should not suffer persecution for Jesus' sake. We should rather stand up and tell them they pushed in and that they should move to the back of the line. There is nothing wrong with being assertive, for being assertive is Christ-like. Christ extended mercy and grace and yet, when it was warranted, He spoke the truth and showed assertion when it was called for.

For example, if we go to a restaurant and we order a T-bone steak but the waiter brings us a hamburger instead, we should not pray about it, but rather make our dissatisfaction known and insist on being served what we had ordered in the first place. Also, living small is not living in humility. Many people use perception as an excuse to be humble. Yet we can be humble and proactive at the same time.

Wherever we are, God wants us to be the head and not the tail. We are not Christian doormats. We serve God. We live according to Godly principles. People see Jesus in us and we will get to where God wants us to go.

Sometimes we must live life on the offensive (not always on the defensive). We do not have to live in a spirit of timidity. We can be humble and bold at the same time. Jesus spoke boldly before Pilate. I call this assertive humility.

# Our Confidence in Christ

*Preaching the Word of God – teaching the things that concerned the Lord Jesus Christ with all confidence.*
– Acts 28:31

We live in an age where confidence is in decline. There are many things that have happened and in the process shaken our confidence. At the time of writing this book, the world's financial system had literally crumbled. People who had put their confidence in it were no doubt shaken. Our country's president had been recalled from office by his party, creating a political crisis that saw the party split. This shook a considerable number of our citizens' confidence in our political system.

Also, we have seen too many government scandals and moral failures by those we looked up to as leaders – both within and outside the Church. The dismissal of the Church by the secular culture as an irrelevant institution has shaken the confidence of many believers. Generally, there is a shortage of confidence in the world today.

Yet in the middle of this confidence crisis, the Bible encourages us to preach and teach the Word of God with confidence, just like the apostles of old did. But then, what is confidence? Confidence is not arrogance and arrogance is not confidence. The confidence the Bible speaks about is confidence in the Lord and not in ourselves. Paul said: 'I do not come in fear and trembling but I come in the power of the Holy Spirit.'

Sometimes people interpret our confidence in God as arrogance. We are assured that God will supply all our needs and it is not arrogance to know and profess that God in us makes us greater than someone in the world. We gain confidence from knowing that if God is for us, no one can be against us.

Our saying so is a demonstration of our confidence in God. It does not in any way make us arrogant to reflect God's promise in our lives. However, while it is important to remember that humility brings us closer to being Christ-like, we must never forget that when humility is twisted and perverted, it can bring destruction. An emphasis on humility without an equal emphasis on our confidence in Christ can lead us into error.

# Humility Inspires Justness and Mercy

*He has showed you, O man, what is good.*
*What does God require of you but to do justly,*
*to have mercy and to walk humbly with your God?*
– Micah 6:8

We do not walk around telling God what to do but instead we get into agreement with what God has said we are and what his Word declares we can do.

Humility does not think one is superior to the other, but equal. Once we are able to identify with all types of people, humility will bring with it compassion, love and empathy. Paul said: 'I am the chief of all sinners' (1 Tim 1:15). That did not make Paul arrogant. Instead, it shows him as a humble man who recognized where he came from.

Saying 'chief sinner' means he acknowledged his faults and imperfections. He understood that he did not deserve anything. He knew it was through the grace of God and by giving his life to the service of God, that he became the great man of God he was. We should never in our lives feel like we are superior to anyone else. The only person we should be superior to is our former self. What Paul said came from a position of humility, in the knowledge of what God had done for him.

Some of us are so bad, not even the devil wants to hang around with us. We become conceited and have an exaggerated opinion of ourselves because of the titles, positions and power we hold. Yet, we fail to understand that it was through God that we were able to achieve the things we did. God requires us to walk humbly with Him. Humility is the quality that will enable you to do justly and have mercy. Pride (the opposite of humility) cannot enable one to do justly and show mercy.

CHOOSE HUMILITY: 21 MARCH

# There Is Greatness in Serving Others

*When he had washed their feet, and put on His garments and had sat down before them, He asked: 'Do you know what I have done to you? You call Me Teacher and Lord and you are right, for that is who I am. If I then your Lord and Teacher have washed your feet, you ought also to wash one another's feet.'*
– John 13:12–14

We need to look at the people around us and how they serve humanity and God. Then we need to recognize that only God can give them the reward they receive. If we believe people will come to the ends of the earth to watch us preach or do something of importance, then that is being arrogant and pompous. Rather look at the people's presence at the event as a reflection of their immense love for God – not for us.

We forget sometimes how blessed we are to be in certain positions where some people serve us. In that oversight we sometimes become arrogant. God created us in his image. Sometimes we return the favour thinking we are these special people. But humility is what will keep us grounded. As Christians, we need to love and serve one another.

The act of Jesus washing the feet of his disciples has a very profound meaning. Here is the Master Himself performing a menial task usually carried out by the lowliest of servants. That tells us we should never get to a position in life where serving others is something beyond us. When you come to think of it, God is the greatest servant in the universe. He sustains life and keeps the universe intact – all on our behalf. And this is God we are talking about!

Through his actions, Jesus demonstrated that He would not instruct us to do something that He Himself was not prepared to do. Though as the Master and Teacher He deserved to be served; Christ chose to serve. This is a characteristic of godly leadership and godly human relationships – the preparedness to serve others.

Sometimes we tend to also lose sight of what is proper Christian behaviour and what is not. Serving others does not make us less of who we are. It certainly did not make Jesus less of a Lord and Saviour.

# Bask in His Love

*And may you be able to feel and understand, as all God's children should, how long, how wide, how deep, and how high His love really is; and to experience this love for yourselves, though it is so great that you will never see the end of it or fully know or understand it. And so, at last you will be filled up with God Himself.*
– EPHESIANS 3:18–19

Although we cannot see or touch God, we know that He is real in spirit. When we communicate with Him through prayer, we are able to understand his deep love for us. That love is also evident in his Word and through our faith in Him. The Bible in many of its parables and verses talks about God's unconditional love for us and the many gifts He has blessed us with – as a result of that love. He desires for that love to be reciprocated from us and He wants us to dwell in that love.

He knows each of us by our name and loves each of us for the person whom He has created in us. Like parents have an insurmountable love for their children and are willing to go to the ends of the earth for them, endure anything for them and provide them with every good thing there is in life, so God wants the same for us. He is our Father and we are his children.

Most of us grew up knowing how to recite John 3:16. Our familiarity with that verse has caused many of us to speak so easily, perhaps even smugly, about the love of God. Most of us believe in that love but I wonder how many of us have even come closer to grasping the length, width, depth and height of God's love. Paul says that we can never see the end of God's love nor fully understand it.

We need to allow ourselves to bask in that love instead of just knowing about it. Many a time we rob ourselves of this love and are afraid or shy to revel in our status as children of the Most High God. We need to choose his love and embrace the values and lessons taught through that love in our everyday lives. Then we can have Him working in us and through us. God's love is available and waiting for anyone who is ready and willing to receive Him. Move in God's love today.

# Living Out God's Love

*Your love must be real. Hate what is evil, and hold on to what is good. Love each other like brothers and sisters. Give each other more honour than you want for yourselves. Do not be lazy, but work hard, serving the Lord with all you heart. Be joyful because you have hope. Be patient when trouble comes, and pray at all times. Share with God's people who need help. Bring strangers in need into your homes …*
– Romans 12:9–13

So many of us take love for granted in all areas of our lives. We tend to misuse love in our marriages, friendships and other relationships. God wants us to realize the sincerity of love and its meaning in our lives. He does not want us to love from our mouths by just saying the word. He wants us to love through our deeds. He wants us to use love to restore broken relationships and to live in harmony with everyone around us.

He wants us to be towers of love to everyone who needs love – in spite of our differences. God wants us to have authentic and real love like He loved us when He gave us the world and into that world his Son. In our loving Him, He also wants us to show humility and a Christ-like character.

Among the things Paul urges us to do in demonstrating our love is being hospitable – given to generous and cordial reception of guests. There are many Scriptures in the Bible where we are commanded to do this (1 Pet 4:9). Paul also commands us to help the helpless, esteem others more, make friends with the unimportant and live peaceably with all men. I see the above passage as a model for Christian living. But we cannot do all of the above without the indwelling of the love of God in our hearts. God has already shared his love abroad in our hearts. All we need to do is to live out (i.e. express it). And in the above passage Paul tells us how we can do this.

If we use love as a daily tool in our lives, we will be able to make decisions based on love. This will ultimately be the better choices to make and it will shun anger, hurt, deceit and pain, because of the love we have inside us. But that love must be real. We need to decide to show and include that authenticity in all we do and say, so that the world will function in an atmosphere of love and peace.

CHOOSE TO LOVE AND BE LOVED: 24 MARCH

# What Love the Father Must Have!

*This is how God showed His love among us: He sent His one and only begotten Son into the world that we might live through Him.*
– 1 JOHN 4:9

The greatest gift of love we could ever have received was God giving us his only Son to die on the cross for us. Only if we put it into a personal context, will we realize the magnitude of that sacrifice.

How many of us will sacrifice our children for sinners and wicked people, all of whom are strangers and have turned their backs on us or refuse to know us? Yet God gave us his Son willingly and without malice. Verse 10 of the same chapter says, 'This is love: not that we loved God, but that he loved us and sent his Son as an atoning sacrifice for our sins.' God communicated his love both in words and deeds.

John reminds us that this was God's only Son, yet the Father sent Him. Can you imagine the pain a parent feels when a child leaves? If you are a parent you know how painful it was the first day your child had to leave for school or the day they moved out of the house into their own flat. Think of the pain God felt when He sent his one and only Son. There were no other sons who could be a source of comfort. What love the Father must have for us that He did this!

Jesus shared his Father's love. Despite knowing the pain that lay ahead for Him and the persecutions He was going to face; He still died for us so that we may live through Him and have life eternally. What greater love is there than when you love someone so much that you are willing to die for them, give your life for them and endure intense pain and heartache for them – just so they will live forever with you in heaven?

God has reached out to us in love and wants us to be his children. We can choose to ask his forgiveness, repent from our past sins, move into his love and make Him Lord and Saviour of our lives. We do need to pause and consider this great act of love by God – certainly the greatest in all of eternity!

# God Cannot But Love You

*Because Your love is better than life, my lips will glorify you.*
*I will praise you as long as I live, and in your*
*name I will lift up my hands.*
– PSALM 63:3–4

When we choose to allow ourselves to experience God's love, we are able to enjoy all aspects of the God-given life we are blessed with. His love completes us and fills us so much so that we can only glorify Him and lift our hands to praise Him.

How many of us feel that way when we are in love? We want to spend every waking moment with the person, talk to them on the phone all the time, and never be separated from them. In the same way, when we experience the love of God, it will create in us a new heart which will sing praises to his Name. We would desire always to be in his presence. Fellowship with God is a measure of your love for Him. If you want to know whether your love for God has grown cold or not, check your fellowship time with Him. God's love is the kind in whose presence we should always want to be and the kind we should never want to be without.

For example, listen to a group of new mothers talking about their babies and all the milestones they have achieved. There is so much pride, enthusiasm and praise for the person they helped create and continue to nurture. It is hard for them to talk or think about anything else. God's love for us is the same. Once we experience it, we are filled with the same pride and enthusiasm as a new mother who is in awe of her child.

God and love are synonymous. Fellowship with God and dwelling in his love are the same thing. When you are in doubt or the enemy accuses you of not being worthy of God's love, it would be worth confirming to your heart (and to the enemy) constantly that God loves you because that is who He is – He cannot but love. That is his nature!

# Nothing Can Separate You from God's Love

*For I am convinced that neither death nor life, neither angels nor demons, neither the present nor the future, nor any powers, neither height nor depth, nor anything else in creation will be able to separate us from the love of God that is in Christ Jesus our Lord.*
– Romans 8:38–39

We are so special to God and because we are his children, He will always be there for us. His love for us is deeper than that of a mother for her child. It knows no bounds and it has no limits. It will intensify day by day and it will survive any trial, temptation or tribulation. Even if we choose to distance ourselves from God's love it will not change how much He loves us. He will just wait patiently for us to open the doors of our hearts so that He can come in and make us brand-new in Him.

As parents we are often in a position where we have to deal with disobedient or even delinquent children who may resent us, criticize us or reject our love. Yet it does not mean that we have to disown them or stop loving them. They will always be our children and our love for them will always remain as great as it was when they were innocent babies, not yet spoiled by the world and its influences, but just waiting for us to love them, teach them and take them on their journey through life.

Similarly, God's love for us continues, regardless of the circumstances. Nothing can separate us from his love. Paul made the point very clear. This was a man who had been imprisoned, persecuted and suffered trials and tribulations. Having once been imprisoned, Paul knew there was no prison that God's love could not penetrate. Having had a shipwreck at sea, Paul knew the tragedy was not so great that God's love could not transform it. Having had many trails and tribulations, Paul knew they were not so crushing that God's love could not change them.

Your bad experiences are not so horrific that God cannot turn them around. Nothing can separate you from his love – not even your bad and shameful experiences.

# God's Everlasting Love

*'I have loved you with an everlasting love;*
*I have drawn you with loving kindness.'*
– Jeremiah 31:3

God's capacity to love us is everlasting and eternal. Wrapped up in that love is his generosity, kindness, strength, compassion and guidance which draws us closer to Him when we choose to receive Him in our hearts and lives.

He delights in being with us as our love-giver. Not only does He just give the love, sometimes, like in the Scripture above, He tells us about his love for us. You see, God is not a secret lover who is shy to express his love. He does not hold back his intimation of love and makes no secret of it. If He has to declare it in order to put it beyond all doubt in our hearts, He will do it.

God says He has loved us with an everlasting love – not just any kind of love. The word 'everlasting' means something which will never finish – it has no beginning and no end. Yes, this love, flowing like a river, has its origin in the heart and sovereign will of God, who Himself has no beginning or end. Whereas our love for God can be traced to a particular beginning (when we were saved) his love for us goes back to the eternal past. How do we know that? Because God is love and He has no beginning.

When we choose to receive his love, He teaches us to share his love with the rest of his children and display it in all we do in our lives. Besides allowing us to witness and experience for ourselves his unconditional love, He teaches us to love by presenting us with people to whom we can display his love. These people will come into our lives as friends, spouses, leaders, family and even children. They will inspire, encourage and give us an opportunity to love. The love and kindness we show them is what God uses to draw us closer to Him.

The people God sends to us will help us grow in areas where we are lacking. Through them we will see the importance of love and begin to grow in it.

# He Never Moves, It's Us Who Do

*'I love those who love Me; and those who diligently seek Me will find me.'*
– PROVERBS 8:17

Sometimes we get so caught up in the challenges of our everyday lives that we allow ourselves to be absent from God and his love for us. We forget to pray and communicate with Him in order to feel his love. We lose our faith and therefore also our way.

But God never stops loving us. He knows our hearts and waits for us to seek Him and call on his Name, so we can find Him again. He never moves away from us. In fact, when you feel as though God has deserted you, it is not Him who has moved but you. His place in our lives is constant and never changing. We are the ones who choose to lose our place in Him. But if we take the time to seek Him, we will find that He is right there where we left Him.

God waits patiently for us to choose Him and life in Him, so He can surround us with his unfailing love. We are the ones who put up boundaries between ourselves and the love of God – especially when we are living a life that is not in line with the Word of God. When we do that, we start to become deficient in the areas of love in which we should be growing. This will in turn become evident in our negative attitudes and in our relationships with others. We become filled with contempt, hatred, envy, anger and despair. However, when we remove the boundaries, start to confess our sins, stand accountable for our actions, and allow God to live in us, He will move through us.

He assures us that when we diligently seek Him, we will find Him. God is not interested in playing hide-and-seek with us. We can seek (and find Him) in his Word and in prayer.

# Obedience: the Measure of Our Love for Jesus

*'He who has my commandments and keeps them is the one who loves Me; and he who loves Me will be loved by My Father, and I will love him and will disclose Myself to him.'*
– JOHN 14:21

Jesus spoke these words the night before He was crucified. The disciples must have sat there feeling sorry for Him. In their minds, feeling sorry for Jesus probably showed their love for Him. But Jesus turned this on its head. He told his disciples, 'If you really love me, you will keep my commandments.' That is the true measure of our love for Jesus: obedience.

We often take God's love for granted and believe we can live the life we want to lead as long as we profess our love for Him. But God wants us to show our love for Him not just through feelings or professing such love for Him but by obeying his Word. In order for Him to work in us and for us to enjoy the rewards of his love, we need to obey his Word and keep his commandments, allowing Him to do in us what needs to be done.

He also wants us to trust in Him and his Son and put Him above all else. He wants us to be committed and show humility and most of all seek Him through prayer and faith – so He can fulfil the promises He made for our lives. When we are able to keep that connection with Him through his commandments, He can draw closer to us and affirm our positions in his Kingdom.

Our obedience also allows God to see our love for Him and the sincerity with which we love Him. God is not our part-time lover and He refuses to assume that role in our lives. He wants us to seek Him always, and have the same constant love for Him that He has for us.

If we make a conscious choice to give back even just a portion of the love He gives us by staying true to his Word, He is prepared to fill our lives with every promise He has for us so we may live the God-chosen life He wants for us.

# The Greatness of God's Love for Us

*Just as it is written, 'Things which eye has not seen and ear has not heard, and which have not entered the heart of man, all that God has prepared for those who love Him.'*
– 1 Corinthians 2:9

We cannot begin to imagine the extent to which God loves us. We simply cannot comprehend the greatness of that love. He reveals to us that love in the grace He gives us every day. Yet it is only a portion of what He wants us to have in Him when we choose eternal life.

We are part of God's Kingdom and if we love Him, we become kings and priests in that Kingdom and are entitled to all the benefits which come with this unique status in Christ.

Imagine this: If God created the heavens and the earth, the magnitude of his power to work in us and allow us to live the life we deserve is nothing short of awe-inspiring. If He is the Lord of all, imagine what our inheritance is. Imagine what is being prepared for those who love Him and choose to let Him into their lives.

He has great plans for each of us, whom He has knitted together in our mother's womb before we even knew Him. He wants us to recognize his ability to work in us and through us so we can enjoy the many blessings He has in store for us. His blessings, glory and grace are more than sufficient for us, as his Word says. He is waiting to do great things in our lives.

No amount of wealth or earthly possessions can compare to the abundance God intends for us in this life and when we reach heaven. What He has prepared for those who love Him shall be fully revealed when the Father shall bid them, 'Come, enter, And My glory eternally share.'

# Love God with All Your Heart

*It shall come about, if you listen obediently to My commandments which I am commanding you today, to love the* LORD *your God and to serve Him with all your heart and all your soul, that He will give the rain for your land in its season, the early and late rain, that you may gather in your grain and your new wine and your oil. He will give grass in your fields for your cattle, and you will eat and be satisfied.*
– DEUTERONOMY 11:13–15

Again, God asks us to love Him with all our hearts and to stay connected to his Word, so He can cause blessings to come our way. Of the many Scriptures which prove that God wants you to prosper, this is one of the most definite.

God wants to give you rain for your land. Rain stood for blessings and increase. For a farmer, when rain comes he knows he is going to have a good harvest. God wants you to have a good harvest in your labour. He wants you to gather (be able to save out of your surplus) and to have new wine and oil. He wants you to eat and be satisfied.

As He did with so many nations, prophets, people and disciples who loved Him in his Word, God is waiting to supply all our needs, so we may live satisfied, joyful and love-filled lives. He wants to dwell in our hearts and not just in our heads as a figment of our imagination. God wants us to reach out to Him, connect with Him, feel his love inside our hearts, and most of all, to allow Him always to be God in our lives. He wants us to be filled with a desire to love Him, a burning desire to worship Him and an unparalleled enthusiasm to serve Him so He can serve us.

He commands us to serve, obey, love and accept Him in our hearts. It is only then that He will prosper us. If you look carefully at the above Scripture, the blessings come after fulfilling certain conditions. Too often we chase after God's prosperity and blessings, instead of hearkening to his Word. When we obey God, we place Him in a position where He can shower us with endless blessings.

# April

## CHOOSE PROSPERITY

*And even one life that bears witness to the truth of the prosperity law will quicken the consciousness of the whole community.*

– Eric Butterworth

## CHOOSE TO BE REWARDED

*The true believer is rewarded in everything, even in affliction.*

– Abu Bakr

## CHOOSE TO BE SATISFIED

*Look at Christ, my dear friend: His life was divine through and through, full of self-denial, and He did everything for mankind, finding his satisfaction and his delight in the dissolution of his material being.*

– Mikhail Bakunin

## CHOOSE VICTORY

*You can stand tall without standing on someone.*
*You can be a victor without having victims.*

– Harriet Woods

# Be Faithful in the Little

*'His master replied, "Well done, good and faithful servant! You have been faithful with a few things; I will put you in charge of many things. Come and share your master's happiness!"'*
– MATTHEW 25:21

God wants us to be faithful over the little He has given us. That is the essence of good stewardship. In this parable, God shows us how a master commended a steward who had shown diligence and faithfulness in what he had been given. The faithfulness and diligence was not shown by how the steward kept what he had been given but by how he increased it.

This is how God wants us to deal with the talents and resources He has given us. He wants us to use them productively and be confident that He will give us responsibility over greater things. Whatever you have and however little it is, show good stewardship by using it productively. One way to do so is to give. It is easy to put things on hold and say we will give the next day, the next month or when we have more money. Yet God wants us to give now, pay now, serve now, reach out now and do what is right now.

If we hold onto the material world, we will never be free from it. We will always be concerned with debt, trends and keeping up with everyone else. In turn, this will negatively impact on our emotional and psychological well-being as we allow ourselves to drown in a cesspit of worry, ego and insecurity about not being good enough.

God is not interested in which suburb we live, how big our house is, how expensive our car is or what position we hold. Instead, He wants us to be able to give. Can we give, pay, serve, reach out and do what is right now?

God said in his Word that if we are faithful over a few things, He will give us responsibility over many things.

# Prosperity Is Relative

*Dear friend, I pray that you may enjoy good health and that all may go well with you, even as your soul is getting along well.*
– 3 John:2

What the above verse reveals is that prosperity is relative to our soul prospering. God does not want us to prosper beyond our spiritual maturity. We need to understand God's love and allow our heart and soul to reflect that love and divine promise.

If God gave us what we wanted when we wanted it, it would destroy us, since we first need to develop the necessary attributes to handle what comes with it. God always connects his fruit to his prosperity. We qualify for more in terms of how we deal with less.

Abraham was almost a hundred years old when God gave him a son, because it was only then that he could fulfil the purpose God had for him. David did not just become king. He had to go through all the stages and levels God needed him to go through before God's plan was achieved. Joseph had to go through a process of character formation before he could become prime minister of Egypt.

If David was made king when he was still a shepherd, he would never have had the life experience and maturity he needed to rule over thousands of people and to make the impact he made on so many. Moses first had to go through the stages of his anger and guilt after he had murdered someone and spend forty years roaming the wilderness. It was only thereafter that God used him.

Even Jesus did not just come down from heaven and die on the cross for our sins. Instead, He was born and lived among people before He fulfilled his purpose. He needed to be here for that period of time to feel and identify with what his Father had created. He also grew to love, understand and be moved to the point where He was ready to give his life so we may be saved and renewed in Him.

# Your Well-Being Doesn't Equal Being Well-Off

*'Do not let this Book of the Law depart from your mouth; meditate on it day and night, so that you may be careful to do everything written in it. Then you will be prosperous and successful.'*
– Joshua 1:8

Every time God talks about his prosperity, He talks about the principles, conditions and lifestyle that go with it. You cannot dissect fruit and prosperity. They go hand in hand. If God wants us to prosper, it must come from Him, his Word and his life. In the Book of Psalms, God asks us to delight in Him as He delights in us and in our well-being.

God cannot have pleasure in our prosperity if He is against prosperity. He is interested in the quality of life we lead, not just concerning our financial means but all aspects of our lives.

There is a difference between your well-being and being well-off. Some of us can be well-off and still live in poverty. Therefore, the quality of the life we lead comes from the quality of our contribution to that life. That is why you need to add value to life and not just to success. A genuinely prosperous human being and a godly person both produce an inheritance for their children's children. Everything in life works in the cycle of a full circle. It is true that the more we give, the more we will receive and the more blessed we will be. This includes our children who inevitably form part of the next generation.

We all know the story of the Good Samaritan and a man who was robbed and left to die at the side of the road. A Levite saw him and walked by but the Samaritan picked him up and took him to a place of restoration. He took care of all the needs of the wounded man, even though he was a stranger to him. He did not do it for a reward but because of his quality of life which came out in his character. His character showed compassion, humanity, kindness and a need to do what is right. We need to live our lives just doing the right thing and leaving the rest to God. In time it will be added unto us.

# God Will Supply All Your Needs

*And my God will meet all your needs*
*according to His glorious riches in Christ Jesus.*
– PHILIPPIANS 4:19

Is prosperity a blessing or curse? I think it is important for us first of all to define godly prosperity. Prosperity is the God-given ability to meet any need at any given time. God wants to meet our needs and the needs of other people, and if it is according to his riches, it can never run dry.

Paul directed this Scripture at the Philippians. The prosperity was not specifically related to material wealth but also to spiritual well-being. Once we understand the true meaning of prosperity, we will be able to see that being rich in all aspects of life (in terms of our emotions, characteristics and psychological make-up), we are able to achieve all the things we need to.

When we have a positive outlook on life, we are able to achieve the things we set our hearts and minds to. This may include achieving monumental material success as well. Prosperity allows us to overcome curses, which can be in the form of poverty, depression and even physical illness.

In the Book of Psalms, God says He is our Shepherd and we shall not want. He will make us lie down in green pastures and lead us beside the still waters. So it is God's idea to make us prosperous. If it is God's idea for us to live a prosperous life, then everything that comes from God is in God.

Even when God created the earth, He created it so that all our needs are met. His original plan for us was to live and be in a place of prosperity. One of the things that stops us from living a life of prosperity is the fear related to our security. We become unwilling to give because we are afraid of having less than we should if we give away what is already ours.

But God multiplies that which we have given and in Him we will never lack anything. He will supply all our needs as He has promised to do – and God does not lie. He stands by his Word and acts on all of his promises.

# Life More Abundant

*'The devil comes to kill, steal and destroy but Jesus came to give life and give it more abundantly.'*
– John 10:10

We will never be exempt from Satan and his intentions to take us away from the will and love of God. He will work fervently to destroy our relationship with God by causing monstrous trials, temptations and disappointments in our lives. Even so, we need to stay connected to God and his strength in us. Regardless of what the devil tries, God will never leave us. He will never allow us to face the devil's attacks alone.

Instead, He will walk beside us, with us and sometimes even carry us. He will then restore all that which the devil has taken and cheated us of. If we live a godly life, nothing will kill our spirit and prevent us from receiving our inheritance. The devil will repeatedly try but he will always fail if we stay focused on God. When we allow Christ to live in us, we will experience life more abundantly.

Psalm 23 gives us an idea of what kind of life this abundant life is. We shall not want. God will refresh us. He will restore our souls. He will give us guidance. He will comfort us. He will provide for us even in the presence of our enemies. And yes, goodness and mercy shall follow us. That is life abundant! When Jesus speaks of giving us more abundant life He is not just talking about livening up an otherwise dreary life. He is saying that because of Him our lives will be worth living. Remember that we lost everything in the Garden of Eden. Satan deceived us and stole our authority, destroying our fellowship with God in the process. Jesus came to fix that. He came to make sure that we once again become what God had created us to be – for in the Garden of Eden we had abundant life and enjoyed fellowship with God. Jesus came to restore all that.

# Look after Your Temple

*For physical training is of some value, but godliness has value for all things, holding promise for both the present life and the life to come.*
– 1 Timothy 4:8

Godliness is profitable for all things, but your physical health is important as well. Therefore, it is critical for you to watch your health because God needs to work with something and not against something. Your temple (your body) is something you should look after so God can work with it while you are in it.

Let us draw a comparison between physical training and training for godliness. For any athlete, there are at least three elements involved in their training: the decision to train, diet and regular exercise. An athlete who does not have these three elements in their plan, will more than likely not achieve their goals. Similarly, if we do not have these elements in our race (remember Paul said we are in a race?), the chances of running a good race are small.

Just like an athlete has to make a firm decision to train and stick to the decision, we also have to make a firm decision to live the Christian lifestyle and stick to it. No athlete wins a race without a commitment to their goal. Jesus said, 'If anyone would come after me, he must deny himself and take up his cross and follow me' (Matt 16:24).

Secondly, no runner wins a medal by eating lots of hamburgers and pizza. Athletes watch what they eat. Their diet is strictly controlled, although they live with family and friends who enjoy this kind of food. As Christians, we have to watch our spiritual diet by feeding our souls with the Word and being nourished in prayer. There is a lot on offer in this world, but a good part of it is non-nutritive to our souls.

The last component is regular exercise. To keep fit and ready for the race, a runner needs to exercise. Similarly, we have to exercise ourselves in the Word of God. We should not just listen to it but practise it. James says, 'Do not merely listen to the word, and so deceive yourselves. Do what it says' (Jas 1:22). That is spiritual exercise.

# You Are Abraham's Seed

*If you belong to Christ, then you are Abraham's seed, and heirs according to the promise.*
– GALATIANS 3:29

If we are in Christ, we qualify for the blessings of Abraham. It is important for us to know what the blessings of Abraham are, how they operated and what requirements accompanied them.

Jesus went to a woman with an infirmity and told her that she was the daughter of Abraham. He told her to go forth and be healed. Likewise, it is important for us to realize that if we are in Christ, then we are Abraham's seed and heirs to the promise. Because this woman was a daughter of Abraham, Jesus said she was entitled to healing. Jesus told her to go and be healed.

God says you must go, yet most Christians tell God to do everything first. 'Before I go, God, you must bless me, provide for me and show me exactly what I must do. Only then will I go.' This is how many respond to God. When God told Abraham to leave his kith and kin, Abraham did not ask God to first give him the details of where He was leading him to. He just went. That is faith and if we are Abraham's seed, we must imitate him.

Jesus says: 'Follow Me and I will make you fishers of men', but we say: 'No, Jesus, You follow me.' That is why some people end up with half-hearted experiences of God – they are not in a place where God wants them to be. How many times do we find ourselves in a place where we are waiting on God when He is actually waiting on us?

CHOOSE TO BE REWARDED: 8 APRIL

# Your Prosperity Goes beyond You

*Behold, children are a gift of the LORD,*
*the fruit of the womb is a reward.*
– PSALM 127:3

One day, while he was working, a poor Scottish farmer named Fleming heard a cry for help. He put down his tools and ran to the bog, where he found a boy who was waist-high in muck, screaming and struggling to free himself. Farmer Fleming saved the lad from what could have been a slow and terrifying death. The next day a fancy carriage pulled up to the farmer's sparse surroundings. An elegant nobleman stepped out and introduced himself as the father of the boy whom the farmer had saved.

'I want to pay you,' he said, 'for saving my son's life,' but Farmer Fleming refused, saying that he could never accept payment for saving a life, waving off the offer.

At that moment the farmer's son came to the door.

'Is this your son?' the nobleman asked.

'Yes,' said the farmer proudly.

'I'll make you a deal – let me take him and give him a good education. If the lad is anything like his father, he will grow up into a strong man that you can be proud of,' said the man, and that he did.

In time Farmer Fleming's son graduated from St Mary's medical school in London and went on to become known as the noted Sir Alexander Fleming – the discoverer of penicillin.

Years afterward, the nobleman's son was stricken with pneumonia and what saved him was penicillin. The nobleman's name was Lord Randolph Churchill and his son's name was Sir Winston Churchill.

When we prosper we can place the next generation in a position to go further than we have ever been before – if we stay focused and purpose-driven.

We should not think about ourselves. The inheritance for the next generation is not just financial but also character-based. We must teach children and youth to grow up in the principles of God. They must know God's Word, character and integrity and be disciplined to work.

CHOOSE TO BE REWARDED: 9 APRIL

# The Motive behind Our Giving

*'I the* Lord, *search the heart; I test the mind, even to give to each man according to his ways, according to the results of his deeds.'*
– Jeremiah 17:10

God is able to make all grace abound towards you so you may have sufficiency in all things and abundance in great works. God wants us to have abundance so that whenever we have the opportunity to give, we will, because it is more blessed to give than to receive.

He will place in our lives all the opportunities to give. At the same time, He will test our willingness to give. Christianity is not about what you get but what you give. When our motive is only to get, then we will definitely stop giving because we will first wait to receive. God searches the heart and tests the mind – He wants to establish the motive behind our deeds. Therefore, we should not give out of selfish motives but because it is more blessed to give than it is to receive.

There are times when we may give and give and give and not receive, but it should still not stop us from giving. If the motive is to give because we love God and we have his nature in us, it *will* come back to us a hundredfold. We will pass the test. Our generosity is pleasing to God, who will bless us richly for it.

We can have abundance for every good work we do since his righteousness endures for ever. He who supplies seed to the sower will supply and multiply the seeds we have sown and we will be rewarded with the harvest from it. But we need to make the right God-filled choices to receive those rewards, as every action results in an outcome. We need to establish as well as choose what we want that outcome to be.

God has already assured us that He will give to us according to the results of our deeds. If our deeds in finances are resulting in people being blessed, then He will give accordingly.

CHOOSE TO BE REWARDED: 10 APRIL

# God Will Reward You

*'Love your enemies, and do good, and lend, expecting nothing in return; and your reward will be great, and you will be sons of the Most High; for He Himself is kind to ungrateful and evil men.'*
– Luke 6:35

All rewards are obtained after a task is completed. God gives us the task to live godly lives. He wants and expects us to love everyone, even our enemies. He expects us to do what is right in his eyes and shun evil. It is easy to love those who love you but loving your enemies is another matter.

However, God will not instruct us to do something He Himself cannot do and for which He has not equipped us. He loved us while we were enemies and has shared abroad in our hearts his love – the very same love with which He loved us when we were still his enemies. We are therefore capable of loving our enemies not because of our human ability but because of divine enablement.

God wants us to be obedient to the Word and act on his commands. When we are able to do that, God sees the righteousness in our ways and will reward us accordingly – sometimes much greater than we could ever have imagined.

He has also blessed us with many talents and wants us to use those talents to live, share and move forward in his Name. He requires us to be faithful to Him so He can multiply what He has given us. We will also be held accountable by God for what we do with those gifts and blessings and how we use them. Our rewards in heaven will be determined by our actions on earth. He wants us not to use our gifts to live of the flesh but to live in Him and in his Spirit.

We must also be careful not to lose that with which God has blessed us by refusing to bless others. For as long as we are hoarders, we will deny ourselves the chance to receive the rewards which await us.

CHOOSE TO BE REWARDED: 11 APRIL

# Don't Trade Your Reward for Short-term Pleasure

*Knowing that from the Lord you will receive the reward of the inheritance. It is the Lord Christ whom you serve.*
– COLOSSIANS 3:24

We are not here to please man but to please God and find favour in his sight. And with that favour comes grace and with that grace we also receive the rewards God has for us. We must refuse to serve idols or give more importance to our earthly possessions, neglecting God and the work He wants us to do.

God is a jealous God who refuses to share our love because He is real and wants us to live in his glory. He wants us to understand that our lives are not just limited to the earth but extend after death as well. If we choose to serve other gods, we deny our reward of eternal life.

If we choose to lose our focus on God and instead focus on earthly pleasures, we deny our reward of eternal life and salvation. As children of God, each of us is entitled to an inheritance in his Kingdom. As long as we serve Him, do what is right in his sight and remain faithful to Him, we will receive the rewards which come with the Father. We are the rightful heirs and God wants us to retain our birthrights as our title deeds to that inheritance.

Esau, despite being his father's favourite child, sold his inheritance to his brother Jacob. In so doing, he lost out on the many blessings of his father Isaac. And this he did for a plate of food. Esau placed more importance on temporary gratification and lost his long-term inheritance. The lesson, therefore, is not to trade our inheritance for short-term pleasure.

We are God's chosen people and of all living creatures, his favourite. Yet if we choose to sell our place in his Kingdom, we will lose all of our intended blessings.

CHOOSE TO BE REWARDED: 12 APRIL

# Our Confidence in Him Carries a Reward

*Do not throw away your confidence, which has a great reward.*
– Hebrews 10:35

What is this confidence the author is talking about here? This verse is from a chapter where the writer describes a painful and tragic situation of persecution and imprisonment that had happened some time ago in the church to which he is writing. He wants them to remember that experience and how their confidence in God and in their faith enabled them to stand, how their love and identity with those who suffered stood. This is the confidence the author is talking about.

We are being encouraged as believers not to look at the temporary cost of love and shrink back from confidence in God. If we do so, we shall lose out on the promises and will be destroyed. The stakes are high, as not only will we lose the promises but we will also suffer the eternal damnation of hell. In verse 39 of the same chapter, it says, 'We are not of those who shrink back to destruction.' That is hell.

So we are warned not to drift away and throw away our confidence but to focus on our great reward. What is this reward? Apart from the crowns in heaven, the reward is that which Christ purchased for us – eternal life in and with God. You see, all people will live eternally but ours will be different in that we shall spend our eternity with God. This is the confidence we must not throw away. The writer knows that if we lose confidence in this truth, it would be easy for us to backslide.

We are worthy in God's eyes – so much so that He sacrificed his only Son for us. We must never doubt his love and good intentions for our lives. We need to stand firm and remain confident in his Name and prepare ourselves to enjoy his many rewards in our lives.

# Have Faith and Be Rewarded

*Without faith it is impossible to please Him,*
*for he who comes to God must believe that*
*He is and that He rewards those who seek Him.*
– HEBREWS 11:6

We can never achieve anything if we do not believe in ourselves and if we are not confident that it can be done. Similarly, we cannot do God's work and live in Him if we have no faith in Him. But what is faith?

Faith is what connects us to God. We are connected to God and please Him when we anticipate the future with certainty. This is what Hebrews 11:1 means when it says, 'Now faith is being sure of what we hope for and certain of what we do not see.' When we look beyond the visible into the invisible and focus on what we know to be true, then we are exercising our faith.

But what do we know to be true? That God rewards those who diligently seek Him, that if we sow a seed God will reward us, that nothing can separate us from the love of God, that He will never leave us nor forsake us, that when we give to the poor we are lending to God. Indeed, there are many principles we know to be true about our God. God is. If we have faith in Him and live lives which are pleasing to Him, then we will be rewarded according to that faith and the work which comes from it.

The gift of eternal life can only be received through faith in Jesus Christ – there is no other way. Before we receive it, we have to perform and complete the works that God has called us to do. And when Christ comes again, He will separate those who obeyed Him from those who did not and then He will reward us accordingly.

If we do not believe in God, we will not enjoy the inheritance we have in Him and we will not experience the life we could have. But by having faith in Him, we are guaranteed a reward.

CHOOSE TO BE REWARDED: 14 APRIL

# Watch Yourself and Receive Your Reward

*Watch yourselves, that you do not lose all what we and you have accomplished, but that you may receive a full reward.*
– 2 JOHN 1:8

John warns us never to have an 'I have arrived' mentality. We always need to be on the alert, lest when we think we have got it all figured out, we stumble. In fact, it is precisely when we think we have got it all covered that we trip and fall.

Here on earth there are rewards we get from God because of our faithfulness and our faith in Him. There are things we accomplish this side of eternity, but we shall get our 'full' reward in heaven. It will be a tragedy to accomplish here on earth but never get our full reward in eternity. It is for this reason that John warns us to watch ourselves. This is sobering.

But losing all that we have accomplished is not only limited to eternity. It is easy to fall into the trap of temptation or to make decisions which can actually prove detrimental to our lives here on earth. We can quickly lose everything we have built up throughout our lives because of one silly mistake. Therefore, the choices we make in our lives are vitally important to the outcomes we shall have, both here on earth and in eternity.

David spent years building himself and a nation through God. He was a king, with a powerful army, had defeated Goliath, had killed a lion and a bear and was ruling over a successful nation. He had arrived but made the mistake of not watching himself. Through one sin with Bathsheba and the killing of her husband, David was denied the privilege of building the holy temple of God – the reward which God had originally ordained for him. We need to be wise with how we handle situations in our lives. We can so easily lose what God has ordained for us if we make the wrong choices.

We need to choose to hold onto our rewards and not allow anything to come in the way of our achievements.

# Benefits of Fearing the Lord

*The fear of the Lord leads to life, and he who has it will abide in satisfaction; he will not be visited by evil.*
– Proverbs 19:23

Those who fear the Lord are blessed with many benefits. The Bible encourages us to live in the fear of the Lord because of the many promises God makes to those who will do so. According to the above passage, when we fear the Lord there are three benefits – we shall have life, live in satisfaction and evil will not visit us. There are other passages in Proverbs that tell us about more benefits when we fear the Lord. Proverbs 10:27 says, 'The fear of the Lord adds length to life, but the years of the wicked are cut short.' Proverbs 14:27 says, 'The fear of the Lord is a fountain of life, turning a man from the snares of death.' There certainly are benefits to fearing the Lord.

God does not desire for us to be afraid of Him, but to revere Him and obey his Word. That is what the word fear means in this context. God wants us to stay connected to Him and not give in to this world's temptations. He wants us to realize that, like a parent disciplines a child, we can also be disciplined by Him when we falter and wander off the path on which He has put us.

But if we continue to retain our Christ-like characteristics and live according to his will, He will give us all the desires of our hearts and ensure that we prosper in the way He wants us to. We will always be satisfied and never have need for anything because God will meet all of our needs. The most important thing for us to be satisfied is to have the Christian character that comes with getting to know the Lord and his Word.

God loves us and wants us to live fruitful lives. He wants us to make in impact. So if we abide in Him and his love, we will be satisfied in his presence and not have to endure the evils of the world.

CHOOSE TO BE SATISFIED: 16 APRIL

# The Key to Contentment

*Godliness with contentment is great gain. For we brought nothing into this world, and it is certain we can carry nothing out; but having food and clothing, let us be therewith content.*
– 1 Timothy 6:6–8

God desires for us to be satisfied in Him. He is glorified when we, as his children, are content. Some of us believe we can only be content if we have whatever everyone else has. Yet materialism and money can never bring joy nor make us content.

Too often we think contentment is determined by physical things. When we have jobs, homes, cars and bank accounts we think we are content. But Paul is giving us a very liberating approach to life and one which I believe is a key to contentment. And that is: We brought nothing into this world and will take nothing out. If we have something to eat and clothe ourselves with, we should be content. The basic principle here is that the source of our contentment should not be the modern society we live in. Even if we were in the poorest country, our contentment should not change. But that can only be possible when we liberate ourselves from material things. Mother Theresa left a wealthy and comfortable life with her family to go and live among the poor. The service she provided to the poor gave her the utmost contentment. Mahatma Gandhi could have made a fortune from practising law, but instead he gained contentment from doing a service to mankind. He walked around in loin cloths and gave up the satiety of food so that he could fulfil his purpose. He died content – having completed what was in his heart.

So God wants us to complete his purpose for us and be satisfied in Him, so we can grow in his glory and love. In so doing, we qualify for all the rewards which come in his Name and through Him – gifts of love, fulfilment, contentment, enjoyment and assurance.

# Give Thanks

*When you have eaten and are satisfied, praise the Lord your God for the good land He has given you.*
– Deuteronomy 8:10

It is easy to take our lives for granted and not appreciate how much we are blessed. We forget to be thankful to the One who has made it possible. In the slightest of inconveniences we, especially those of us who live in relatively prosperous countries, complain about all the things we have and do not have. Not for a moment do we think about the people who are worse off than us, instead we carry on and whinge as if we are in the worst possible situation. There is a poem, written anonymously, which explains the simple things we have to be thankful for. It goes as follows:

> Even though I clutch my blanket and growl when the alarm rings, thank you, Lord, that I can hear. There are many who are deaf.
>
> Even though I keep my eyes closed against the morning light as long as possible, thank you, Lord, that I can see. Many are blind.
>
> Even though I huddle in my bed and put off rising, thank you, Lord, that I have the strength to rise. There are many who are bedridden.
>
> Even though the first hour of my day is hectic, when socks are lost, toast is burned, tempers are short, and my children are so loud, thank you, Lord, for my family. There are many who are lonely.
>
> Even though our breakfast table never looks like the pictures in magazines and the menu is at times unbalanced, thank you, Lord, for the food we have. There are many who are hungry.
>
> Even though the routine of my job often is monotonous, thank you, Lord, for the opportunity to work. Many have no job.
>
> Even though I grumble and bemoan my fate from day to day, wishing my circumstances were modest, thank you, Lord, for life.

Give thanks to Him and be satisfied for all that we have and are blessed with. Once we are able to do that, we will see the glory of God in our lives.

# Get Direction from the Right Source

*You will make known to me the path of life; In Your presence is fullness of joy; In Your right hand there are pleasures forever.*
– Psalm 16:11

In order for us to experience the happy life God wants us to have, it is important that we have a heart that is longing and desiring a close relationship with God. It does not matter how many times we carry a Bible or go to church, or how much we try to convince ourselves and others that we are Christian. If we do not have a close and loving relationship with God, we can never fully experience God.

If our spiritual life is lacking, then we will lack in all other areas of our lives as well. We need to have a relationship with God which will fill our soul. Once our soul is filled with his Spirit we will be able to bear the authentic fruit of the Spirit. If we choose to follow the ways of the world and still believe we are followers of Christ, we are lying to ourselves and our souls will be starved of the love, joy, fulfilment and satisfaction that only God can provide. It will also lead to us losing the very purpose God has for our lives.

The psalmist says it is God who makes known to us the path of life. And He does so when we are for ever in his presence. It is amazing how we sometimes look for direction in life from different sources when the Bible is clear as to who gives direction. It is He who makes known to us the path (direction) of life. So, stop asking for directions from man and from whoever has styled him- or herself as someone who can provide direction. Get your direction from the right Source.

It is God who will direct you to the fullness of joy that is found in his presence, and to the pleasure that is in his right hand. You can't find that joy and those pleasures without Him making known to you the path of life.

# Be Content with What You Have

*Keep your life free from love of money, and be content with what you have, for He has said, 'I will never leave you nor forsake you.'*
– HEBREWS 13:5

The world's population is at almost 6 billion people, and the bigger it grows, the bigger our need to survive. But with this need for survival comes an urge to compete with one another. But, if we focus on God and appreciate what we have, we will live a contented life.

Stanford University of Medicine in the United States of America, under the leadership of medical doctor Phillip M Harter, carried out research which asked the following question: If the earth's population was shrunk into a village of just 100 people with all the human ratios existing in the world still remaining, what would this tiny, diverse village look like? These were their findings:

> 57 would be Asian, 21 would be European, 14 would be from the Western Hemisphere, 8 would be African, 52 would be female, 48 would be male, 70 would be non-white, 30 would be white, 6 people would possess 58,9% of the entire world's wealth, and all 6 would be from the USA, 80 would live in sub-standard housing, 70 would be unable to read, 50 would suffer from malnutrition, 1 would be near death, 1 would be pregnant, 1 would have a college education and 1 would own a computer.

So, if we have the small but necessary comforts and we are not starving, we need to realize that we are living a life of satisfaction and that we are richer than 75 per cent of the world's population. Furthermore, if we are in a position to have whatever we want without having to beg, steal or borrow, we are among the top 8 per cent of the world's wealthy.

Many people in the world who are living in dire conditions will give everything they have to get just one small part of what we have. Appreciate and savour every moment of it without forgetting the underprivileged.

# Living Life Abundantly

*'I came that they may have life, and have it abundantly.'*
– John 10:10

So many people have tried to define life, but most of them tend to diminish the meaning of life. There are those who say life is difficult. Some say life is like a box of chocolates, you never know what you will find inside. Some just see life as the drudgery of existence between birth and death. Some define it as a rat race!

But Jesus spoke about having life and having it abundantly. Now, there is a thought: Jesus says life can be abundant. Life is not small in size, as human beings define it. It surely can't be a box of chocolates or a rat race! Life is bigger than that. But that kind of life, only Jesus can give. Anything that man can give is not life.

The car and the holiday house you have is not life. Man can give that. The money you have is not life. Man can give money. The career you have is not life. Man can make your career. What then is life, abundant life? It is not about God giving you all the money in the world, neither is it about having all the material things you desire. Far from it.

Abundant life is about people. We have found abundant life when we share God's love for people and his desire to see them saved. We have found abundant life when we live a lifestyle of service, finding God's life as we give of ourselves. We have found abundant life when we live a life of giving. If we want to see what abundant living is, we only have to look at the life of Jesus when He was on earth. No more and no less. In Him we have a perfect example of abundant life.

CHOOSE TO BE SATISFIED: 21 APRIL

# Learning to Be Content

*I have learned the secret of being content in any and every situation, whether well-fed or hungry, whether living in plenty or in want.*
– PHILIPPIANS 4:12

The apostle Paul talks about ultimate and complete satisfaction in God by appreciating what he has and rejoicing in the fact that he leads a life of contentment. But we prevent ourselves from achieving that level of satisfaction because we concentrate too much on the things we do not have, rather than on the things we have.

In fact, Paul was not referring to the material things of the world but he was actually talking about his heart, which was filled with the spirit of God and its righteousness. He knew that he was never alone even when it seemed like the world was against him. He also knew that if he rested on the mercy and love of God, God would supply all his needs. He also had the confidence of knowing that he had someone to depend on for all things – someone not of this world but the Creator Himself. What better assurance is there than that?

The significance of Paul's words never really hit home until you discover that Paul was writing this letter while on death row. You see, it is easy to tell people to be content when you are living in comfort. But Paul was in prison because he had been falsely accused of starting a riot in Jerusalem. And he knew what his fate was: He was going to get the death penalty. And it is in that circumstance that he tells us to be content in any and all circumstances.

Paul could be content because he had learnt to distinguish between the temporal and the eternal. His imprisonment was not eternal but temporal. In fact, in so far as eternity was concerned, he was a free man. He could be content because he had learnt to discern the limits of his power. We would be much more content in life if we could leave to God the things we cannot change.

# Be of Good Cheer, You Have Overcome the World

*For everyone born of God overcomes the world.*
*This is the victory that has overcome the world, even our faith.*
– 1 JOHN 5:4

When we accepted to have God in our lives and said the sinner's prayer, we were immediately born again. When we are born again in Him, we immediately become victors in overcoming the things of the world. This new birth is also possible because of the faith we place in Him.

As soon as we allow God into our lives, we choose to reject our past mistakes, failures and the darkness in it. Instead, we choose to live in faith and in the light of God. We start to enjoy life because of the blessings which come with having God in our hearts. While the world may be filled with trouble and grief, we are able to overcome and find peace in God's presence. This in turn allows us to live according to God's will. Then we are able to claim victory in all aspects of our lives.

You see, God is not a Survivor. He is an Overcomer. In John 16:33 Jesus said, 'These things I have spoken unto you, that in me ye might have peace. In the world ye shall have tribulation: but be of good cheer; I have overcome the world.' That is how we know Jesus – an Overcomer of the world. And guess what? We too have overcome the world because we are born of God. Jesus is the Firstborn among those born of God and that is why He could boldly say He has overcome the world.

Our new spiritual life in Christ allows us to have victory over our physical lives. With and through Christ, we have overcome the allurements and pleasures of this world. With and through Christ, we have overcome the physical weakness of the flesh. With and through Christ, we have overcome the temptations of this world. He is in us and we are in Him and we have overcome. 1 John 4:4 says, 'Ye are of God, little children, and have overcome them: because greater is he that is in you, than he that is in the world.' For this reason, we are of good cheer.

# Helping Others Gives Us Strength

*What shall we say then to these things? If God be for us who can be against us? Nay, in all these things we are more than conquerors through Him that loved us.*
– Romans 8:31

Through God's promise for us to be conquerors, we are able to be confident about the future. The following story is the perfect example of this:

A monarch of long ago had twin sons. As they grew up, the king sought a fair way to choose one as crown prince. All who knew them thought them equal in intelligence, wit, charm, health and strength. Being a keenly observant king, he thought he detected a trait in one which was not shared by the other.

One day he said: 'My sons, the day will come when one of you must succeed me as king. The weight of sovereignty is very heavy. To find out which of you is better able to bear it cheerfully, I am sending you to a far corner of the kingdom. One of my advisors there will place equal burdens on your shoulders. My crown will one day go to the one who first returns bearing his yoke like a king.'

In a spirit of friendly competition, the brothers set out together. Soon they overtook an aged woman struggling under a heavy burden. One of the boys suggested that they help her. The other protested: 'We have a saddle of our own to worry about,' and hurried on while the other helped the aged woman. All along the road, he found others who needed help. A blind man took him miles out of his way and a lame man slowed him to a cripple's walk.

Eventually he reached his father's advisor, where he secured his yoke and started for home. On his arrival at the palace, his brother met him in dismay: 'I don't understand. The weight was too heavy for me. However did you do it?' The future king replied thoughtfully: 'I suppose when I helped others carry their yoke, I found the strength to carry my own.'

– Author Unknown

# Our Victory Is Not Stale But Fresh

*Thanks be to God, who gives us victory through our Lord Jesus Christ.*
– 1 CORINTHIANS 15:57

Jesus was a conqueror but He did nothing without first seeking God and depending on Him. He did what was pleasing to his Father and fulfilled the plan God had for Him to save his world.

We too need to depend on and seek God and surrender all of ourselves to Him. Prior to us accepting God into our lives, we lived lives of sin and, like Adam and Eve, were absent from God. God is omnipresent but sin can take us away from his presence. When Adam and Eve had sinned, God came down from heaven asking their whereabouts. That is what sin had done in our lives – it had separated us from God's presence.

But as soon as Jesus died on the cross, shed his blood and we allowed Him into our hearts, we were given a new life, which was already pleasing to God. If we allow ourselves to forget our salvation, we will forget the sacrifice God made when Jesus was crucified and will lose our victory.

Pay attention to what Paul is saying. God gives us the victory. We don't earn it but He gives it to us. It is not our abilities and human efforts that give us the victory but God. It is important to keep a correct perspective in this regard because when we have victory in life we are sometimes deluded and think it is because of how smart we are. Also, God gives us victory, not defeat. We should not therefore carry ourselves in life as though we are a defeated lot. Defeat is not what God gives us.

Is it not amazing that the Bible does not say He gave (past tense) us but that He gives (perfect present tense) us victory. The victory is fresh and applies to our everyday living. We don't live on yesterday's victory but on fresh victory. Lastly, Paul says the victory is given to us through our Lord Jesus Christ. We know of no victory outside Christ.

CHOOSE VICTORY: 25 APRIL

# You Have Victory over Satan

*The God of peace will soon crush Satan under your feet. The grace of our Lord Jesus be with you.*
– Romans 16:20

The devil, like God, has many plans for our lives. However, unlike God's plans, his are not plans to prosper us. Jesus said the devil comes to steal, kill and destroy (John 10:10). Only we can allow him to come into our lives and take what God has given us. That is what happened in the Garden of Eden – Adam and Eve allowed Satan to take what God had given them. The Garden was their domain and they had authority over every living thing.

We have to learn to resist the devil so he cannot carry out the disparaging plans against our lives. James admonished us to 'resist the devil' (Jas 4:7). The word 'resist' means to stand against, oppose, or to set oneself against. Therefore, whatever tricks or temptations the devil comes with, we are to resist and oppose him. He secures his triumph against us through deception and craftiness – that is what he did to Adam and Eve, and his strategy has never changed. But we are to make our way against him through courage and the Word of God. When he sees that direct resistance, he most assuredly will flee.

We are enabled to push back and reject his temptations because Christ, when He died on the cross, made us conquerors over Satan. Through his death our sins were forgiven, the curses annulled and the path set for us to walk in victory. The power of God is within each of us, and through Him we can be victorious over all things.

It is only natural for us to sometimes feel overwhelmed by the devil and the things of the world. However, we must choose never to allow ourselves to fall into the trap of insecurity, hopelessness and despair. God's grace is more than sufficient for us. Through Him we have already overcome Satan. All we need to do is resist him.

God's plans for us are far more important than those of the devil. If we choose to abide in God's plan, nothing the devil does can separate us from it. God will present us with all the opportunities to be victorious. We need to choose to triumph.

CHOOSE VICTORY: 26 APRIL

# Buckle Up, Prepare Yourself for Victory

*Finally, be strong in the Lord and in His mighty power. Put on the full armour of God so that you can take your stand against the devil's schemes.*
– Ephesians 6:10–11

In order for us to be victorious, we need to embrace Christ-like characteristics. Jesus overcame Satan through the Word. When the devil approached Jesus with all the allurements and false promises of glory, Jesus hit back with the Word. In every instance, He answered back to the devil by saying, 'It is written.' The Word of God is like a sword of the Spirit.

Satan is a spirit and you can only fight him with spiritual weapons. That is why Paul admonishes us to put on the full armour of God. Satan is not intimidated by anything other than God's full armour. You cannot fight him using the things of this world. Although the devil was defeated, it has not stopped him from attacking the children of God. So great is his need to destroy the work of God that he will try and try again to attack us. That is why we need the full armour of God – the breastplate of righteousness and truth, shield of faith, helmet of salvation, sword of the spirit and feet shod with the Gospel of peace. We are to leave no part exposed to attack from the enemy.

Sometimes we take our focus off God and remove his armour from ourselves. When we do that, we live in the flesh and can never defeat the devil. Our weapons cannot be of the flesh because we are fighting spiritual battles. When we don't have God's armour on, we will never be able to conquer the obstacles which the enemy puts before us. Also, if we put on other people's armour we can never defeat the enemy.

But like David did with Goliath, if we put aside armours that are not of God and choose to remain bold, keep our focus and faith in God, then victory is ours.

CHOOSE VICTORY: 27 APRIL

# What God Will Do and Won't Do

*You are of God, little children, and have overcome them, because He who is in you is greater than He who is in the world.*
– 1 JOHN 4:4

Sometimes in life, we feel lonely and as though God is not hearing us. We feel abandoned, rejected and neglected by the Father who promised to care for us, protect us and love us. We forget the many gifts God has given us. We tell ourselves that we are in hopeless situations. We cry out to God and wait on Him but feel like He is ignoring us. The truth is He is not.

God is aware of every trial in our lives, every obstacle and all the pain. It pains Him to see his children in pain. He desires to see us use the tools He has given us to be victorious. He will not fight our battles for us but He will help us fight them to claim the victory we deserve. David fought his battle with Goliath, but God empowered him. That is the principle. The following poem illustrates what God will and won't do:

I asked God to take away my pain. God said, 'No. It is not for Me to take it away, but for you to give it up.'

I asked God to make my handicapped child whole. God said, 'No. Her spirit is whole, her body is only temporary.'

I asked God to grant me patience. God said, 'No. Patience is a by-product of tribulations. It is not granted, it is earned.'

I asked God to give me happiness. God said, 'No. I give you blessings. Happiness is up to you.'

I asked God to spare me pain. God said, 'No. Suffering draws you apart from worldly cares and brings you closer to Me.'

I asked God to make my spirit grow. God said, 'No. You must grow on your own, but I will prune you to make you fruitful.'

I asked for all things that I might enjoy life. God said, 'No. I will give you life so that you may enjoy all things.'

I ask God to help me LOVE others, as much as He loves me. God said, '… Ahhhh, finally you get the idea.'

– AUTHOR UNKNOWN

# God Will Not Push You into a Corner

*'A bruised reed He will not break, and a smouldering wick He will not snuff out, till He leads justice to victory.'*
– Matthew 12:20

Regardless of how hurt we are, how broken or how bad the situation seems, God will always give us a way out of it. You see, God is not like man. He will not kick a person who is down – that is what Matthew means when he says He will not break a bruised reed. In fact, He specialises in straightening bruised reeds. I like The Message translation of this verse, 'He won't walk over anyone's feelings, won't push you into a corner.'

God does not cause the trials we face in life. He does, however, leave space for them in our lives and allows us to face them because He knows He has given us the victory over them. He will lead us through trials, carry us and help us find our strength in them. There is a lesson to be learnt in everything we face. God does not waste the experience we go through in life, whether they are good or bad. That is why Paul says, 'All things work together for good for them that love the Lord, and who are called for his purpose' (Rom 8:28). Paul did not say 'some' things but 'all' things. A desirable outcome will follow from every situation provided we choose God to direct us to the victory which awaits us.

We will find that even though we thought we were broken, our ability to overcome will repair in us all that was crushed. It will also lead us to God's purpose and love and allow us to dwell in his grace, confidently knowing that He will never leave us alone.

The darkness will lead us to his godly light, but it will also add and equip us with other godly characteristics in order to deal more boldly with further trials. If we choose to be led by Him, we will have victory – emotionally, mentally and physically – to conquer the world over which He has dominion.

CHOOSE VICTORY: 29 APRIL

# Submission to God Causes Satan to Flee

*Submit yourselves therefore to God.*
*Resist the devil and he will flee from you.*
– James 4:7

The worst thing we can do in our lives is not submit to the power and grace of God. Once we choose to have that void inside us, we leave the door open for the devil to attack. And attack he will. He is quick to see our insecurity and knows all our weaknesses. He will use it against us to gain power over us.

We sometimes believe that as Christians we are automatically immune to the devil's attacks, but this is far from the truth. A life in Christ will never be without trials, temptations and obstacles. It is in fact those very trials which make us stronger in our faith and in the Lord. But we need to choose to stand strong and submit to God, his Word and his promises in our lives. Once we choose to take that stand, God will place us in a position where we can have the victory we deserve.

Satan will never succeed in his attempt to bring us down, because we are able to fight him with the power of God placed in us. We will defeat him with the blood of Christ and through the Word of our testimony. When we have unconditional love for God, we will put up the hardest possible fight to stay in God's light. Nothing the devil attempts will be able to move us from it.

But we must be conscious that putting the devil to flee does not just start with resisting him. It starts with submitting ourselves to God. So many of us want to put the devil to flee but are not prepared to submit ourselves to God. Well, we can't have it our way. The two go together. When we resist God (instead of submitting to Him), it means we are submitting to the devil and he cannot flee from us.

# The Lord Gives You Power and Strength

*He gives power to the faint; and to them that have no might He increases strength.*
– Isaiah 40:29

God promises to be with us through everything we endure and to give us the strength and ability to go through it. By drawing strength from Him, nothing will keep us down – even when we feel we cannot go on. He will take us to victory and by his might the very things we thought were impossible for us will suddenly become possible.

How then can we doubt our ability to overcome? It does not matter how tired or how down and out we are. When the Israelites were defeated by the Midianites and Gideon felt down and defeated, an angel of the Lord appeared to him and said: '… The Lord is with you, mighty warrior' (Judg 6:12). The angel found Gideon threshing wheat not in an exposed and breezy place but in a winepress. The man was so depressed and afraid that he would not thresh wheat in the open.

Gideon was faint and had no might. His people had been humiliated by the Midianites. But listen to the Lord giving him an assignment, 'The Lord turned to him and said, "Go in the strength you have and save Israel out of Midian's hand. Am I not sending you?" "But Lord," Gideon asked, "how can I save Israel? My clan is the weakest in Manasseh, and I am the least in my family." The Lord answered, "I will be with you, and you will strike down all the Midianites together"' (Judg 6:14–16). God was seeing something in this 'mighty warrior' that the warrior himself was not seeing – strength.

God knows us personally and believes in us. If God is confident in us, who are we to lack confidence in ourselves? We must choose to see his power working in our lives. We must choose to allow his strength to fill us, his love to endure in us and his mercy to abound in us – for when we make that choice we become victors in his Name. Gideon conquered when he chose to see himself as God saw him.

# May

## CHOOSE COMFORT

*For in a dearth of comforts, we are taught to be contented with the least.*

– Sir William D'Avenant

## CHOOSE JOY

*Sometimes your joy is the source of your smile,*
*but sometimes your smile can be the source of your joy.*

– Thich Nhat Hanh

## CHOOSE HOPE

*The grand essentials of happiness are:*
*something to do, something to love, and something to hope for.*

– Allan K Chalmers

## CHOOSE PEACE

*Peace has to be created, in order to be maintained. It is the product of Faith, Strength, Energy, Will, Sympathy, Justice, Imagination and the triumph of principle. It will never be achieved by passivity and quietism.*

– Dorothy Thompson

## CHOOSE FAVOUR

*Seek not the favour of the multitude; it is seldom got by honest and lawful means. But seek the testimony of few; and number not voices, but weigh them.*

– Immanuel Kant

# Jesus Comforts Us According to Our Needs

*'How then will you vainly comfort me, for your answers remain full of falsehood?'*
– JOB 21:34

Giving someone in despair the right kind of comfort is so important to the healing process.

Many times, in our efforts to provide comfort we end up pushing the person further down the black hole in which they already are. A friend of mine, who was recently widowed after her husband died tragically in a car accident, complained about the well-meaning people who wanted to comfort her but said all the wrong things.

She said she wanted to scream when people said to her: 'Shame! It is such a tragedy and should never have happened to you, you are so young' or 'Life goes on' or 'You cannot stop the will of God' or 'It was his time' or 'It could have been much worse – what if he lived and was in a wheelchair so you would have had to spend the rest of your life caring for him.' She explained: 'I don't want to see anyone who can't smile and share the wonderful memories I had with my husband. I don't want sympathy.'

Suffering is very unique to a person. In the case of my friend, she wanted to mourn her husband by celebrating the person he was, talking about the fun times they had together and laughing at his love for life. She did not want to cry, feel sorry for herself or have people feeling pity for her. She was confident in whom she was and in the strength she possessed to overcome the grief. She continued to live physically without the man she loved because she knew they were spiritually still together. So people have different needs when it comes to how they seek comfort. The only proper way to comfort someone is to recognize his or her need.

Job knew that his only source of comfort was the Lord because no one knew his heart like the Lord did. In the same way, Christ knows each one of us and the unique states of our hearts. He is waiting to move in and fill it with his love and comfort, but we have to choose to let Him in.

CHOOSE COMFORT: 2 MAY

# God Always Watches Over Us

*Yeah though I walk through the valley of the shadow of death, I will fear no evil: for thou art with me; Thy rod and Thy staff will comfort me.*
– Psalm 23:4

In this most famous Psalm, God reiterates his presence in our lives and assures us that we are never alone. He is always walking alongside us and waiting to carry us through the sadness and grief we may experience in life.

In his presence there is fullness of joy and when we walk with Him, He is our greatest Comforter. He will take care of us because He truly loves us. We know for certain that He will watch over us and move into our hearts when we are grief-stricken. You see, we all walk through the valley of the shadow of death when we lose a loved one. Though death to us is a shadow (Jesus has overcome death) and no shadow is dangerous, we are still shaken when we lose a loved one. But even in that situation, He is there to comfort us.

God will never abandon us and will remain faithful to his Word that He will never leave us nor forsake us. David reiterates this when he says, 'I will fear no evil, for thou art with me.' God's mercy, grace, love comfort and peace endure for ever.

The saying that God will never give us more than we can handle is true. He will always give us the strength and comfort to face any situation. But what is even more blessed is that He does not give us the strength and the comfort and then turn his back to us. He never leaves us to face tough situations alone. He will always be with us, everywhere and through everything – because we are his children and He will never allow us to remain hurting while He is alive in us.

CHOOSE COMFORT: 3 MAY

# Look for Comfort from the Right Source

*Reproach has broken my heart and I am so sick, and I looked for sympathy, but there was none, and for comforters, but I found none.*
– Psalm 69:20

Throughout the Bible we are given examples of the failure of humans to comfort sufficiently, like God is able to. Job complained about the vain people who comforted him. David was saddened that, regardless of his stature, he failed to get the desired comfort he required from the many people who surrounded him.

If we choose to seek comforters on earth, we will always be disappointed. The world today is full of people who are so busy in their own lives that they have no time to give to anyone else who may need it. The world is a selfish place and has literally become self-centred. People focus on surviving and achieving wealth and success, so much so that they neglect to see the value in providing comfort, companionship or love to someone who may need it. Everyone just wants to keep it all for themselves and they are afraid of letting go of it because it will then deplete whatever they had stored up in the first place.

And still we depend on people to give us comfort and provide us with peace. Even as Christians – who have full knowledge of the comfort which comes with God – we are quick to ask deacons, pastors and everyone else to pray for us, instead of just falling on our knees and seeking God ourselves. We are too lazy to invite Him to come in and restore us, comfort us and fill the voids which were left by our grief. We choose to leave it up to everyone else to do.

But we must choose to find comfort in Christ and in the Word of God. Also, because we are not of this world, we eschew the self-centredness we see around us. We are blessed so that we can be a blessing to others. We are comforted so that we can comfort others. God loves us so that we can show love to others. Let us never lose sight of the fact that we are God's conduit.

CHOOSE COMFORT: 4 MAY

# His Word Produces Hope in Us

*For whatever things were written before,*
*were written for our learning, that we through the*
*patience and comfort of the Scriptures might have hope.*
– Romans 15:4

One of the best gifts God has given us is his Word. Even in our darkest times, if we turn to the Word of God, we will find the comfort we are seeking through every page in the Bible, which is filled with God's promises and love for us. The Bible is God's Word, a testament of who He is and what He wants us to know.

It is his love letter to us because He foresaw our needs, desires and doubts and wanted to give us the blessed assurance we would need in our daily lives. For everything that we go through in life, we can find solutions, answers and assurance in the Scriptures. So great was God's need to ensure that we would have his assurance and presence in our lives, through his Word, that He gave us a book with 1 189 chapters to find the comfort we seek.

God never wastes any experience. Whatever the saints of old went through and is recorded in the Bible, that is for our learning. Right from Adam and Eve in Genesis to John in Revelation getting a glimpse of eternity when he was on the Island of Patmos, the Bible is full of life's lessons. And that is what makes the Word of God dynamic in our lives – the contemporary application of things that happened in the past.

In every story of the saints of old, there are innumerable godly principles we can learn. Yes, the Scriptures produce in us patience and comfort that we may have hope. Of all living people, we as children of God are the only ones who have true hope – the hope of eternal life, hope of salvation, hope of resurrection from the dead, and the hope of his calling. And it all comes from his written Word. All we need to do is embrace his Word and keep it close to our hearts. God promises always to be there with and for us. This is our blessed hope.

CHOOSE COMFORT: 5 MAY

# Comforted to Comfort

*Blessed be the God and Father of our Lord Jesus Christ, the Father of mercies and God of all comfort, who comforts us in all our affliction so that we will be able to comfort those who are in any affliction with the comfort with which we ourselves are comforted by God. For just as the sufferings of Christ are ours in abundance, so also our comfort is abundant through Christ.*
– 2 CORINTHIANS 1:3–5

One of the greatest comforts we have through Jesus is his own experience through his life on earth. We know that He is not looking at situations through the eyes of his Godly stature, but as one of us, one who walked the earth and suffered greater pain, affliction and persecution than any of us ever will.

He walked in our shoes and understands our pain in the various situations we are faced with. He is able to empathize and provide exactly what we need to be restored and resurrected like He was. The Hebrew writer puts it this way, 'For we have not a high priest which cannot be touched with the feeling of our infirmities; but was in all points tempted as we are, yet without sin' (Heb 4:15). That is comforting to know – that we are led by Someone who has been there before.

The Bible says He comforts us in ALL (not some) our afflictions. And there is a purpose behind that – so that we can comfort those who are in ANY affliction. I have put these two words in capital letters because at times we limit God. We think there are certain afflictions in which God will not comfort us and we want to reserve these for our privacy. He comforts us even in our self-inflicted afflictions. God wants us to comfort those who are in any affliction. It is amazing as Christians how we pick and choose who we will comfort based on the nature of their affliction. God say we must comfort those who are in any affliction.

God will pick us up when we are at our lowest points and raise us up to glory just like He rose. He will move in us and fill us with his presence. He loves it when we lean on Him and leave our burdens on his shoulders, for He is eager to give us rest and to strengthen our spirits.

CHOOSE COMFORT: 6 MAY

# Don't Complicate Matters, Use God's Principles

*I sought the Lord, and He heard me,*
*and delivered me from all my fears.*
– PSALM 34:4

Whether it is human nature or not, we always tend to opt for the more difficult way out of something, before we look at the easier option. As human beings, it would seem we find some sort of pleasure in making our lives more complicated because there is a greater sense of accomplishment that comes with successfully conquering through more difficult means.

And when we fail, we are quick to blame God instead of just doing what He told us to do in the first place. God gives us clear instructions to seek Him and his Kingdom first and then all the basic necessities of life will be added to us. But for some reason, we choose to take the more difficult options by seeking first the basic necessities of life and making God our last option.

He tells us to seek Him and He will deliver us from all our fears. But what do we do? We nurse our fears and keep them to ourselves instead of bringing them to Him. Even though He assures us that He will never fail us and that He will give us the comfort we need, we still attempt to proceed through our hurt and grief on our own, instead of just looking to Him. If we could obey and follow God's Word we would not be entangled in the situations in which we sometimes find ourselves.

Even so, God does not turn his back on us. He sits in the wings waiting for us to come to Him. When we do, He is ready and willing to give us the comfort that we need and deserve. We will never fall short of the glory that comes with Him, but we first need to choose Him so that He can work through us and in us.

# Seek God First

*Be still, and know that I am God.*
– Psalm 46:10

Nothing should give us more comfort than knowing we have God – the Creator of the heavens and the earth, of all humankind and the living world – as our Father.

Instead of wallowing in our sadness and despair and complaining about all the things that have gone wrong, God wants us to be still, to stop right where we are, to stop the negativity in our thinking, to stop doubting, to stop questioning, to stop the ranting and look to Him. Listen to his voice, feel his presence, see his glory and know that He is God – the King of Kings and the Lord of all.

He is omnipotent and omnipresent, the beginning and the end. He is *Jehovah El Elyon* – the God Most High. He is *Jehovah Jireh*, our Provider; *Jehovah Rophe*, our Healer; *Jehovah Shalom*, our Peace; *Jehovah Elohim*, our Preserver; *El Shaddai*, our God who is more than sufficient; *Adonai*, our Master; *Jehovah Nissi*, our Banner; *Jehovah M'Kaddesh*, our Sanctifier; *Jehovah Tsidkenu*, our Lord of Righteousness; *Jehovah Rohi*, our Shepherd; *Jehovah Shammah*, our ever-present God; *Jehovah Sabaoth*, our Lord of Hosts; *Jehovah Tsemach*, our Branch; *Jehovah Kadosh*, our Holy One; *Jehovah Shapat*, our Judge; *Jehovah El Roi*, our God who sees; *Jehovah Palet*, our Deliverer; *Jehovah Yeshua*, our Saviour; *Jehovah Gaol*, our Redeemer; *Jehovah Magen*, our Shield; *Jehovah El-Berith*, our God of covenant; *Jehovah Gibhor*, our Warrior; *Jehovah Zur*, our Rock.

He is our Messiah, Wonderful Counsellor, Everlasting Father and Prince of Peace. He is *Melekh*, our King. He is our Baptizer, our Truth, our Advocate, our Grace. He is merciful, holy and He is the God of Life. Do we need anything else or anyone else to find comfort? No! Seek God first and He will listen and give you more comfort than you could ever imagine. When you know Him in relation to the above-mentioned names, you cannot but be still.

CHOOSE JOY: 8 MAY

# Focus More on Joy Than on Mourning

*His anger lasts for a moment, but His favour lasts a lifetime! Weeping may go on all night, but joy comes with the morning … You have turned my mourning into joyful dancing. You have taken away my clothes of mourning and clothed me with joy.*
– Psalm 30:5, 11

How beautiful and reassuring that is – God's anger lasts for a moment but his favour lasts a lifetime! As God's children, there are things that we do at times that anger God – like when we sin and disobey his Word. But because of his nature, that anger is outlasted by the boundless love He has for us.

God wants us to experience joy which will fill us and shine through us. Yet we become so entrapped by the evils of the world that we aspire not to the joy which should fill our lives but to the things of the world.

As Christians we are supposed to have the joy of the Lord as our strength. We have to reflect – through our words and actions – the joy that the Lord has placed in us. People look to us to share that joy with them. But at times we focus more on the weeping instead of the joy. As Christians, we sometimes spend so much time thinking about what is not allowed that we do not take the time to rejoice in what is. We completely miss the point when it comes to what Christianity is and how we should behave.

We spend so much time focusing on how the other person is not following the so-called 'rules' of Christianity that we forget the basis of our own faith – that it is God who has made us righteous. There are no 'rules' for Christianity. All God requires from us is to love everyone as He has loved us and to have a righteous, Christian character that shows godly characteristics such as generosity, kindness, patience and a passion to minister to others.

By living the life that is righteous in his eyes, we will live a life that is blessed by God. We will experience more joy than we could ever imagine. That joy will live in us, move in us, resonate from us, and therefore impact on the world.

CHOOSE JOY: 9 MAY

# Joy to the World!

*Make a joyful noise unto the LORD, all the earth: make a loud noise, and rejoice, and sing praise … Let the floods clap their hands: let the hills be joyful together before the Lord; for He is cometh to judge the earth: with righteousness shall He judge the world, and the people with equity.*
– PSALM 98:4–9

The greatest moment of joy on the earth was when Christ was born, because He came to save us from the world and from sin. There was great rejoicing in the heavens because never before was there a greater display of God's love for humanity.

One of the songs to come out of that birth was the Christmas carol, 'Joy to the World', which describes the joy Christ's birth brought to humanity. During that time, people had yearned for centuries for God to reveal Himself personally. It was at that moment that the Word became flesh and dwelt among them. The song is a paraphrase of the last part of Psalm 98.

So today, choose to put a song in your heart that speaks of the joy God has brought to the world. Spend your day in the glory of God and in the fulfilment of his promise to us, when He gave us his Son.

Joy to the world! The Lord is come! Let earth receive her King;
Let every heart prepare Him room, and heaven and nature sing.
Joy to the earth! The Saviour reigns;
Let men their songs employ,
While fields and floods, rocks, hills, and plains
Repeat the sounding joy.
No more let sins and sorrows grow, nor thorns infest the ground;
He comes to make his blessings flow
Far as the curse is found.
He rules the world with truth and grace,
And makes the nations prove
The glories of his righteousness, and wonders of his love.

– ISAAC WATTS

CHOOSE JOY: 10 MAY

# Rejoice in the Lord Always

*Always be full of joy in the Lord. I say it again – rejoice! Let everyone see that you are considerate in all you do.*
– PHILIPPIANS 4:4–5

The highest appreciation we can show to God for his grace, mercy and love in our lives is by allowing others to see God's character and the joy of the Lord in us. He wants us to let go of pain, hurt, worry, anxiety and the problems we face. He wants us to have faith in Him and his power to take care of it.

We must choose to be joyful in all things and never let our guard down, for we are victors in the Name of our Lord God Almighty. We have salvation, the promise of eternal life, protection and prosperity. One of our greatest challenges is to experience joy in our lives. Paul reiterated to the Philippians what he had instructed the Romans, 'Rejoice in the Lord always, and again I say rejoice' (Phil 4:4). In both instances, Paul said rejoice or be full of joy in the Lord – not in people, possessions or your position but in the Lord.

Although rejoicing in people, possessions or your position may be nice, there will come a time when they will let you down. Joseph was let down by his own people. Yet despite the trials he faced, he remained joyful in God. Through that joy he was able to forgive his brothers who had persecuted him. He recognized that it was all part of God's plan for his life and something that He had to undergo in order to reach the destiny God had ordained for him.

In the same way, we need to look at the bigger picture and remain joyful always – regardless of the circumstances which befall us and the situations in which we find ourselves. If we look back on our lives we will find that everything we endured in the past led to a greater purpose. God will sooner or later reveal the destiny He has for us, so there is no reason to be sad.

Like the famous song goes: 'Don't worry – be happy.'

# God Smiles on You and Wants You to Smile

*Blessed are the people who know the joyful sound! They walk, O Lord, in the light of your countenance. In Your name they rejoice all day long and in Your righteousness they are exalted.*
– Psalm 89:15–16

Life has become so busy that we forget to smile. We get on with our everyday lives and our routines without enjoying the many blessings and the beauty with which God has surrounded us.

We allow ourselves to become trapped in a cycle of joylessness and darkness, which in turn denies us the chance to shine the way God wants us to. We allow ourselves to feel trapped in our jobs, cycle of unemployment, marriage, singleness, divorce, widowhood, parenthood and in life as a whole. We go through the years without smiling and experiencing the joy of the Lord, which the Bible says is our strength. When we do not let ourselves experience that joy, we rob ourselves of having any hope. We then immerse ourselves in a state of loneliness and fear.

Yet God smiles on us every day through so many things that surround us – the sunshine, the bright blue sky or even the soft touch of raindrops. He smiles at us through the gentleness of the animals and people around us and through the way He fills our heart with love when we let Him in. We need to make sure that we enjoy each day and live our lives to the fullest. The psalmist says we have to be a people who rejoice in God's name 'all day long'. Now, talk about leaving no room for sadness!

CHOOSE JOY: 12 MAY

# Our Joy Is of an Elevated Kind, Superior in Quality

*… Do not grieve, for the joy of the Lord is your strength.*
– Nehemiah 8:10

'The joy of the Lord is our strength' must be one of the most popular Scriptures in the Bible. Yet, despite how many times we repeat the verse, we tend to forget its true meaning. It becomes mere words to us instead of an affirmation of our faith and belief in God.

But if we have God in us and live the life that God wants us to live, we will have the joy of God in us. That joy will then remind us of the promises God made us. These are promises to love, protect and take care of us so that we can leave the anxieties of the world behind us and rejoice in Him.

When we have that joy, we will have the strength to overcome all that confronts us because God has instilled in us the assurance that He will never fail us. Even when we are battered and mourning, we can take comfort in knowing that God is right there in our midst. He will embrace us and keep us in the palm of his hand.

It is good to know that no matter where we go, what we do and what we are experiencing, we are never alone. We are never crushed and never left weak, for the joy of the Lord is our strength. This is a different joy, a joy of divine origin. It is of the Lord, it springs from the Lord as the Source and is therefore of superior quality. What man describes as joy does not compare to the elevated nature of the joy of the Lord. It is precisely because of its Source and quality that it can give us strength.

This joy can be our strength because we know and are assured that our future is underwritten by the goodness of the Lord. Yes, we are confident that goodness and mercy shall follow us all the days of our lives.

# Weeping Is for Now But Joy Will Come

*'... God blesses you who weep now, for the time will come when you will laugh with joy.'*
– Luke 6:21

The only time we can ever truly appreciate the blessings of God and the way He comes through for us is when we go through trials ourselves. When things go wrong in our lives it is hard to feel blessed. We then go through what we are going through because we are living in the moment and cannot see the outcome. Yet God knows our beginning and our end. We may be weeping today but God knows that the time will come when we shall laugh with joy.

There are reasons why He allows certain things to happen in our lives because He knows how He will use it in the future to prosper us. And when He does, we will experience the fruits of those hard lessons. We will then experience more abundant joy than ever before.

He will also give us time to grieve and wallow so in the future we can differentiate between that low feeling and feeling 'high' when we are filled with God's joy. God wants us to get high on Him and He wants us to get addicted to that joy through learning from the lows and letting go of them, so we can steadfastly aspire to the highs.

Those of you who have children can relate to the sweet sound of their laughter. It pleases you as a parent to see and hear your children laughing. The same applies to God. The sound of our joy and our laughter is the sweetest sound He hears. If we choose Him, we will spend our lives in laughter and joy – not in sorrow and rebuke.

CHOOSE JOY: 14 MAY

# It's up to You to be Joyful

*The fruit of the Spirit is love, joy, peace, patience, kindness, goodness, faithfulness, gentleness and self-control. Against such things there is no law.*
– GALATIANS 5:22–23

The fact that joy is one of the fruits of the Spirit tells us how spiritual joy is. There are children of God who frown at others when they are joyful. To them, God is serious and cannot be associated with joyfulness. But as we can see in the letter to the Galatians, joy is a serious spiritual affair. Those who are joyful are not in the flesh but in the Spirit. God wants us to be happy and full of joy. When we choose to have God in our lives, we can develop our faith and grow the fruit of the Spirit so we can be joyful.

Joy is a characteristic that allows us to look at our lives positively and share optimism with everyone around us. God will use the joy in us to bless others who are in need of comfort and happiness. The more we impart joy to others, the more God will replace it with a greater joy in our lives.

But in order for us to experience the joy of the Lord, it is vital that we do the work of the Lord. In the Book of Matthew, Jesus said there are different ways to be happy. These ways include being pure of heart, being humble, being gentle, being peacemakers, being righteous, being merciful and having a positive outlook on our lives.

Jesus tells us that joy is possible at all times and in all areas of our lives if we choose to live according to God's will. Having joy is a choice. The difference between fruit and gifts is that the former require us to grow them where the latter are just given to us. Therefore, it not up to God whether you will have joy or not – it is up to you. We need to choose to let Him give us joy. We must also choose to rest in Him, love Him, worship Him and trust that He will always come through for us.

CHOOSE HOPE: 15 MAY

# Our Hope Is in God

*But now faith, hope, love, abide these three;*
*but the greatest of these is love.*
– 1 CORINTHIANS 13:13

Without the gift of hope in Christ, many of us would find it hard to look forward to the future – even if we have God's strength and love behind us.

Hope is defined as looking forward to something with confidence or expectation. But looking forward to something that we expect someone else to do (even if it is God) is sometimes difficult. We would hold on to what we have in the world, rather than hold on to God and his promises. It is easier sometimes to believe in what you have and can have, by seeing in the physical realm, than to believe and hope that God will provide. Naturally, we do not want the stresses of wondering whether God will provide or when He will do so. But then we are no longer natural – we are born-again.

A famous catchphrase says: 'If you want something done or done properly, do it yourself.' That is how natural people think – that they have to be in control. In the same way, instead of placing our hope in God and then wondering and wishing it will happen, we rather choose to do it ourselves so we can see it happen and not doubt whether it will. But by doing so, we deny the power of God in our lives. It is not us who are in control but God. Let us put our hope in Him. We become hopeless when we put hope in ourselves and in others.

However, when we choose to hold fast to the hope we should have in God, we will be able to let go and let God do the work for us. We must choose to hope and expect a miracle, because when we have faith, hope and love through God, we will always find and receive what we are searching for.

# The Hope of the Righteous Does Not Perish

*When a wicked man dies, his expectation will perish, and the hope of strong men perishes.*
– Proverbs 11:7

God despises wicked men who deliberately ignore the salvation He has given them. Such people choose to set their hopes in the world and not in God. Because they choose to turn their backs on the promises of God, they will be judged accordingly. They will never experience victory in the world or in their lives because they choose to live selfish and ungodly lives. But when they place their hope in the Lord, they are instantly entitled to the productive and blessed life which comes from God.

However, when we choose hope in the Lord and live a life that is righteous to Him, we will experience all of God's glory. We will be conquerors over all things. When we look at the current state of the world – the disease, poverty, war and endless strife – we realize how important hope is. The world is in the state it is because of lack of hope in God. Humanity chooses to place hope in politicians, wealth, success and vanity.

Instead of building nations like ancient Israel, we choose to fight with one another, compete with one another and blaspheme God. We do this in the worldly hope that we will rise up above the rest and be better than the next person. This kind of greed for false power and security has put us in the hopeless situation that the world is currently in. The only way we can create any change is by placing our hope back in the promise of God and in the salvation of Christ.

It may seem hopeless and as though change from the current state is impossible. Nevertheless, we are told over and over that nothing is impossible with God and that we can do all things if we believe in Him. We simply need to make the choice to keep our hope in God. Hope of strong men perishes but hope of the righteous does not perish.

CHOOSE HOPE: 17 MAY

# Fixing Our Eyes on His Grace

*Fix your hope completely on the grace to be brought to you at the revelation of Jesus Christ.*
– 1 PETER 1:13

Nothing and no one is able to fulfil us and give us the grace and love that only God can. Regardless of the relationships we have and despite how successful we are, if we don't choose to live and walk in God, we will eventually run into trouble in our lives.

We were created by God and He knows what makes us stay in good shape. Any car that does not regularly go for a service, at a mechanical centre that knows that brand, will eventually experience problems. Indeed, it may even break down. The same applies to us. God is our manufacturer. No one else knows this 'product' called a human being better than God. Therefore, if we want to stay in good condition, we have to be regularly serviced by Him – in prayer, in fellowship and through his Word.

There are certain things in life, like the sudden death of a child or spouse, which can never be explained by anyone or anything on earth. The more we search for answers, outside and without God, the more we will find ourselves sinking deeper into an abyss of despair and grief. Only God can effectively comfort and minister to us during such times. God will restore and help us find the peace we need.

This is his promise to us. But that can only happen if we fix our hope completely on his grace. It has to be done completely, not half-heartedly. The writer of Hebrews put it somewhat differently, though meaning the same, 'fixing our eyes on Jesus, the author and perfecter of our faith' (Heb 12:2). Then the Lord will ensure his plans and purposes in our lives are fulfilled. God will also guide us down the path we need to take in order to do the things He wants us to do, live the lives He wants us to lead and be the people He wants us to be.

CHOOSE HOPE: 18 MAY

# God Has Planned for You to Prosper

*'For know the plans I have for you,' says the LORD. 'They are plans for good and not for disaster, to give you a future and a hope.'*
– JEREMIAH 29:11

We are so blessed and privileged to know that even before we were born, God had his hand on our lives and had a plan for us. Like any father wants what is best for his child, God too wants the very best for us. God has a plan for our lives. We might try to live our lives the way we please, but we will only really be of great value to ourselves, humanity and God's kingdom when we do what He has planned for us. He has a very important plan for each of us and wants us to find it and fulfil it.

When we discover what God's plans are for our lives, we find great joy in being what God intended for us to be. As a matter of fact, we'll find a lot of satisfaction in doing things we never dreamed of before. There is nothing as fulfilling as doing what you were called or born to do.

Yet, in order for God to help us find the plan and achieve it, we need to have faith and hope in Him. He wants us to have hope and trust in Him. He wants us to believe that we are never alone. He wants us to dwell in the hope for our future and what He wants to do in our lives.

Sometimes certain things may happen in our lives which we do not understand because we had faith in God and his Word. When that happens, we usually lose our hope in Him and in life. Nevertheless, God wants hope to remain within us throughout any trial or battle – for He will restore us.

He wants us also to remember our rewards in heaven and never to lose that inheritance. The only way to keep it is to choose to stay hopeful always.

CHOOSE HOPE: 19 MAY

# God Is Our Confidence

*For You are my hope; O Lord God,*
*You are my confidence from my youth.*
– Psalm 71:5

When we realize that nothing can be achieved in the world, except through God, we will be able to place our hope in Him alone, and that hope will give us the confidence we need to live the best life we can under his authority.

Just knowing that God is with us in everything will give us the hope we need to live. David knew what he was talking about in this psalm. From the time he was a boy shepherding his father's sheep to when he killed a lion, a bear and defeated Goliath, God had been his confidence. We need to teach and encourage our children to place their confidence in God right from their youth.

God never changes, He remains the same yesterday, today and for ever. That is what gave David hope when he faced new challenges. He knew that the God who gave him victory yesterday was the same God today. That is why when he faced Goliath he recounted his past experiences. That is what gave him hope and confidence in tackling whatever new challenge he faced. He knew he could never be disappointed or let down by God.

God will always be there when we are facing situations we need to deal with in our lives. He will be present through all our troubles, as our salvation, as a source of peace that surpasses all understanding, as a source of truth, and as our redeemer and counsellor. As long as we have hope in Christ, we will need or want for nothing.

CHOOSE HOPE: 20 MAY

# Stay in Hope, Your Isaac Is on His Way

*Let us hold fast the confession of our hope without wavering, for He who promised is faithful.*
– HEBREWS 10:23

We must never forget that if there is anyone we can depend on to come through for us, it is the Lord. As long as we remain in his presence and hold on to the confession of our hope in Him, He will never fail us. Having hope in the Lord requires us to be patient and not be double-minded but confident that He will do what He has promised – because He is faithful. God is not man that He should lie. What He promises, He delivers.

A typical example in the Bible of someone who held on to hope and remained patient for God to fulfil his promise was Abraham. God promised to bless him and give him many descendants – except God made the promise when Abraham was 75 years old. In the flesh, it would be easy to doubt God's promise and lose hope – after all, how can someone so old be told that he would have many descendants?

But Abraham held onto God's Word and never lost his hope. He waited 25 years for God to bring the promise to pass. That is why I made the point earlier that hope requires patience, because what you are hoping for could take time before it manifests. At the unbelievable age of 100, Abraham had a son. He never lost his faith in God, even when it would have been easy to do so.

Paul says of him, 'In hope against hope he believed, so that he might become a father of many nations according to that which had been spoken, 'SO SHALL YOUR DESCENDANTS BE' (Rom 4:18). We must have the same hope in our lives and believe that God is faithful and will bring to pass what He has promised. Hope is future-oriented and requires that we indeed trust God with what is yet to come. Your Isaac may have yet to arrive but he is definitely coming.

# Depending on God in Difficult Times

*And hope does not disappoint us, because God has poured out his love into our hearts by the Holy Spirit, whom he has given us.*
– Romans 5:5

Thank God today. Though it is arduous to rejoice as we wait for hopes to be fulfilled, rejoicing enables God to perfect us in ways we are unable to see at the time. And this kind of hope, purified in the crucible of waiting, and sometimes suffering, does not disappoint. The apostle Paul, in his writings, spoke about rejoicing in God and the hope He allows us to have in Him. Paul talks about rejoicing in the hope of the glory of God, rejoicing in our tribulations and rejoicing in God. Paul encourages us to rejoice at all times, for we serve a living God, who will give us grace through the tribulations we face. This will ultimately lead to perseverance, which will lead to proven character. The latter will then evolve into hope, which will never disappoint us.

God works in us – even when we believe He is not there, not listening and not part of what we are going through. Like the story of the man who had dreams about footsteps in the sand – he wondered why through most of the good times in his life there were two sets of prints, evidence that God was walking beside him, but at the worst times in his life, there was only one set of prints in the sand. He questioned why God left him when he needed Him the most.

God replied by saying it was then, through those bad patches, that He carried him. That is why there was only one set of footprints – they were God's. He was safely nestling in God's arms in the difficult times. In our lives too, we may think that God is not there, while in fact He is.

Throughout the Bible God proves his faithfulness to his people by leading them safely through, or delivering them from all their predicaments and troubles. He did so for the children of Israel in Egypt and as they journeyed through the wilderness. He will never leave or forsake us.

Throughout the bad patches in our lives, if we have our hope in Him, He will never leave us to face it alone. Instead, He will build us and make our character grow. Ultimately, He will lead us to victory.

CHOOSE PEACE: 22 MAY

# Retaining God's Peace in Our Lives

*This is what the Lord says – your Redeemer, the Holy One of Israel: 'I am the Lord your God, who teaches you what is best for you, who directs you in the way you should go. If only you had paid attention to My commands, your peace would have been like a river, your righteousness like the waves of the sea.'*
– Isaiah 48:17–18

In order to do the work of God effectively, one of the most important characteristics to have is inner peace. Inner peace enables us to carry ourselves confidently and to face whatever adverse situation without panicking.

We can achieve inner peace by having the right kind of relationship with God and the right kind of relationships with other people. This relationship, in which we have to trust God, obey Him and let Him control our lives, will give us a sense of well-being and make us safe and secure in Him.

But we can lose that inner peace if we do not listen to God and take heed of his Word. If we do not allow Him to plant his Word in us and if we do not obey his instruction, we will struggle to fulfil our purpose – because the inner peace which gives us the confidence and strength to do things will disappear as well. God, through the prophet Isaiah, tells us that if we obey his commands we can have peace like a river and righteousness like the waves of the sea. These are powerful images. A river is for ever flowing and waves always push the debris to the shoreline. That is the effect of God's peace in our lives.

We must also be careful not to lose our peace through destructive relationships with people. We must respect everyone but not compromise our beliefs. We can also lose our peace when we allow fear to take over. We must trust God and allow Him to work in our lives. Let us retain God's peace in our lives – and have it flowing continuously – by paying attention to his commands.

CHOOSE PEACE: 23 MAY

# Jesus Has Given You His Peace

*'Peace I leave with you; My peace I give you. I do not give to you as the world gives. Do not let your hearts be troubled and do not be afraid.'*
– John 14:27

We all experience trials, problems and heartaches in our lives. Such experiences make it difficult for us to find or have peace. Finding that peace in the world is impossible. In fact, when we try that route – of finding peace in the world – we draw further and further away from God. As a result, we are robbed of the extraordinary peace that only Jesus can give.

We should not forget that we are so special that it took God to send his only Son to save us. By sending Jesus – our Prince of Peace – God ensured that we would have peace. After the fall of man in the Garden of Eden, there was no peace between man and God. By dying, Jesus reconciled us with God and now there is peace between us and our Creator. Jesus filled the space between man and God and allowed us to go to the Father through Him so we could receive our many gifts and blessings from heaven.

This does not mean we will not face new challenges because we have Jesus, but we are given the comfort of knowing that, regardless of what those challenges are, God will give us the peace we need to overcome them. We must choose to walk with Him in order to experience his peace. Jesus says He has given us peace, not just any kind, but 'His' peace. He said, 'I leave you with My Peace.' But what kind of peace is that? It is the kind that He had at sea when He was with his disciples in the middle of a storm. Yes, it is the kind He could pronounce on the raging sea when He said, 'Peace, be still.'

He has given us that kind of peace – of knowing that He will protect our hearts and minds from worry, fear and anxiety. He will give us the confidence to trust in Him. The peace that comes from God is a deep and lasting peace, a peace beyond human understanding. It enables us to face the future without any fear.

CHOOSE PEACE: 24 MAY

# Let Not Sin Disturb Your Peace

*Dear friends, I urge you, as aliens and strangers in the world, to abstain from sinful desires, which war against your soul.*
– 1 Peter 2:11

God wants us to remain faithful to Him and in no way risk losing the peace He has promised us. The devil is waiting to cause torment and delights in our misery, but God wants us to keep our eyes on Him. The devil has, since the beginning of time, tried to destroy the peace that is our right.

He tempted Adam and Eve in the Garden of Eden to sow enmity between God and mankind. He tempted Jesus in the desert in an attempt to destroy peace between the Father and Son. He tempted Jonah to run away from his assignment because he (the devil) did not want to see Nineveh reconciled with God. He tempted David to commit adultery and by that single act sowed discord in David's family. He tempted Ananias and Sapphira, he tempted Judas – the list goes on.

He will also try to tempt us through every possible means because he does not want to see harmony between our body and soul. The devil delights in strife and tension – whether between our soul and body, or between and among us as brethren or between us and God. He will even try to mess with our thoughts and emotions but we have to resist him as Jesus did. When we do that we are able to find favour in God's eyes and therefore retain the peace He has given us.

You see, Satan knows that he can steal your peace by getting you to succumb to sinful desires which battle against your soul. No person can live in sin and have peace. Read the psalms and see how unsettled and restless David's soul was after he had sinned against God. Abstain from the desire of the flesh, and when you do so, God will care for you, wrap you in his love and surround you with his perfect peace.

CHOOSE PEACE: 25 MAY

# Adopting God's Perspective to Your Trials

*'You intended to harm me, but God intended it for good to accomplish what is now being done, the saving of many lives.'*
– GENESIS 50:20

We often face things in our lives that we do not understand and we question God as to why it happened. Sometimes we behave as though there is a time limit to suffering and obstacles in our lives. We are too quick to ask: 'Why me, Lord?' Joseph never asked that question as he was going through difficult times – sold to slavery, falsely accused of rape and thrown in jail. He saw his trials, as the verse above attests, from God's perspective.

I have heard many people say after going through a trial in their life, that they would not wish it on their worst enemy. Yet they fail to realize that by saying that, they have accepted their own strength to overcome the trial. They would not want anyone else to go through it because they recognize the pain which comes with it. We know that if God allows it to happen, He will also provide a way out of it.

God never promised us a life free of trouble but He did promise to help us in those times of trouble. We need to wait on Him because God has perfect timing and knows exactly when to intervene in our lives. He will make everything come right in time and we will be rewarded. It is this promise that gives us the peace to face life and its challenges without fear.

We all know that life is not fair and we will all go through battles before we are able to claim victory. Indeed, sooner or later, challenges will cross your path. But instead of looking for someone to blame, we should trust that God will guide us through our deepest valleys and lead us to a place of peace.

# His Peace Guards Our Hearts

*And the peace of God, which surpasses all comprehension, will guard your hearts and your minds.*
– PHILIPPIANS 4:7

We will never fully comprehend the might, power and peace of God. In life, the more life experience we have, the more wisdom we possess, so we can deal with further trials and situations. If we had a bad relationship in the past which hurt our spirits and the very essence of who we are, we will tread more carefully the next time when we get into a relationship. And should that relationship fail, we will be able to endure the suffering more easily than we were able to the first time around, because we have been equipped with lessons from the first one.

Therefore, we must have the peace of knowing that whatever we go through, that same peace will guard our hearts and minds. We need to trust God to keep us strong. We need God to renew our strength, keep us calm in our spirits even when everything around us looks hopeless. Paul speaks about the 'peace of God' – not our peace. Ours is based on circumstances and as soon as these change for the worse, it crumbles.

But God's peace is eternal because God is eternal. Even in the midst of a storm or crisis, God's peace remains unshaken. That is why it surpasses all understanding. Human comprehension says when there is a crisis, there must be panic. God's peace says when there is a crisis, be still and know that He is God. God knows everything and He knows what He is doing in our lives and what He wants for us. He knows even before we do. He wants us to lean on Him and have faith in his ability to see us through.

God knows what He is doing and He is in control. He also loves perfectly. Thus, rather than try to understand all that comes our way, we should rather trust our God completely and give thanks that we have access to his peace at all times. We must remain faithful because He is always faithful.

CHOOSE PEACE: 27 MAY

# Fixing Our Eyes on Jesus

*Let us fix our eyes on Jesus, the author and perfecter of our faith, who for the joy set before Him endured the cross, scorning its shame, and sat down at the right hand of the throne of God.*
– Hebrews 12:2

It is not abnormal to sometimes struggle to find peace. Nonetheless, God says in his Word that we need to keep our eyes fixed on Jesus and He will make us complete. We need to change our focus and concentrate not on our failures, problems and shortcomings but directly on the Lord's peace to fill our lives.

We also need to initiate change in the circumstances of our lives. It is true that God helps those who help themselves. In all the miracles involving man that we read about in the Bible, it was the beneficiary of the miracle who had to take the initiative. David had to advance to Goliath and throw the stone for the miracle to happen. Peter had to step out of the boat for him to experience the miracle of walking on water. The people attending a wedding at Cana had to fill the pots with water for the wine miracle to take place. Moses had to strike the Red Sea with his rod for it to open. God requires you to take action for Him to intervene.

If we choose to stay fixed to the place we're in, then nothing God does will move us from there. We need to be willing to accept his will, his work and his peace in our lives so that He can help us to change the circumstance we're in. We also need to change our attitudes about the situations we find ourselves in. Adopting a different attitude could just be the saving grace to finding our way out of a difficult situation.

Also, we must never stop thanking God because through our continuous thanksgiving to Him, we will be able to experience a peace like no other – even though we might feel like we are in the midst of the worst storm.

CHOOSE PEACE: 28 MAY

# Peace Starts with You

*'Blessed are the peacemakers, for they shall be called sons of God.'*
– MATTHEW 5:9

The world we live in is so devoid of peace and so ravaged by war, hatred and contempt that we find it hard to focus on the simple essentials in life. Since World War 1, there has never been a day of peace in the world. If it is not a big war involving the developed nations, then it is some civil war in the underdeveloped or developing nations.

Statistics show that there are more than 33 wars going on right now (cbn.com), with more about to start. Military historians also tell us that the 20th century was bloodier than all of man's history combined. Peace has been one of the most elusive attributes in the past century.

The lack of peace is not confined to the relationship between nations, but pervade all human relationships. Hundreds of thousands of unborn children are murdered every year and the rates of divorce, suicide and murder as well as depression are at an all-time high. This is an indication that even at an individual level, people lack inner peace.

And it does not matter how many wars nations fight in an attempt to bring peace: peace actually starts with each of us as individuals. It begins in our hearts when we allow God into our lives. Before Jesus ascended to heaven, He said He was leaving us with his peace. If we embrace his peace, our hearts will change. Once our hearts change, our behaviour towards fellow people will begin to change and we will view others as God's creation whose lives have value. This perspective of other human beings promotes good neighbourliness, a sense of community and solidarity as humanity. Only then can peace be possible, but it all starts with the change of heart.

Therefore, we need to make a decision to invite God into our hearts so He can fill us with peace and we can become peaceful individuals, in peaceful nations and in a more peaceful world.

CHOOSE FAVOUR: 29 MAY

# Being Esthers of Our Generation

*Now when the turn of Esther, the daughter of Abihail the uncle of Mordecai, who had taken her for his daughter, was come to go in unto the king, she required nothing but what Hegai the king's chamberlain, the keeper of the women, appointed. And Esther obtained favour in the sight of all them that looked upon her.*
– ESTHER 2:15

Esther, meaning 'star', was an orphaned Jewish child. Originally named Hadassah, which means 'the myrtle', Esther is the heroine of the Biblical book that bears her name. She was raised in Persia by her cousin, Mordecai, and was chosen by king Ahasuerus to replace the vacillating and adamant queen Vashti. Hadassah received the name of Esther when she entered the royal harem.

The prime minister in the land Haman asked the king for authority to kill all the Jews in the Persian Empire after Mordecai refused to bow to him. The king agreed, but upon Esther hearing this, she risked her life and position as queen to go to the king on behalf of her people. She reasoned with him and he overturned the decision to kill the Jews. Esther is a prime example of someone who won the favour of God. She was a person of faith, goodness, devotion and courage. She built upon these characteristics, combining them with a sense of watchfulness. Esther was also devoted to her cousin, Mordecai. Her grace and beauty gave her the favour amongst everyone she came into contact with. She especially won favour from God.

In order for us to have favour from Him, God wants us to live the life Esther did and adopt the values she had. She was lifted up in the eyes of God and became an instrument for God through her devotion and willingness to listen to his voice. She was also able to prevent the devastation and destruction of her people because of her willingness to obey Him. We need to be the Esthers of today and have faith that God will deliver us. We must have the courage to stand up for what we believe and then God will grant us his favour and use us as his instruments.

# Peace and Favour Are Ours

*'Glory to GOD in the highest, and on earth peace to men on whom His favour rests.'*
– Luke 2:14

The birth of Christ was evidence of God's favour on us. He sent his Son to earth through Mary, who also found favour in the sight of God through living a life of righteousness, so we could be saved from all our sins.

The favour of God, the angel announced, rests on us. What an assurance! It rested on us when we were sinners – Jesus had not been born yet when the angel made this announcement. Our sins had not been paid for then. Yet, we already had the favour of God. How much more now that we are his children? The angel also declared peace upon us. The birth of Jesus also marked the beginning of peace between us and God. Sin had made us enemies of God but with the birth of Jesus we were to be reconciled to God.

As Jesus walked the earth, He won the same favour from God through his character and obedience to the Father. That favour manifested in the anointing and power Jesus displayed in his ministry. His ministry had results and demonstrated the awesomeness of God's Kingdom. Jesus wants to do the same for us. The favour of God was on Jesus throughout his life and ministry and it was evident wherever Jesus taught. Those who came into his presence with an expectation and hunger for God experienced his power in their lives. It is God's desire that whoever we come into contact with should see and experience the God who lives in us.

When we are in the will of God, we are able to see things through his eyes. So, whatever we go through in our lives, we are able to wait on God and do what is right in Him. This will ultimately bring glory to God. Whenever his favour rests on us, we and those around us will see the manifestation of his power in our lives.

CHOOSE FAVOUR: 31 MAY

# Receiving God's Favour through Obedience

*'But go and learn what this means:*
*"I desire mercy and not sacrifice." For I did not*
*come to call the righteous, but sinners, to repentance.'*
– MATTHEW 9:13

Many of us believe that just by being Christians we have earned our place in heaven. Yet this is not true. We may have accepted Jesus into our hearts but we may not be living the Christian life. God wants us to have a Christ-like character both for our benefit and in order to please Him. We find favour in God by obeying his Word and doing what is pleasing to Him.

We can never be righteous based on our own understanding, but we can be righteous when we listen to God – for righteousness comes from Him. Even if we do good works, we could lack in our spiritual life and our relationship with God. There are many people on earth who are doing good works, but that does not necessarily qualify them to be righteous. Man's righteousness or goodness is like a filthy rag before God.

For us to finish the race well and enter into God's eternal life we need to obey his Word and not draw back in our relationship with God. However, if our spirituality is not strong and we find ourselves sliding back in our relationship with God, then we can never receive our reward of eternal life and salvation because we become poor in Christ.

We must also be careful not to do good works to score points with God. Our goodness should come from our hearts and without expecting a reward for ourselves. We should love freely, give freely and accept everyone as God accepts them. Then and then only will we receive God's favour that is fitting for us. But again, finding favour comes from making choices which will impact on our lives and on others. We first need to choose to be unconditionally good and lead upright lives in order to receive the rewards in heaven.

# June

## CHOOSE FRIENDSHIP

*What a Friend we have in Jesus*
*All our sins and grief to bear!*
*What a privilege to carry*
*Everything to God in prayer!*

– Joseph M Scriven

## CHOOSE OBEDIENCE

*Unwavering obedience to the true principles we learn will assure us spiritual survival.*

– Anonymous

## CHOOSE PASSION

*Chase down your passion like it is the last bus of the night.*

– Glade Byron Addams

## CHOOSE PERSEVERANCE

*Perseverance is not a long race; it is many short races one after another.*

– Walter Elliott

# No Greater Love Than God's Love

*... God is love.*
– 1 John 4:8

There is no better description of God in the Bible than this one which describes exactly what God is and what being a Christian is about – love!

God loves us more than anything and we are his elected people. He is always good and wants us to be good too. He wants our hearts to be filled with the love He has. That is why the Bible says He has shared his love abundantly in our hearts. But He does not just want the love to reside there and lie dormant – He wants us to exercise that love. It would not have helped us if God said He loves us but did not put that love into action. By sending Jesus to earth to come and die for our sins, God put his love into action. And that is what He wants us to do – exercise his love.

God's love for us is so great that He sacrificed his only Son so we may be saved from the world and its sin. Through that love we were transformed from the kingdom of darkness into the Kingdom of Light and are now called children of God. That love also means that God is compassionate. He sees our pain and hurts. He wants to help us. It does not matter to Him what evil we may have done in the past, for his love knows no bounds and He is waiting to forgive us and let his mercy fall on us – if we choose to confess our sins to Him and trust Him.

He loves us because He is our Abba Father, our Daddy in heaven, and therefore He is also our Protector, Healer and Provider. He has given us an identity and put us in a place of security. His love means He wants to bless us with many good gifts and a life with Him that is eternal. What greater love is there? None!

CHOOSE FRIENDSHIP: 2 JUNE

# Love Is a Choice, Choose To Love

*We love because he first loved us.*
– 1 JOHN 4:19

Love is not only a powerful word but also a powerful feeling and emotion. It can drive people to two extremes. Firstly, it can drive a person to a point where they are willing to die for love – like Jesus did when He gave his life for us. Secondly, it can drive a person to madness – like when a man 'loves' a woman to a point where he is extremely jealous and will not let the woman speak to any man. That is not godly love.

But the love that comes from God is pure and wholesome. God's love will not drive you to madness but to acts of compassion and consideration for others. We are able to feel that kind of love and share it with everyone around us – or that is what God hopes we will do.

Love is also a choice – a choice to be set free by putting the needs of others ahead of our own. Love is sacrificial; a choice to give of yourself without expecting anything in return and a choice to love with all you have without malice. Frankly, when we walked away from God there was nothing He could lose by not pursuing us. God is self-sufficient and complete in Himself. But He chose to pursue us and put our needs (for salvation) ahead of Himself.

God loves us so much that He has given us a new nature which allows us to love others sacrificially and unconditionally, regardless of how much love we get in return. God wants us to grow in love and continue receiving his love. He wants us to be grounded in his love.

As they say: 'Love makes the world go around.' If we have the love of the Lord in us, we will be able to shine in that love and start a wave of love to surround the families of the world.

CHOOSE FRIENDSHIP: 3 JUNE

# Love: the Key to Producing the Fruit of the Spirit

*But from everlasting to everlasting the* Lord's *love is with those who fear him …*
– Psalm 103:17

God is with us, leading us, guiding us, loving us, providing for us – all with his unlimited resources. What do we need? Do we need strength, peace, love, joy, or hope? He has it all. He is longing to pour out his favor and blessing upon us. We need to be open to Him and to trust Him. We need, by faith, to receive what He has for us. It is essential that we realize how much He loves us and that He has a good purpose and plan for us.

Once we experience the love of God, receive it, and respond to it, we will develop a godly character that is pleasing to Him. And when we are changed as new people, we are able to live according to his will and commands, the greatest of which is to love Him and our neighbours as we love ourselves.

With this love come the fruit of the Spirit, which are joy, peace, patience, kindness, goodness, self-control, faithfulness and gentleness. Today's verse says if we need these fruit of the Spirit, God has them all. All of these can be produced if we walk in love. For example, having patience with someone is not difficult if you love that person. Also, being faithful comes naturally when you walk in love. For example, the spouse who loves their partner will be faithful to them.

When we are able to bear that fruit, then our lives will be a testimony and can affect the people around us. The fruit of the Spirit are never just for us to enjoy – they always impact other people's lives. Peace, for example, is important in so far as your relationship with others is concerned. The same applies to kindness, goodness, gentleness and all the other fruit.

The devil will always try to prevent us from experiencing or walking in God's love by reminding us about past hurts, rejections and disappointments. Even so, we must never allow these thoughts to deny us the love of God. His love will allow us to forgive, accept and repent. It will also allow us to live less selfishly by helping and loving those in need.

# Love Is a Verb, a Doing Word

*... love one another deeply.*
– 1 PETER 1:22

This kind of love is not a noun, not an adjective, it is a verb. It is a very deliberate action. That is the love of our Father and the love He wants us to have for one another. A verb is referred to as a 'doing word', a word of action, and that is how God wants us to see love. He does not want us to hoard it and keep it inside just as an emotion. Instead, He wants us to use the love He has so graciously given us to help, comfort and support others.

The greatest lesson we can learn from the Bible is to love everyone as God loves us. When we are able to understand this kind of love, we will be able to embrace other virtues that come with it. When Jesus died on the cross, it was his love that enabled Him to say: 'Father, forgive them.' Even in his worst pain, He still begged for mercy for those who caused the afflictions on Him. If we can show the same love, the world will be a better place. The following description of love says it all:

> Perfect love is gentle and teachable, kind and easy to be entreated. It enters the school of Christ, as a pupil, not as a master, realizing how much is yet to be learnt, rather than how much has been attained. Perfect love shows us our ignorance and begets the inextinguishable desire to dissipate that darkness, and to enter the realm of real and reliable knowledge. If you find yourself growing wise above all your teachers, inclined to become dogmatic, to criticize your fellow disciples and set yourself up as a standard for the whole church, you have no little reason to fear that you are not controlled by the Spirit of God. Self-wisdom may easily assume the place of divine wisdom; and Satan may appear as an angel of light even in one who concerns himself with the most holy things. In no way are his ends more effectually secured than by inducing people to promote the subject of holiness by exceptional methods, and in an unreachable and arrogant spirit.
>
> – SOURCE UNKNOWN

CHOOSE FRIENDSHIP: 5 JUNE

# Love Puts the Interest of Others First

*Rather, in humility value others above yourselves …*
– PHILIPPIANS 2:3

Love is such a real emotion that it impacts greatly on our actions and reactions to the world.

Do you remember the story of Solomon and the two mothers who came to him with a baby? They lived in the same house and both had babies within a few days of each other. But one child died and the mothers both insisted that the child that was alive was theirs.

Solomon knew that the only way to come to a solution was through a test of love. He ordered for a sword to be brought to him. He then asked for the child to be cut in two so each woman could get a half. While one woman thought it was the best idea, the other was filled with compassion for her son and begged the king not to kill the child but to let the other woman have him instead. The king gave her the baby, confident that only a mother's love for her child could allow her to give him up just to save him.

In life, we will also be put through tests of love. Those of us who have children know exactly what it means to go through a test of love. So do those who are married. As long as you are a human being and have people around you, whether it is in church or in the workplace, you will go through tests of love. If we never lose that love, we will not only pass the tests but will, like the mother in the story, also find grace and victory before God.

King Solomon knew that motherly love would put the best interest of the child first by sacrificing whatever it took to save the child. This defines love – the choice to put another person's best interest first. That is what God did. He put our interest first and did whatever it took – the death of his Son – to save us.

CHOOSE FRIENDSHIP: 6 JUNE

# God's Love Is Blind to Our Unrighteousness

*But God commands His love for us, in that, while we were yet sinners, Christ died for us.*
– Romans 5:8

Is it not wonderful to know that God accepted us just as we were and allowed Jesus to die for us, regardless of our sin? Would it not be wonderful if we could have the same kind of love? God's love is not meant for perfect people. Martin Luther described Christian love as:

> Love [that] does not let itself be embittered, does not cease to love, does not cease to do well, and does not cease to put up with evil. In short, love cannot hate or be hostile to anyone. No one can commit greater evils than love can bear. No one can commit more sins against it, than love can cover. It cannot be so highly enraged that it refuses to forgive. It acts like a mother does toward a child who is sickly, foul, and filthy. She has no eyes for these defects, even though she sees them. Love makes her blind. In fact, the eyes with which she looks upon her child, as a beautiful fruit of her body, given by God, are so pure that she is unmindful of all the imperfections and considers them as nothing. She even excuses and adorns them. If the child is far sighted, it must not be said to squint, but to wink cutely with its eyes. Even a wart must be considered very becoming.

That is exactly how God views us. He is unmindful of our unrighteousness. That is why He calls us his righteousness.

What is Christian love? As Christians, the kind of love Martin Luther describes here is exactly the kind of love that God wants us to have – a love that is unconditional and has no expectation, ulterior motives or conditions. Christian love is a daily choice and an imperative to a Christ-like character.

CHOOSE FRIENDSHIP: 7 JUNE

# Taking God's Love beyond Our Circle

*For Christ's love compels us, because we are convinced that one died for all, and therefore all died.*
– 2 CORINTHIANS 5:14

One of the words Christians like to use in reference to the unsaved is 'heathen'. Often, we use the word in a derogatory and arrogant context. As Christians, it is sometimes easy for us to be prejudiced against anyone who does not fit into our perfect 'Christian' circle. And because of that mindset, we confine ourselves only to 'Christian' people. We surround ourselves with those who belong to our 'Christian subculture' and live our lives thinking that we are superior to everyone else.

But that is not what God wants us to do. God does not want us to have a superiority complex over any person but to have a 'Christ-like complex'. His desire is that we should increasingly conform to Christ's character. His love ought to compel us to love everyone. Jesus did not die for Christians. He died for everyone – us the former heathens and those we still refer to as such.

As Christians, we need to show the same kind of love towards everyone by accepting them as they are – whether they are saved or not. We must stop the habit of only being with believers because we do not want to be seen with so-called 'heathens'. How can we make a difference if we refuse to move out of the 'saved' circle we are in? We should not waste all our love on the 'saved'. They already have God's love. Rather, like Jesus, we should go into the world and impart love to everyone.

Jesus walked among the poor, wicked, prostitutes and those living in the worst kind of sin and yet He still loved and accepted them. He knew that if He showed them love, they would experience the Father's love. We need to move outside of ourselves, our mindsets and current circles to be among the world. We need to show people in the world how honoured, special and privileged they are and that Jesus loved them enough to die for them – despite their sins.

CHOOSE OBEDIENCE: 8 JUNE

# Obedience, That's What It's About

*Whoever has My commands and obeys them,*
*he is the one who loves Me.*
– JOHN 14:21

One of the best ways for us to show God our love for Him and to live the best possible life in Him is to obey his Word. His Word has many life lessons, rules and commandments which, if we obey them, will ensure that we lead prosperous and God-filled lives.

Obedience was one of the most repeated teachings of Jesus. He urged his disciples to obey his commandments and his Word. When we do that, we make it possible for God's purpose for our lives to be fulfilled. Imagine what the world would be like if some of the great heroes of faith chose not to obey God?

Abraham obeyed God despite his misgivings and loss of comfort and security. He left his country and was prepared to sacrifice his son Isaac as God had commanded him. He was therefore blessed beyond comprehension and ultimately became known as the father of all nations because of his obedience to God. Noah, despite being ridiculed, also put his faith in God and obeyed Him. That obedience saved his family at a time when the world was full of sin. Jacob was also blessed when he obeyed God. He had the honour of God changing his Name from Jacob to Israel (the loved one of God).

Various books in the Bible, like Leviticus and Deuteronomy, are about obedience to God. By keeping God's commands and following his instruction, the people referred to in these books were blessed in body, mind and spirit. Joshua and Moses obeyed God despite their shortcomings and were blessed by Him. Daniel, Joseph, Jesus, Mary, David, Solomon, Ruth, Esther and so many others all obeyed God and He gave them great honour and blessings in his Name.

If we want to be in God's favour and love, the best way to achieve that is through obedience to Him. Our obedience is the sign of our faith in Him and an expression of our love for Him. So, choose to be obedient and live in God's grace.

CHOOSE OBEDIENCE: 9 JUNE

# Obedience Is Better Than Sacrifice

*And Samuel said, 'Hath the LORD as great delight in burnt offerings and sacrifices, as in obeying the voice of the LORD? Behold, to obey is better than sacrifice, and to hearken than the fat of rams.'*
– 1 SAMUEL 15:22

The worst thing we can do is to disobey God. When we do that, we will be judged because our disobedience is a blatant display of our disregard for God, our lack of faith in Him and our lack of love for Him.

After the many sacrifices God has made to ensure that we are saved and blessed, the greatest non-appreciation we can show is not to obey his laws. Our disobedience also leads to us living ungodly lives and being absent from God's presence and his will for us.

Adam and Eve were the first to disobey God by eating the forbidden fruit. God was angry because He had created them and given them a perfect paradise to live in but they were ungrateful and chose to disobey Him. They were consequently banished from the Garden of Eden and sent out into the world to toil and work in order to survive.

Cain was punished for killing his brother, and so were the Israelites, when they disobeyed God. David fell short of the glory of God when he sinned. So many of God's greatest prophets were first blessed when they obeyed God and then punished when they disobeyed Him.

The above passage records the circumstances that led to God's rejection of Saul, the first king of Israel. Saul had been instructed through the prophet Samuel to enact complete judgement upon the Amalekites. This was because of what the Amalekites had done to the Israelites years before, when they came up from Egypt. But Saul disobeyed God. He spared Agag and the best of the sheep and cattle, the fat calves and lambs – everything that was good. Because of his disobedience, the Lord rejected Saul as king (1 Sam 15:23).

Often our disobedience comes after God has blessed us. We then become engrossed in those blessings and lose sight of who blessed us and why we were blessed in the first place. We need to choose to be obedient in all aspects in our lives so the blessings can remain constant.

CHOOSE OBEDIENCE: 10 JUNE

# Accepting God's Terms and Conditions

*Now that you have purified yourselves by obeying the truth so that you have sincere love for your brothers, love one another deeply, from the heart. For you have been born again, not of perishable seed, but of imperishable, through the living and enduring word of God.*
– 1 PETER 1:22–23

Although Jesus died to save us from sin, the only way we can truly be saved is through obeying God's truth. It is the only way we can have the salvation God intends for us to have. We have to be obliging to his commands. Obedience is essential to our lives in God and the rewards He has stored up for us. To accept God we have to accept his terms.

The passage above says we purify ourselves by obeying the truth. But what is truth? It is the Word of God. When we obey the Word of God, it is like applying soap on dirt – it purifies us, and for a purpose. It is when we are purified that we can have sincere love for our brothers and sisters in Christ.

Imagine one of us wanted to buy our dream house but did not have that amount of cash to purchase it. The best way would be to take a home loan from the bank. How it works is that an application has to be made first to establish whether we qualify for it. Then we have to prove that we are able to honour it and then we have to commit to abide by the terms and conditions which come with it. So great is our desire for that house that we go through the entire process. However, we have to adhere to the terms and conditions that come with it. If we ignore them, we would firstly not qualify, then not get the money and not achieve our goal of owning a house. But when we accept those terms and conditions, we will be able to receive the money as well as purchase our dream house.

In the same way, in order to qualify for our rewards, we need to honour God and obey his Word by complying with the terms and conditions in his commandments and instructions in the Bible.

CHOOSE OBEDIENCE: 11 JUNE

# Jonah: Lessons in Obedience and Disobedience

*God commands us to believe in Jesus; we must keep His commands to abide in Him. If we recognize the importance of faith, we must recognize the importance of obedience, since faith itself is a command from God that we must obey.*
– 1 JOHN 3:23–24

Having faith is vital to obedience. God commands us to have faith. If we choose to be faithless, we have effectively made a choice to disobey God. The Bible says without faith it is impossible to please God.

Let us look at Jonah. He chose to be faithless and disobey God because he looked at his own strength and did not believe he was capable of doing the work that God wanted him to do. He did not have the faith that Nineveh could be saved. If we were all capable to do what God has called us to do, we would not need Him. It is in Him and through Him that we have the strength to do what He has called us to do.

Jonah failed to grasp this truth and that is why he was intimidated by the task before him. He decided to run away from his assignment and God became angry with him because of his disobedience. Although Jonah hid on a boat, God revealed him to the crew. God sent a storm which put fear in them. Jonah was thrown off the boat and was swallowed by a whale. While he was in the whale's belly, God gave him time to reflect and understand his power. Finally the whale spewed him out on dry land and Jonah promised to obey God.

In the same way, we cannot run away from the purpose God has for us. It will always catch up with us. And the more we run, the harder our lives become. Yet, if we remain faithful and obey his Word, commandments and instructions, God will enable, empower and render us worthy of doing what He wants us to do. We will then be capable to do all things in his Name and live a life that is both rewarding for us and pleasing to God.

CHOOSE OBEDIENCE: 12 JUNE

# Repentance Is a Command

*God commands all men everywhere to repent.*
*So, repentance is a command that must be obeyed.*
– ACTS 17:30

Another way to obey God is to repent your sin. God wants us to be accountable and responsible for the lives we lead and the choices we make. We cannot just confess to the Lordship of Jesus and call ourselves God's children if we do not first let go of the past lives we led. Repentance means making a U-turn and refusing to live a sinful life.

If we do not repent, we can never walk in the life of God and become new creatures in Him. We have to first choose to repent, confess our sins and make a commitment to change in order to inherit what God has for us. So repentance is a choice we have to make to walk away from our past. This means we have to acknowledge our sinful state, ask for forgiveness and then invite the presence of God in our lives. Thereafter, we have to learn his Word and live according to his commandments.

Repentance does not stop when we become children of God. Even as we walk this journey of faith, there are instances when we will miss God. Instead of running away from God, we have to run to Him. There is no solution for sin outside God. When we have sinned, God wants us to confess and ask for forgiveness. The Bible says He is faithful and just to forgive us our sins and to cleanse us from all unrighteousness.

When we repent, it will allow us to obey God and live in his Word, walk with Him and do the work He wants us to do. Only then can we receive the rewards He has stored up for us. David once missed God in a big way when he committed adultery with Bathsheba and then killed her husband. But thereafter he ran to God and asked for forgiveness, and that is why God could still say of him that He has never seen a man whose heart was after Him, like David.

CHOOSE OBEDIENCE: 13 JUNE

# Loving One Another: Our Seal As God's Children

*If a man says he loves God but hates his brother, then he is a liar. For how can you love God whom you have not seen and not love your brother whom you can see? And this is my commandment to love your brother as you love me.*
– 1 JOHN 4:20–21

Love is an essential form of obedience which so many people choose to ignore. So many of us come to church and proclaim our love for God when there is so much strife in our own homes and families.

I know one family which professes to be committed Christians; one of the brothers is even a pastor with his own church. They are in church almost every day and they attend every service, pay their tithes and even give food to the missions and the poor. Yet, they do not speak to each other. They compete with each other and display hatred and contempt towards each other. How, then, can they be called Christians when they are disobedient to a simple commandment God has given them?

Charity begins at home and if we cannot have peace, love and acceptance in our homes and in our families, how can we go out into the world and claim to love them? How can we come into the presence of God and claim to love Him when we so blatantly disregard his law?

Someone once said: 'We are not simply readers of some old book. We are not the custodians of some ancient tradition. We are participants in the drama of divine love! We love one another, because we are on intimate terms with the God who is love. We are inhabited by God'. God's love is not complete until we, his children, can express it to others.

Choose today to be obedient to God by showing love. The first place to show love is in our home and in our families – especially to our siblings, spouses and children. Regardless of how much of God's work we do in the world, we will never win God's favour if we don't walk in love. Our efforts in doing God's work become futile when we do not display love in our homes and within our families first.

CHOOSE OBEDIENCE: 14 JUNE

# We Don't Reserve the Right to Be Obedient

*God renders to each man according to His works. Those who continue patiently in doing good will receive eternal life. Those who do not obey the truth but obey unrighteousness and work evil will receive tribulation and anguish … But glory and honour await all who work well. The things we do determine our eternal reward.*
– Romans 2:6–10

How more clear can God be about how essential obedience is to our salvation? It does not matter if we said the sinner's prayer or if we even were baptized and it certainly does not matter how often we go to church. What matters to God is the state of our hearts, the love inside us, the faith we have, the commitment we have to Him and, most importantly, our obedience in doing his will.

Our reward of eternal life and salvation can only be gained by obeying God's instructions and by the work we do as his children through his commands. In giving us life, He has blessed us with purpose. However, if we are disobedient to Him, we can never fulfil his purpose or complete what He has planned for us in our lives.

By disobeying Him, we give up our right to eternal life and the grace which comes with the Lord. Our disobedience distances us from the will of God and his glory. The issue of obedience is pure and simple. It means doing what God asks us to do rather than what we have decided He wants us to do. It is so easy to do what we think God wants us to do when it is actually our own plans and ambitions that are at play. Many times we are so willing to do anything for the Lord, except what He asks us to do. When we do that, we are in effect reserving the right to decide for ourselves what we think God's will is or isn't.

But if we live a life in accordance to his Word and which includes love, faith, hope, patience, kindness, generosity and repentance, we will be obeying the Lord and living a life which is pleasing in his eyes. That will put us in a position to receive our eternal reward in heaven.

# Making the Right Choice

*This day I call heaven and earth as witnesses against you*
*that I have set before you life and death, blessings and curses.*
*Now choose life, so that you and your children may live.*
– DEUTERONOMY 30:19

We must find what we are passionate about and wrap it in the destiny around us. When we disconnect our circumstances from our choices, we make a choice to live a powerless life.

It is wisdom when we have a proper view of cause and effect in our lives. It is very simple – we can never separate our lives from our choices. If we disconnect ourselves from our choices, it means that we have no wisdom and do not understand that whatever we choose will have consequences. Everything in life that has to do with our lives demands choice and every choice will have a cause and effect in our lives. So what we sow we will reap. What we do today will determine what we do tomorrow.

If we want to change our future, we have to create it. We have to make the right choices in the present. If we keep on making the wrong choices, we will continue to get the wrong results. There is tremendous power in the choices we make. Our choices not only affect us but also the generations to come. This principle is demonstrated in Deuteronomy 30:19, where God urges us to choose life.

We are faced with choices daily. Some may seem unimportant: what to wear, when to sleep, what to eat. Other choices are significant, having implications for the future: schooling and career choices, where we will live, whom we will marry. Yet of all the choices with which we are faced, there is none so important as how we will respond to our Creator. When we sort through the implications of our choices, be they major or minor, how does God factor into the equation? In other words, how would He like us to choose? There is perhaps no greater choice facing us than an answer to this question.

CHOOSE PASSION: 16 JUNE

# Passion: the Prerequisite for Success

*Let us fix our eyes on Jesus, the author and perfecter of our faith, who for the joy set before him endured the cross, scorning its shame, and sat down at the right hand of the throne of God.*
– Hebrews 12:2

Jesus achieved what He did, because He was passionate about those things. He was passionate about saving the lost – to a point of laying down his life for them. He was passionate about training his disciples and He did a good job at it. He was passionate about his relationship with God and that is why He always sought to do the will of the Father. Looking at Jesus' life, we should learn an important life principle about passion.

Passion opens the door for achievement. Passion motivates. Passionate people are inspired people who are initiators. They are here to create and not only maintain. Jesus' passion for mankind achieved for heaven many sons and daughters. His passion for mankind motivated Him to face the cross. Because He was passionate about his relationship with God, Jesus lived an inspired life. His act of sacrifice created a whole new family of God's children.

Do not wish that things could be different. Do not have big jaw bones that talk a lot and do nothing – we should not always be talking about what we are going to do. We should just do it. That is what Jesus did. He did not just talk about going to the cross, He actually went there. We would achieve a lot if we stop merely talking about what we are going to do and just do it.

Passionate people make things happen and do not settle for mediocrity or the standards that other people create for them. Passion produces commitment. People of passion enjoy the climb as much as they enjoy reaching the summit. In addition, passion turns the 'have to' into 'want to'.

We should not do anything because we have to but rather because we want to. That is what Jesus did when He went to the cross. Passion will keep us committed when the chips are down, the obstacles many, the odds high and resources few. Passionate people are positive about life and the goals they have set themselves. We need to be passionate about God and the things of God.

# Getting a Passion for God

*Who have I in heaven but You? And there is none upon earth that I desire besides You.*
– Psalm 73:25

God must stimulate us more than anything else. As believers we should not be motivated or cranked up; we should be *passionate* about God. The opposite of being passionate is being lukewarm. And we know what God does with people who are lukewarm; He spews them out (Rev 3:16).

Passion is not produced by our own ability. We have the Spirit of God, who, if we allow, will produce the passion in us. In Acts 2, the Spirit of God came upon the disciples and there was no doubt thereafter about the passion they had to preach and spread the message of salvation. God desires for us to be passionate about Him and He has given us the ability to develop such passion. This ability does not only come through the Holy Spirit but through knowing and growing in the knowledge of God.

Simply put, one cannot develop passion for someone without knowing that person. If you are going to have passion for God, then get to know Him and what He has done for you. The better you get to know God and what He is like, the easier it will be for you to be passionate towards and about God – to love Him with your whole being. This also involves getting to know what He has done for us. Interestingly, children appreciate their parents more when they get to know what Daddy or Mommy has done for them. Some of the most adoring praises I have received from my children came when they got to know and understand what Daddy had done for them. The same principle applies to our relationship with God. To be passionate about God, you need to know what He has done for you.

God has revealed Himself in nature, but so much more through his Word. We need to make daily Bible study so much of a habit as eating every day. We would do well to remember that the Bible is more than a book; it is God's love letter to us. It is only through his Spirit and his Word that we can develop our passion for God.

# Choose to Be Filled with Passion

*And every man that had this hope in Him,*
*purified himself that he is pure.*
– 1 John 3:3

No one epitomizes passion for purpose and mankind like Jesus did when He died on the cross for us. The pain He endured will never truly be understood by us. He was kicked, spat at, maimed, beaten, whipped, stabbed and insulted. The pain He suffered was greater than anything we could ever imagine, but still He endured because He was passionate about the plan God had for Him. He was determined to save his children from the sin of the world. His passion allowed Him to go through the affliction and his passion saw Him complete and fulfil the purpose that He came to the world for.

In life, we need to have the same passion that Christ had. Nothing should come in the way of achieving and fulfilling the promise and plans God has for us. We must also show the same kind of passion for our fellow human beings that Christ shows for them. We must, more than anything, have passion for Christ and God's Word. We must be passionate Christians who are eager to follow Christ's example, striving to do what He commanded us to. When our lives are filled with passion, we immediately start to love and appreciate everything we have. We begin to see the blessings in even the smallest things and we are able to be content and complete in the Name of God. God has given us everything we need to be passionate. All we need to do is to make a choice to be filled with that passion.

CHOOSE PASSION: 19 JUNE

# Seek God and Depend on Him

*'For I did not speak of my own accord, but the Father who deny me commanded me what to say and how to say it.'*
– John 12:49

In order for Christ to complete what He came to do, He had to depend on the presence of his Father in his life. When He felt low, scared and doubted Himself, his passion was renewed and restored when He depended on and sought the Lord.

In the same way, we need to seek God and place our dependence on Christ so we may be filled with the same passion He had. Depending on Him will also allow us to be restored with the passion we may lose along the way whenever we face hurdles.

Christ's passion came from his love for us and by obeying the instructions his Father had given Him. In the same way, if we lean on the Lord and not our own understanding, we will be able to receive the passion Christ had. We will do what we are required to do in his Name.

CHOOSE PASSION: 20 JUNE

# Don't Lose Your Passion

*'Do you think I cannot call on my Father, and He will at once put at my disposal more than twelve legions of angels?'*
– MATTHEW 26:53

We will never lose our passion if we stay fixed on God's commands and if we remember his blessings, promises and the grace we have through salvation.

When we choose to remind ourselves of God's power in our lives, we instantly become energized by his power and our passion grows and allows us to do great things – just like Jesus did.

Our passion will never cease if we place our faith in God and believe that even when the road ahead seems long, dark and full of obstacles, we are never alone to face it, for God is always with us. Christ is with us, the Holy Spirit is with us, legions of angels are behind us and God's grace abides in us.

When we remember the power we have behind us, we will never lose the passion to do what we are called to do.

For we are never alone, weak, weary or without back-up from God. All we have to do is call on Him to restore us. If we do that, we will do great things through Him who is in us.

CHOOSE PASSION: 21 JUNE

# Let God Be Your Director

*'Now my heart is troubled, and what shall I say? "Father, save me from this hour?" No, it was for this very reason I came to this hour.'*
– JOHN 12:27

Like the great writer Sir William Shakespeare said: 'The world is a stage and we are all actors on it playing a role.'

Just like that, we all have a role to play in the world and in God's purpose. When Shakespeare referred to us as actors, he did not mean we were meant to put on facades and assume different characters. Instead, he was talking about our actions which allow us to fulfil the roles we have for us.

We find that the greatest actors in the world are those who are passionate about the roles they play and they go to great lengths to do it to the best of their abilities. With that kind of passion, they are willing to take direction from someone who has more experience, authority and knowledge than they do.

Likewise, we need to have direction in our own lives so we can play the roles that God has for us. Our passion to do that will come from our willingness to take direction from God – just like Christ did when He walked the earth.

God will direct us according to his will. Through obeying his direction with passion, we will be able to live a life of purpose in Him. Our passion, coupled with God's direction will allow us to accomplish God's plan for us and live a life of purpose.

CHOOSE PERSEVERANCE: 22 JUNE

# Persevere and You'll Receive Your Promise

*Therefore do not cast away your confidence, which has great reward. For you have need of endurance, so that after you have done the will of God, you may receive the promise: 'For yet a little while, and He who is coming will come and will not tarry. Now the just shall live by faith; But if anyone draws back, my soul has no pleasure in him. But we are not of those who draw back to perdition, but of those who believe to the saving of the soul.'*

– HEBREWS 10:35–39

Between the time that we do the will of God and the time we receive the promise, we have to persevere.

Nothing should stop us from persevering in order to do what God has called us to do.

Satan tried on numerous attempts to tempt Jesus away from God's will but Jesus remained faithful to his role on earth. He rejected Satan and persevered.

In the same way, we can only do what God wants us to do if we remain focused on his will and persevere in everything we do.

Nothing should stop us, not fear, doubt, or temptation, and certainly not the world and its many traps.

We are not of those who shrink back, who step back and who sit back. Instead, I stand up and will receive my promise.

# Perseverance Requires Determination

*Indeed we count them blessed who endure. You have heard of the perseverance of Job and seen the end intended by the Lord – that the Lord is very compassionate and merciful.*
– JAMES 5:11

We know of the perseverance of Job and we have seen the end intended by the Lord. We also saw that the Lord is very compassionate and merciful. Also, because Job persevered and never allowed his afflictions to come between him and his salvation, God allowed his grace to fall on him.

To persevere means to be determined. Many times we battle to find the balance but we must never allow it to stop us from what we have to do.

I can take my hand, which is my natural hand, and then God can take his supernatural life and imprint his super power on the natural – and this hand will then become the supernatural, because they come together. God cannot lay hands on somebody unless there is a natural hand. My responsibility is to provide the natural while God's responsibility is to provide the supernatural. But some of us believe that to be spiritual means that we can keep our hands in our pockets and God will come along and do what He wants to do. No. We have to take the natural and the supernatural and bring the partnership together. That is why perseverance and endurance are essential for God to work and do the works that He has to do through us. He does what He has to do through us and He creates what He has to create through us.

CHOOSE PERSEVERANCE: 24 JUNE

# If God Is for Us, Who Can Be against Us?

*'I have fought the good fight. I have finished the race.'*
– 2 TIMOTHY 4:7

Do not think the Gospel will be preached. It will not be – unless someone is sent. The two have to come together. There has to be the miracle of God's divine manifestation and the natural person called mankind. This is why many people miss it.

To be determined means to be single-minded. We have to be patient. Godly patience is not about waiting but about how we wait. Whatever it is that we are facing, we need to have patience by waiting in a godly manner. Rejoice in the Lord anyway. Have faith, love, hope and be in a place of encouragement rather than discouragement. Have confidence in God to not draw back but make a stand. Whatever comes or goes – remember, if God is for us, then who can be against us?

I will be able to endure through the Holy Spirit in me. When we are weak, He is strong. We can do all things through Jesus Christ who strengthens us.

# Don't Be a Quitter!

*'The one who endures to the end, he will be saved.'*
– MATTHEW 24:13

If we look into the Bible and seek counsel from it we will realize that if we persevere, God will never allow us to fail.

A perfect example of perseverance in the Bible is Moses who never gave up on his purpose to free his people from Egypt. He fought and challenged the king until his people were set free. And even when they were met by the sea, he never lost hope; he knew he had the power of God with him and so he endured. He placed his staff upon the water and the water moved so that they could walk through. Time and time again, Moses endured and his perseverance took them to victory.

It is hard to persevere sometimes when we are faced with adversity. It seems that an easier choice would be to just give up. Yet, no one likes a quitter. Like Moses, we need to persevere and endure everything that comes our way so we can achieve the great victory and sense of pride in our ability, which comes with it.

Perseverance will only add to our potential, capabilities and strength. Unless we choose to persevere, we can achieve nothing and we will find ourselves distanced from God's grace.

CHOOSE PERSEVERANCE: 26 JUNE

# God's Power Will Help You Follow Through

*'Watch and pray so that you will not fall into temptation. The spirit is willing, but the body is weak.'*
– MATTHEW 26:41

It is only natural that as humans, we will get tired and become distracted by life and the challenges that come with it.

There are times we will put things off until later and allow ourselves to procrastinate – believing that we will get to it at a later stage.

But perseverance is not about putting things off until later or about allowing how we feel in the flesh to hinder our progress, work and actions.

Instead, we need to seek God and depend on Him to give us the strength, wisdom and power we need to achieve.

We need to go deep into ourselves and dig deeper into our spirits because even though we may feel weak, Christ in us is strong. His power, and not our own, will help us follow through.

CHOOSE PERSEVERANCE: 27 JUNE

# Nothing Is Impossible with God

*I can do all things through Christ who strengthens me.*
– PHILIPPIANS 4:13

How comforting it is to know that we can do all things through Christ – all things.

What better motivator is there for us to persevere? It is also such an inspiration to know that there is nothing that we cannot achieve and do because Christ is in us. We do not have to depend on others or even on our own willpower. All we have to do is to focus on Him and remind ourselves of his presence in our lives. We need to choose to allow Him to work in us and then we will do ALL THINGS through Him.

Nothing is impossible with God. We need to repeat this and allow it to be planted in our hearts – the knowledge that nothing, absolutely nothing is impossible with God. Knowing that we have Christ in us, how can we ever doubt our success if we persevere to achieve and attain it?

God ensures victory. He led nations and great prophets to victory because they persevered and endured. So what makes us think that He cannot do the same for us? All He wants us to do is to abide by his will and not allow anything to stop us from doing and fulfilling his will for our lives.

Choose to persevere today. Choose to say: 'I can do all things – ALL THINGS.'

Feel empowered, be energized and rejuvenated to do his will. Persevere, for nothing is impossible with God.

CHOOSE PERSEVERANCE: 28 JUNE

# Lean on God, and He Will Do Great Things for You

*But He said to me, 'My grace is sufficient for you,*
*for My power is made perfect in weakness.' Therefore I will*
*boast all the more gladly about my weaknesses, so that Christ's*
*power may rest on me. That is why, for Christ's sake, I delight*
*in weaknesses, in insults, in hardships, in persecutions,*
*in difficulties. For when I am weak, then I am strong.*
– 2 CORINTHIANS 12:9–10

It is so important for us to lean on God, for there are times when our own strength fails us. Depending on God is actually so vital that there are even times when God will remove all the comforts and allow us to become weak – just so we can depend on Him. When we depend on Him, God can start to fill us with his strength. In addition, He will provide, protect and bless us once we allow Him to work inside us and through us.

We will then be able to recognize the power of God's strength in us. This will encourage us to persevere in God's will for us – for we will know that we have a supernatural power behind us which will let us have complete success. We will never be able to confront and fight battles on our own, regardless of how much we persevere, unless we allow God to come into our lives and help us through it. Only God can help us conquer and only God can satisfy our needs. He knows us and knows what our weaknesses are because He created us. Only He can restore and replenish us. So we need to put our trust and faith in Him. Lean on Him and know that He will do great things through us.

# Let's Win the Race for Him

*Therefore, my beloved brethren, be steadfast, immovable, always abounding in the work of the Lord, knowing that your toil is not in vain in the Lord.*
– 1 Corinthians 15:58

Even when a situation seems hopeless, we should never lose hope. When it seems helpless, we should never forget that we have the greatest help we need. When it seems dark, we should remember that we are always in his light. When it seems impossible, we should know that all things are possible. When it seems useless, we should know that God chose to use us because He believes in our potential. When it seems worthless, we should know that nothing which comes from the Lord lacks value and purpose. When it seems futile, we should know that God knows our beginning and our end as well as the purpose He has for us. When it seems senseless, we should know that everything that comes from God has meaning. So we should never allow ourselves to be distracted. Instead, we must persevere and hold fast to what God has ordained us to do because nothing that comes from Him will be done in vain. He has promised us great rewards and eternal life and is always there to ensure that we will win the race for Him.

CHOOSE PERSEVERANCE: 30 JUNE

# He Will Never Fail Us

*He gives strength to the weary,*
*and to him who lacks might He increases power.*
– Isaiah 40:29

Christ is always with us and promises to give us strength, even when we are at our weariest. He will never forsake us. He will never allow us to do his work based on our own strength but will be with us and help us, even when we are confronted with gigantic adversities.

Let us look again at David. Even though the situation seemed impossible, futile and hopeless when he was confronted by Goliath, he never allowed it to deter him. He knew he had the power and strength of God with him and in him. He knew that his own strength and power would fail him, but that that which came from the Lord would never fail. His faith and willingness to accept God's power in him at that moment won him victory over Goliath, a man who made an army shudder and cower back in terror.

So, we too need to believe in the power and strength which comes from God. We must never allow our weaknesses in the flesh to take us away from what we were called to do. God is gracious and merciful and will always protect us – even in the worst kind of trouble or danger.

All we need to do is remain faithful and persevere, for He will never fail us.

# July

## CHOOSE GRACE

*Grace is but glory begun, and glory is but grace perfected.*

– Jonathan Edwards

## CHOOSE GOD'S HELP

*Man's extremity is God's opportunity.*

– John Flavel

## CHOOSE GOD'S MERCY

*Mercy stood in the cloud, with eye that wept essential love.*

– Robert Pollok

## CHOOSE FAITHFULNESS

*Faithful servants never retire. You can retire from your career, but you will never retire from serving God.*

– Rick Warren

CHOOSE GRACE: 1 JULY

# Don't Be a Part-time Christian

*If we confess our sins, He is faithful and righteous to forgive us our sins and to cleanse us from all unrighteousness.*
– 1 John 1:9

God's grace is sufficient for all of us but only when we prove ourselves worthy of it.

We cannot expect God's grace to fall on us if we insist on hiding things from Him.

It may sound stupid to say 'hiding' but many of us believe we can deceive God and hide things from Him and then make up for it by doing something that is required of us. We also believe that we are safe and have eternal life as long as we have accepted God into our lives. We then think that we can still do whatever else we want to do in our lives, as long as we read the Bible, go to church and do some of the things Christians are expected to do. But we cannot be part-time or partial Christians and expect to have God's grace.

God wants us to be honest with Him and lead Christ-like lives. He wants us to be able to stand up and confess our wrongdoings and accept that He will judge us and hold us accountable for them.

Only when we choose to have a responsible relationship with God will we be entitled to have God's grace in our lives, which is more than sufficient to cleanse us and place us back in a position of righteousness.

CHOOSE GRACE: 2 JULY

# Grace upon Grace

*For of His fullness we have all received, and grace upon grace. For the law was given through Moses; grace and truth was realized through Jesus Christ.*
– JOHN 1:16–17

When we are in need of God's grace, it is already sufficient for us. God is able to increase that grace so we can have grace upon grace. In saying that, God wants to assure us of that grace. He wants us always to remember how great his grace is. Christ's crucifixion is an example of grace upon grace. How much more grace can God give us than the life of his Son so we may be saved?

And the deeper the spiritual relationship that we form with God, the greater the grace that we receive from Him. Grace will abound in our lives in the form of endless blessings, greater understanding, sustenance and strength. We are redeemed through Him and because of that, we will receive his fullness and favour – but only if we choose to have a deeper spiritual relationship with God that is pleasing to Him.

CHOOSE GRACE: 3 JULY

# God's Grace Is Abundant

*He predestined us to adoption as sons through Jesus Christ to Himself according to the kind intention of His will, to the praise of the glory of His grace, which He freely bestowed on us in the Beloved. In Him we have redemption through His blood, the forgiveness of our trespasses, according to the riches of His [God's] grace.*
– Ephesians 1:5–7

There is such an abundance of grace in God that it allowed us to be saved from sin and death. We can rest assured that the richness of his grace will provide for us the deliverance we need from temptation, bad habits and affliction. His grace will put us in a place of prominence.

Without God's grace we can never have eternal life. We would be confined to extinction after death, but instead we are forgiven through his grace and made heirs to his glory and riches in heaven. We have the promise to receive our inheritance of eternal life if we remain obedient to Him.

He has predestined a rich and successful life for each of us, as well as a promise of provision to fulfil our needs. Nevertheless, we can only receive it if we walk this life in Him and not in the world. If we seek his grace, we will find it and if we seek God, He will guide us to lead the best possible life we can. Apostle Paul sought his grace and God gave it to him. God actually gave him a wealth of grace because Paul decided to walk a life in Christ and reject his past sins.

If we choose Him first, we will be redeemed. Next, we should give thanks for our salvation by praising Him and obeying Him. If we do that, we will never be short of the grace of God.

# Let's Not Take God's Grace for Granted

*See what this godly sorrow has produced in you: what earnestness, what eagerness to clear yourselves, what indignation, what alarm, what longing, what concern, what readiness to see justice done. At every point you have proved yourselves to be innocent in this matter.*
– 2 CORINTHIANS 7:11

It would be easy to take God and his grace for granted, but we would be making a mistake if we do that. Many people think they can do whatever they like, because all they need to do is confess and ask for forgiveness and everything will be forgiven again.

But that is not how God works. His grace is not an excuse to sin. If we choose to abuse it, we will be held accountable. We forget that God knows our hearts and He can see deep into our souls how authentic we are. If we believe we can deceive Him, He will and can hold back his grace.

We must never be mistaken by thinking we can continuously ask for forgiveness and God's grace will continue to fall on us. God has an advantage that we do not have. He knows how sincere we are; He knows our thoughts and our innermost being better than we do. So we can never deceive Him.

When we choose to disrespect God, we choose to dishonour Him and when we dishonour Him, we choose to discredit his power over us. This will make us fall short of his glory.

# Forgive, Forgive, Forgive ...

*Then Peter came and said to Him, 'Lord, how often shall my brother sin against me and I forgive him? Up to seven times?' Jesus said to him, 'I do not say to you, up to seven times, but up to seventy times seven.'*
– Matthew 18:21–22

God wants us to live a life in which we display grace towards our fellow human beings in the same way as He gives us grace. Forgiving someone is not a sign of generosity but a sign of love and grace that can only be found in the Lord. God does not support killing someone because they have killed, nor punishing someone in the same way they have sinned. Instead, He wants us to forgive and give people a chance to change and repent through that forgiveness.

It is a case of showing love – even in the midst of hatred – so that we do not rob ourselves of salvation. We do not need to behave like sinners. We have authority through God to take a different stand in life and show a different character in Him. It also does not mean that our grace should stop after seventy times seven times. It means we should show God's grace in our lives by imparting his grace at all times, no matter how long it takes. But we must not do so simply because God commanded us to, but because our hearts tell us to and because it is part of who we are in Christ. In order to have God's grace, we need to be graceful people. This is pleasing to God and what God expects from us.

The more we forgive and love those who persecute us, the more grace we will receive from God, and the more opportunity we give them to repent and seek God in their lives as well.

CHOOSE GRACE: 6 JULY

# Don't Let Your Faith Dwindle

*Timothy, my son, I give you this instruction in keeping with the prophecies once made about you, so that by following them you may fight the good fight, holding on to faith and a good conscience. Some have rejected these and so have shipwrecked their faith. Among them are Hymenaeus and Alexander, whom I have handed over to Satan to be taught not to blaspheme.*
– 1 TIMOTHY 1:18–20

Faith is essential to stay in the grace of God. As God's children we must do all we can to ensure that we never strain the relationship between us. Sometimes as believers, it is still easy to fall victim to the world and its many pleasures. If we choose to allow it, we will lose faith. We will allow our weaknesses to overtake our strengths and allow the devil to have his way. We need to remind ourselves of God's grace in our lives and never be in a position where we lose the grace that God means for us to have. If our faith grows weak, we will fall, and getting up will be a lot harder than if we had kept our faith intact in the first place.

Despite Peter's belief in God, he still denied knowing Him when the pressure was on. If we deny the Lord in our lives through our words and actions, we will only receive his grace when we rebuild our faith in Him and allow Him back into our lives. David sinned against God by committing adultery and murder. While he was enjoying the fruits of his sin, his faith in God dwindled. It was only when he had to face the consequences of his sin and accept that he would have to face discipline from God that he realized how his sin had taken him away from God's grace. That is when he begged God for forgiveness.

God did not fail him and he was forgiven. He received God's grace and faith allowed him to be restored. We need to ensure that we do not lose faith so we will never have to fall into the depths of despair which comes with losing faith. Although God's grace is sufficient, suffering is unnecessary in the first place.

CHOOSE GRACE: 7 JULY

# Win God's Favour

*'You gave me life and showed me kindness,*
*and in your providence watched over my spirit.'*
– Job 10:12

Grace is winning God's favour and, as we already know, the only way to win God's favour is by living a life that is pleasing to Him.

Grace is a precious gift God has given to each of us, so we can have salvation. Through his grace, God has already given us all things that pertain to life and godliness. He has already given us all the things we need to live out the plan He has for our lives. Job went through endless afflictions and trials and suffering, but he never stopped thanking God for his grace, which guided him (Job) through all these hardships in his life.

We also need to remain thankful for God's grace that will always be with us.

He has a plan and purpose for our lives and will always give us his grace and power so we may fulfil our plan and purpose.

The only time it will not happen is when we choose not to have his grace with us.

But Jesus is willing to share all of who He is with us, so we can be like Him in our attitudes, love, thoughts, faith and purity – as well as in our power.

CHOOSE GOD'S HELP: 8 JULY

# Safely in the Palm of His Hand

*God is our refuge and our strength, an everlasting help in trouble.*
– Psalm 46:1

Not one of us is devoid of affliction. Life would be abnormal if we sailed through it without any problems. It also means that we will never learn to grow, never learn any lessons and never build on our character by adopting new and positive characteristics. But while we have to be realistic about the trials we will face and the fact that life will never be perfect, we can take solace in knowing that we have a divine and supernatural force that will help us when we are in trouble. It is a power that will ensure our victory and make us stronger and wiser through the trial and thereafter. We are always under the shadow of God's wings and He keeps us safely in the palm of his hand. He is always there in times of trouble. After all the trouble He has gone through to ensure that we are saved and have salvation in his Name, He will never cease to provide the help we need when we need it. All we have to do is dwell in Him, cast our burdens onto Him, and know that He really is an everlasting help in troubled times.

CHOOSE GOD'S HELP: 9 JULY

# God Will Provide a Way Out

*No temptation has seized you except what is common to man. And God is faithful; he will not let you be tempted beyond what you can bear. But when you are tempted, he will also provide a way out so that you can stand up under it.*

– 1 Corinthians 10:13

God will not allow you to face a temptation that is beyond your ability to endure. Every temptation will be accompanied by a way of escape so you can endure it.

There may be times when it seems that there is no way out and as if the problem is bigger than anything we can imagine or cope with. In such times we often choose to be overwhelmed by our problems, leaving us feeling helpless. Yet we are never helpless. God will never allow us to face anything beyond what we can bear.

He knows each one of us. When we have difficulty enduring, He is right there in our hearts, in our thoughts and in our presence to support, help and rescue us.

God has promised to help us endure, but we must make use of the help He provides. Let us summarize the way in which God helps: He does not promise that He will remove our problem; He does, however, promise that He will provide the strength we need to be faithful despite the problem.

CHOOSE GOD'S HELP: 10 JULY

# Let God Empower You

*Say with confidence: 'The Lord is my helper,*
*I will not be afraid. What can man do to me?'*
– Hebrews 13:6

Being confident about God's power in our lives is so important, because it will determine how we face the trials in our lives. If we lack confidence, we will ultimately lack faith and when we lack faith, we will allow ourselves to sink into hopelessness.

But if we remain confident about the power we have behind us, we will boldly face the challenges and trials in life without a doubt whatsoever that we will overcome, because we are empowered to.

At times we tend to give more importance to the power of man than to the power of God, allowing ourselves to be intimidated and trampled on. But God's power is greater than any other power. He is greater than any man or power in the flesh, regarding all things on earth He created and knows them intimately.

No weapon formed against Him or us can prosper. He will fight for us with the promise of a two-edged sword.

He will trample our enemies under his feet and crush them with his might. So we have nothing to fear, for we have the risen God as our Helper and Protector, our Saviour and our Shield.

CHOOSE GOD'S HELP: 11 JULY

# God Will Prosper Us

*'But when the Comforter is come, whom I will send unto you from the Father, even the Spirit of truth, which proceeded from the Father, He shall testify of Me.'*
– JOHN 15:26

God knows all. He is the author and finisher of our faith. He knew that we will have to face various different situations in our lives, which may cause us to stumble. So He sent us help beforehand, so that we will know we will never be alone.

The Holy Spirit is always with us and is our voice of reasoning and reckoning. Remember the story of Pinocchio, when he heard Jiminy Cricket as a voice in his ear, a sounding board, a counsel and a help in times of trouble? So, too, is the Holy Spirit our help, our counsel, our reasoning and our comfort.

If we allow ourselves to grow spiritually, we will feel the presence of the Holy Spirit in our lives. And if we listen close enough, we will hear his voice helping us when we need it most and giving us the peace of mind to know that we will conquer whatever we are going through. We will know that nothing can harm us because of God's perfect plan to prosper us.

CHOOSE GOD'S HELP: 12 JULY

# God Will Never Let Us Down

*'I will not in any way fail you nor give you up nor leave you without support ... [I will] not in any degree leave you helpless nor forsake nor let [you] down ...'*
– HEBREWS 13:5

It is easy to become discouraged and allow ourselves to be weighed down. When we go through low points in our lives, we must look to God and remind ourselves that He will never leave us alone nor fail us. Never. He promised us. God honours his promises and his Word.

He will always be with us and is always willing, ready and able to pick us up from the deepest pit and place us alongside his throne of glory.

Instead of wasting our energy on our problems and allowing them to discourage us, we can focus on God and bring our problems to Him by praying and telling Him exactly what we need. We must humble ourselves before Him and be truthful about our fears and expectations. We must feel honoured that there is always someone we can go to for help, who will hear us and answer our call.

We may fall but never have to stay there. We can dust ourselves off, get up, and try again, because we have help from a divine source. We can rest assured that if we cast our burdens onto Him, He will never let us down.

CHOOSE GOD'S HELP: 13 JULY

# Why Does God Allow Suffering?

*We are hard-pressed on every side, yet not crushed; we are perplexed, but not in despair; persecuted, but not forsaken; struck down, but not destroyed – always carrying about in the body the dying of the Lord Jesus, that the life of Jesus also may be manifested in our body.*
– 2 CORINTHIANS 4:8–10

It is human nature to question God. If He is that powerful, why do we have to face the trials and tribulations we do? If we are his children, why does He allow us to suffer? We will never allow our own children to suffer, because we love them too much. Instead, we will want to feel the pain for them, take on their burdens and problems, and do whatever is necessary, so that they do not have to endure suffering. How, then, can God allow us to suffer? He can easily stop it from happening because He has all the power to do it.

However, there are many times when we as parents are forced to watch our children endure certain situations in life, which they brought on themselves. We do not interfere because we love them. We realize that there are certain lessons to be learned from their mistakes and that it will build their character to deal with problems in the future.

God does the same for us. We may feel hard-pressed, perplexed, and persecuted, but because God is with us, we are never crushed, in despair or forsaken. Instead, we develop the character of Christ, who suffered more than any of us ever will.

CHOOSE GOD'S HELP: 14 JULY

# We Are in Good Hands

*'Rejoice and be glad when you are persecuted, because you are suffering as God's people always have – for great is your reward in heaven.'*
– Matthew 5:12

God never wants us to lose our joy, regardless of what we are going through, because He promises us that we will be rewarded at the end of everything.

He is always there for us and will always help and protect us. I found a wonderful description of God on godisgroovy.com:

> A fifth-grade teacher in a Christian school asked her class to look at TV commercials and see if they could use them in some way to communicate ideas about God. Here are some of the results: God is like BAYER ASPIRIN – He works miracles. God is like a FORD – He has got a better idea. God is like COKE – He has the real thing. God is like HALLMARK CARDS – He cares enough to send his very best. God is like TIDE – He gets the stains out that others leave behind. God is like GENERAL ELECTRIC – He brings good things to life. God is like SEARS – He has everything. God is like ALKA-SELTZER – try Him, you will like Him. God is like SCOTCH TAPE – you cannot see Him, but you know He is there. God is like DELTA – He is ready when you are. God is like ALLSTATE – you are in good hands with Him. God is like VO-5 HAIR SPRAY – He holds through all kinds of weather. God is like DIAL SOAP – are you not glad you have Him? Do you not wish everybody did? God is not like the US POST OFFICE – no rain, nor snow, nor sleet, nor ice keep Him from his appointed destination.
>
> – Author Unknown

So be comforted. We are more than taken care of.

CHOOSE GOD'S MERCY: 15 JULY

# God Is Ready to Forgive Us

*If we say that we have no sin, we deceive ourselves, and the truth is not in us. If we confess our sins, He is faithful and just to forgive us our sins and to cleanse us from all unrighteousness. If we say that we have not sinned, we make Him a liar, and His Word is not in us.*
– 1 John 1:8–10

The one guarantee we have is that God is ready to forgive us. He will forgive us, regardless of the number of times we ask for forgiveness. He is abundant in mercy but He also wants us to be responsible for our actions and not use his mercy as an excuse to sin.

The only requirement for forgiveness is our genuine confession and repentance. We can be grateful that God has so much mercy.

Imagine the kind of life we would have if we were not assured of God's mercy and grace.

Through his mercy, He wants us to be reminded of our actions, learn our lesson and not do it again.

Let us look at the story of Cain and Abel. Cain committed the first murder in the world, but God forgave him when he came forth before God and confessed his sin.

Even so, when God forgave him, Cain was marked and that mark was not a sign of punishment from God but a sign of God's mercy so that he would be reminded not to sin again.

In life there are consequences for all our sins and actions against God.

The mistakes we make will leave scars in our lives that will never be removed, but it will serve as a reminder of what we would never want to experience again.

# Mercy Is God's Choice

*'... I will have mercy on which I will have mercy,*
*and I will have compassion on which I will have compassion.'*
– Exodus 33:19

If we are sincere about our transgressions, God will forgive us and we will find favour in Him. But it is up to Him whether we are worthy of that mercy or not. We all know the parable of the prodigal son (Luke 15) who demanded his share of the inheritance, and then squandered it all, ending up feeding pigs and wishing he could have some of the pig food to eat:

> 'But when he came to himself, he said "... I will get up and go to my father, and will say to him, 'Father; I have sinned against heaven and before thee ...'" And he arose and went to his father.
>
> But while he was yet a long way off, his father saw him and was moved with compassion, and ran and fell upon his neck and kissed him ... the father said to his servants, "Fetch quickly the best robe and put it on him, and give him a ring for his finger and sandals for his feet; and bring out the fattened calf and kill it, and let us eat and make merry; because this my son was dead, and has come to life again; he was lost, and is found."'

His older brother was not happy and refused to join the celebrations:

> 'His father, therefore, came out and began to entreat him. But he answered ... "Behold, these many years I have been serving thee ... and yet thou have never given me a kid that I might make merry with my friends ..." But he said to him, "Son, thou art always with me, and all that is mine is thine; but we were bound to make merry and rejoice, for this thy brother was dead, and has come to life; he was lost, and is found."'

There are times when, although his mercy is abundant and available at a moment's notice, we will not be worthy of that mercy.

CHOOSE GOD'S MERCY: 17 JULY

# Like a Father, He Will Look for Us

*When the scribes and Pharisees complained that Jesus consorted with sinners, He told them these parables, illustrating his love and compassion: 'What man of you having a hundred sheep, and losing one of them, does not leave the ninety-nine in the desert, and go after that which is lost, until he finds it? And when he has found it, he lays it upon his shoulders rejoicing. And on coming home he calls together his friends and neighbors, saying to them, "Rejoice with me, because I have found my sheep that was lost." I say to you that, even so, there will be joy in heaven over one sinner who repents, more than over ninety-nine just who have no need of repentance. Or what woman, having ten drachmas, if she loses one drachma, does not light a lamp and sweep the house and search carefully until she finds it? And when she has found it, she calls together her friends and neighbors, saying, "Rejoice with me, for I have found the drachma that I had lost." Even so, I say to you, there will be joy among the angels of God over one sinner who repents.'*

– LUKE 15:2–10

There are times when God will allow us to wander off, but He will never let us get lost. Like a father will look for a child, He will look for us, because regardless of how far we wander, his mercy is great and his love is even greater, and He will look for us, find us and bring us back into the fold and then rejoice.

It is such an honour to know that we will never be left alone in the wilderness but will have none other than the Lord look for us.

# Enjoy the Fruits of God's Mercy

*'Blessed are the merciful, for they shall receive mercy.'*
– MATTHEW 5:7

We are God's elect and his chosen people. When we are able to display a Christ-like character, we will be able to act in the likeness of God. When we are able to do that, God will be most merciful over us and will ensure that He is our caretaker.

When we are able to be in his likeness, we will experience the fruits of his mercy.

First, we will be able to love everyone as He has loved us and He will continue to allow his love to abound in us.

We will have the peace of God's mercy as well as the joy of the Lord which is our strength. His mercy will also allow us to trust Him more, and our faith in Him will grow. When we are blessed with the fruits of mercy, we will experience less worry, anxiety and conflict in our lives, because He will be by our side and will never leave us. We will live a life full of God's presence.

# Are You Ready To Forgive?

*Then Peter came to Jesus and asked, 'Lord, how many times shall I forgive my brother when he sins against me? Up to seven times?' Jesus answered, 'I tell you, not seven times, but seventy-seven times. Therefore the kingdom of heaven is like a king who wanted to settle accounts with his servants. As he began the settlement, a man who owed him ten thousand talents was brought to him. Since he was not able to pay, the master ordered that he and his wife and his children and all that he had be sold to repay the debt.'*

– Matthew 18:21–25

The story about the unforgiving servant is the perfect example of how God's mercy works in our lives and how we become worthy of receiving that mercy.

The story relates how a king, while settling accounts with his servants, finds that one owed him 10 000 talents. Normally, the servant would be cast into prison and his family sold into slavery until all was paid. But when the servant entreated the king to have mercy on him, the king, 'moved with compassion', wrote off the entire debt!

The forgiven servant then found one who owed him 100 denarii's (or about $15). This petty debtor begged for additional time to pay off the debt, but the servant, without mercy, had him jailed until all was paid. The king found out and was furious and dealt with the servant.

Sometimes in life, we just expect God to have mercy on us when we deny others of our mercy. God wants us to be merciful so we can receive his mercy. He also wants us to treat his children as we want to be treated. God is ready to forgive if we are ready to do the same.

# A Perfect Example of Our Need for God's Mercy

*Have mercy on me, God in Your kindness.*
*In your compassion, blot out my offence.*
*O wash me more and more from my guilt*
*and cleanse me from my sin.*
*My offences truly I know them;*
*my sin is always before me.*
*Against You, You alone, have I sinned;*
*what is evil in your sight I have done …*
*Give me again the joy of Your help;*
*with a spirit of fervor sustain me,*
*that I may teach transgressors Your ways*
*and sinners may return to You.*
– Psalm 51:1–4, 11–12

When we allow ourselves to experience God's mercy by being honest about our shortcomings, his mercy will allow us to be free from the burden of guilt.

A friend who was on a diet was shattered when she pigged out one day because she was tempted by the feast that was before her. She felt so guilty that she went home and into the bathroom where she made herself bring up the food. All that did, literally, was leave a bad taste in her mouth and it made her feel worse.

In life, guilt can sometimes consume us, causing us to do things that make the situation worse and that provide no relief. However, if we receive God's mercy, we will receive his peace, comfort and freedom from guilt, so we can put our past mistakes behind us and move forward.

CHOOSE GOD'S MERCY: 21 JULY

# God Is a God of Mercy

*... 'The LORD, the LORD God, merciful and gracious, longsuffering, and abounding in goodness and truth.'*
– EXODUS 34:6

God is a God of mercy. When He appeared to Moses, He declared his Name before Himself, saying to Moses that He is a God of mercy and grace.

There are various times in the Bible when God reaffirms who He is by describing the extent of his mercy. His mercy led the people of Israel out of Egypt. It was his mercy that fell on David, his mercy that fell on Jonah, his mercy that fell on Lot, and on Noah and his family, his mercy that fell on Joseph, and his mercy that fell on his children to lead them to victory and freedom.

In life, we must never choose to disregard God and his power. He tells us over and over again what He is and the gifts which come forth from Him. He wouldn't repeat it as often as He does, if it is not important to our lives and our salvation.

When we choose to forget God's power, we choose to live a life that is absent of Him and therefore we choose to stay in many of the situations we face, instead of allowing his mercy to carry us through.

# Go Out And Use Your Talents

*His Lord said to him: 'Well done, good and faithful servant; you were faithful over a few things, I will make you ruler over many things. Enter into the joy of the Lord.'*
– MATTHEW 25:21

In the parable of talents, a man going on a journey called his servants and entrusted his property to them.

> 'To one he gave five talents of money, to another two, and to another one … The man who had received the five talents went at once and put his money to work and gained five more. So also, the one with the two talents gained two more. But the man who had received the one talent went off … and hid his master's money.
>
> After a long time the master returned … The man who had received the five talents brought the other five. "Master," he said, "you entrusted me with five talents. See, I have gained five more."
>
> His master replied, "Well done, good and faithful servant! …"
>
> The man with the two talents also came. "Master," he said, "you entrusted me with two talents; see, I have gained two more."
>
> His master replied, "Well done, good and faithful servant! …"
>
> Then the man who had received the one talent came. "Master," he said, "I knew that you are a hard man … So I was afraid … and hid your talent in the ground. See, here is what belongs to you."
>
> His master replied, "You wicked, lazy servant … you should have put my money on deposit with the bankers, so that when I returned I would have received it back with interest. Take the talent … and give it to the one who has the ten talents. For everyone who has will be given more and he will have an abundance. Whoever does not have, even what he has will be taken from him …"'
>
> – MATTHEW 25:19–29

God gives each of us talents and wants us not to keep it to ourselves but to go out into the world and use it.

# The Value of Faithfulness

*'So if you faithfully OBEY the commands I am giving you today then I will send rain … so that you may gather in your grain, new wine and oil, you will eat and be satisfied.'*
– Deuteronomy 11:13–15

The Bible places great value on faithfulness. With faithfulness comes obedience to do the work of God and ultimately receive our rewards in heaven.

Once we are able to remain faithful to God in all things He will ensure that we are blessed beyond comprehension.

Our faithfulness is central to the rewards we receive in heaven. God will judge us according to our faithfulness.

Like Noah, Abraham, David, Elijah, Eli, Solomon, Jacob, Moses, Joseph and so many other great examples in the Bible, who remained faithful despite the circumstances in their lives and the trials they faced, their faithfulness saw them receive huge rewards. It is true what they say: 'With great victory, comes great sacrifice,' and the best way to ensure the victory, even in the midst of the sacrifice, is to remain faithful.

CHOOSE FAITHFULNESS: 24 JULY

# Be Faithful and God Will Honour His Promises

*You found [Abram's] heart faithful to you, and you made a covenant with him to give to his descendants the land …*
– Nehemiah 9:8

God honours his Word and the promises He has made to us if we remain faithful to Him and his commandments. We need to have a godly heart and attitude because this is indicative of a sincere and faithful heart, which is a heart where God is.

By having hearts filled with God we will be faithful in all things and God will honour his many promises to us so we can receive his choicest and richest blessings.

When we are faithful, nothing will stop us from acting on the Word of God, and doing the will of God. But we need to be faithful not only with our mouths, but with our actions as well, so God can use us the way He wants to and reward us accordingly.

God wants us to be able to be faithful over the little He has given us and to be confident that He will reward us with many more things to come. It is all too easy to put things on hold and say we will do it tomorrow, next month or when we have more money, but God wants us to give now, pay now, serve now, reach out now and do what is right now.

If we hold onto the material world, we will never be free from it. We will then always be concerned with debt, trends and keeping up with everyone else. In turn, this will negatively impact on our emotional and psychological well-being as we allow ourselves to drown in a cesspit of worry, ego and insecurity about not being good enough.

God is not concerned with the suburb in which we live, how big our house is, how expensive our car is, or what position we hold. Instead, He wants us to be able. Can we give now and pay now, serve now, reach out now, and do what is right now?

God said in his Word that if we are faithful over a few things, He will make us faithful over many things.

CHOOSE FAITHFULNESS: 25 JULY

# God Rewards Our Faithfulness

*For he guards the course of the just*
*and protects the way of his faithful ones.*
– Proverbs 2:8

The story of Daniel is such a prefect example of faithfulness to God and the way God rewards us for it:

> Although Daniel won favour with the king for his wisdom, he was still thrown into the lion's den when he disobeyed the king's orders to not worship God. It is not important to obey man but God. Daniel refused to disobey God's commandment by not praying and interceding with Him and God saw his faithfulness. So when Daniel was thrown into the lion's den, he fearlessly waited for death. He was quite ready to die if it was God's will. He waited for the great, fierce beasts to spring at him in the darkness; he listened for the sound of their feet. Instead, there was the sound of an angel's wings, and the light of an angel's face shone in the darkness. And when he looked at the prowling beasts, lo! their mouths were shut by the angel's hand, and they could do him no harm, because God rewarded Daniel's faithfulness.
>
> The king came in the morning and he called out to Daniel. Daniel answered: 'O king, live for ever. My God hath sent his angel, and hath shut the lions' mouths, that they have not hurt me: forasmuch as before Him innocence was found in me; and also before thee, O king, have I done no hurt.'

In the same way, we will be kept safe and protected, but it is imperative to remain faithful to God, regardless of our circumstances.

CHOOSE FAITHFULNESS: 26 JULY

# Where Does Your Loyalty Lie?

*'If anyone comes to Me and does not hate [love less] his father and mother, wife and children, brothers and sisters, yes, and his own life also, he cannot be My disciple.'*
– LUKE 14:26

Faithfulness is evident in what we value in life and the things to which we remain loyal and committed. Many of us choose to be faithful to things that are not of God.

We allow ourselves to be consumed by money, power and earthly things. In order to retain that, we remain faithful to our employers, companies, and friends – even if they are a bad influence – our cars and everything else. Yet God wants us to be faithful to Him, so we can be his disciples.

We cannot do his will if we are loyal to things of the world and not to God.

We must choose today where our faithfulness and loyalty lie. It is only God who can establish his blessings and rewards for us.

CHOOSE FAITHFULNESS: 27 JULY

# Get Rid of Your Doubt

*People will be lovers of themselves, lovers of money, boastful, proud, abusive, disobedient to their parents, ungrateful, unholy, without love, unforgiving, slanderous, without self-control, brutal, not lovers of the good, treacherous, rash, conceited, lovers of pleasure rather than lovers of God …*
– 2 TIMOTHY 3:2–4

Man is generally faithless to any standard that can be considered as truly godly.

If being faithful is defined as maintaining conscientiousness, being reliable and having a sense of responsibility, then being faithless means being someone who chooses to be unreliable, undependable and dishonest. These characteristics are not desirable when we are God's children, as they will prevent us from experiencing God's presence in our lives.

Even as the most dedicated children of God, we allow certain elements of faithlessness to abide in our lives. It is that which allows us to go through what we go through. In the Book of Job, he says that the very thing he feared had come upon him. Regardless of his faith in God, he feared for his family and that fear caused his downfall.

God requires us to be completely faithful. When we reach that level of faithfulness, we can rest assured that we will be in the grace of God and He will take care of us.

In today's negative world, it is easy to become faithless. Yet, regardless of how small that doubt is, God sees it and it will affect our lives. Life is about the law of attraction; what we feel, think and believe is what we attract. Even if we are ninety-nine per cent faithful but have just one per cent of doubt, somewhere in our lives that doubt will bring consequences that we will have to face.

So we need to make a conscious choice to be one hundred per cent faithful and to know that God is in control and that He will take care of everything.

CHOOSE FAITHFULNESS: 28 JULY

# With Faith Comes Possibility

*'And the Lord said, If ye had faith as a grain of mustard seed, ye might say unto this sycamore tree, be thou plucked up by the root, and be thou planted in the sea; and it should obey you.'*
– LUKE 17:6

Again God is establishing his power in life. He reminds us that if we remain faithful, there is absolutely nothing we cannot do, regardless of how impossible it may seem.

We just have to believe we can. With faith comes possibility. Nothing of greatness in the world was ever achieved without faith.

For a moment in every day – even if it is for just a moment – we need to look around us, at our homes, families and lives and see how our faith allowed us to achieve all that we have. We may believe that it came from hard work and money, but it was actually our faithfulness in ourselves and our abilities that allowed us to work hard, earn money and acquire the many things we have.

God wants us to know that power does not only belong to Him – it is in us as well because He dwells in us. If we just take a little time to exercise just a little bit of it, we can do anything in which we have faith. We are able because He is able and our faith will ensure that there is nothing we cannot do or achieve.

# He Wants the Very Best for Us

*Now may the God of peace Himself sanctify you completely;*
*and may your whole spirit, soul, and body be preserved*
*blameless at the coming of our Lord Jesus Christ.*
*He who calls you is faithful, who also will do it.*
– 1 THESSALONIANS 5:23–24

God has sanctified us and through salvation He has made us whole. Just as we have every faith in our children to do great things, for we see the potential in them, so God too has faith in us, for He knows our potential and what we can do if we have faith in ourselves. He is faithful always and calls us faithful as well, because if we are his children we have inherited his characteristics. We were made in his image and therefore He made sure that we would have faith built into us, but it is up to us whether we choose to be faithful or not.

God guarantees that we will live a life which is fulfilling if we remain faithful like Him. He will never stop the work He has begun in us because He has faith that we can overcome and achieve. He wants the very best for us, He wants us to be happy and He wants us to live perfect lives. Most of all, He wants us to remain faithful to complete those works in our lives.

CHOOSE FAITHFULNESS: 30 JULY

# Are You 'Surviving' Life Or Are You Living Life?

*[He upholds] 'all things by the word of His power.'*
– Hebrews 1:3

There are times we will feel like we are just going through life from day to day without any will or purpose. We choose to allow ourselves to survive instead of live the life God has given us and make the most of it. Many of us 'survive' life, waiting for the day it will all end and we will be in God's house. But if we live life like that we will never reach our destination because it is not what God wants for us. He does not want us just to survive faithlessly because that is not who He is. He wants us to live and live faithfully in the knowledge that all things are possible in Him. God never disappears from our lives. He keeps track of everything we do. He coaches us through his Word and carries us through our trails. He comforts us, gives us peace, anoints us, ordains us and moves through us. All He expects in return is our faithfulness to live the life He wants us to live.

There is no trial or loss or pain we will ever experience that is greater than what Jesus went through when He died for us, and because He remained faithful, He rose again and was able to do what God ordained Him to do in that He brought salvation to the world.

We too can live a purposeful life if we choose never to allow our trials to leave us faithless.

CHOOSE FAITHFULNESS: 31 JULY

# Making the Right Choices

*A faithful man will be richly blessed.*
– Proverbs 28:20

When we choose to be faithful and obedient to God, we are guaranteed a reward. However, if we choose to be disobedient, we will have to deal with the consequences thereof.

Being faithful is all about making the right choices with regard to everything in our lives, especially our relationship with God. Being faithful also means doing everything we can to ensure that nothing and no one comes in the way of our faith and fellowship with our Father in heaven. Those choices may mean that we are not always accepted by society, our family or the people of the world, but the most important thing is that we will be accepted by God. We will never fall short of his grace despite being rejected by the world.

I remember talking to a friend of mine once who complained about being lonely because she stood up for what she believed in, and as a result no one spoke to her. She also thought it would be better just to be nice, conform to everyone else's characters and be two-faced, because it is more acceptable than to be rejected because of one's honesty.

Nonetheless, Jesus also stood alone among the Pharisees. He was also rejected, despised, abandoned and persecuted. But He was not moved. He allowed nothing to come between Him and his will. He remained faithful and we have to do the same, despite the bleakness of the situation and how lonely we may feel. Just like God expects us to be faithful, He is always faithful to us and we can trust Him to deliver us in all things in our lives. We will never be lonely and there will be nothing we will not be able to endure. Our faithfulness in Him will lead us through.

# August

## CHOOSE GOD'S ACCEPTANCE

*Lord, grant me the serenity to accept the things I cannot change, the courage to change the things I can, and the wisdom to know the difference.*

– Saint Francis of Assisi

## CHOOSE TO TRUST GOD

*It is impossible to go through life without trust:*
*That is to be imprisoned in the worst cell of all, oneself.*

– Graham Greene

## CHOOSE GOD'S PROTECTION

*The Lord is faithful, and He will strengthen*
*and protect you from the evil one.*

– 2 Thessalonians 3:3

## CHOOSE GOD'S PRESENCE

*His centre is everywhere, his circumference is nowhere.*

– Henery Law

CHOOSE GOD'S ACCEPTANCE: 1 AUGUST

# You Are a Winner

*'I am your Creator. You were in my care even before you were born.'*
– Isaiah 44:2

Our birth was not a mistake or a mishap, and our life is no stroke of luck. Our parents may not have planned us, but God did. He was not at all surprised by our birth. In fact, He looked forward to it.

Tony Campolo once said: 'Do not ever call yourself a loser. Consider the fact that you were once a sperm and you were once with 45 million sperm at the starting line, and at the end of the tunnel there was an egg. There was a race and you won. Do not ever call yourself a loser. The odds were 5 million to one and you came through. You are not a loser. You make the Olympics seem insignificant. You are here by divine intervention.'

God chose us to be winners. We are not here today because we are insignificant; we are here because God planned for us to be here. He knew us before we were in the womb, and we are here to make an impact. When we are weak, He is strong – and when we are discouraged, He will encourage us. He will heal us. He will pick us up when we are tired.

His grace is sufficient and He will make us run like rabbits and fly like eagles. We shall overcome and be winners. We will achieve our destiny through Him.

# We Are a Great Work of God

*For we are God's workmanship, created in Christ Jesus to do good works, which God prepared in advance for us to do.*
– Ephesians 2:10

It is important for us to realize that if God wants us to stay somewhere, we must stay, and if God wants us to go, we must go. Yet we must know also where we must be so that we can stay connected to our destiny.

We start to walk with Him because when He begins to deal with our hearts and says 'turn left' we will go left, and then God will reveal his plan for us.

And when He reveals his plan, He gives us the understanding and wisdom to fulfil that plan so that we may lead a life that is pleasing to Him. Like great artists produce great works, so too are we a great work of God, and He has ordained a life for us that is fitting and in keeping with that workmanship.

He has chosen us to do his works and, unless we stop it, He will let nothing get in the way of what He has already planned for us.

# God Has Chosen You

*'You have not chosen me, but I have chosen you and I have appointed you, that you might go and bear fruit and keep on bearing, and that your fruit may be lasting, so that whatever you ask the Father in My Name, He may give it to you.'*
– John 15:16

God has chosen us – individually – and it is vitally important because that means we were born for an assignment, and it was not born for us.

Our destiny was created before we were born. God has preplanned our lives before we came unto the earth. We existed in his mind before we came unto the earth, and that is why we have a gifting, an anointing and a special strength. Whatever it might be, God says He has chosen us and planted us where He wants us to be. God chose for us to be alive right now on the earth at this time. This means that what God has begun, He will complete.

He is on our side and wants us to reach our full potential. His responsibility is to make us a great nation. Ours is to obey, and to go where He wants us to go.

CHOOSE GOD'S ACCEPTANCE: 4 AUGUST

# He Will Take Us out of the Storm and into the Sunshine

*'Can a mother forget the baby at her breast and have no compassion on the child she has borne? Though she may forget, I will not forget you! See I have engraved you on the palms of my hands.'*
– Isaiah 49:15–16

We are royal priesthood and we are chosen. We are not accidents. We were chosen by God to be a holy nation, his own special people.

God created us in his image, and we decided to return the favour. We think we are doing Him a favour by serving Him. But there is nothing that compares to the marvellous light. When we look into the darkness of the world and we see famous people falling on their heads, depressed people, purposeless people, we need to recognize what a privilege it is to be called out of the darkness of hatred and bitterness and resentment and out of the darkness of lack. We can see who to trust and who not to. We can see into the marvellous light.

We have to walk in the marvellous light of the Lord and know that it is a privilege to obey God. He will never leave nor forsake us. He will take us out of the storm and into the sunshine – He will never turn his back on us but walk us through our trials. We have a God who has written our lives up. Our lives are light and the joy of the Lord is our strength.

And we are called into that marvellous light. Thus, we are his most accepted people and we must thank Him.

CHOOSE GOD'S ACCEPTANCE: 5 AUGUST

# We Are Special to Him

*How great is the love the Father has lavished on us, that we should be called children of God? And that is what we are!*
– 1 JOHN 3:1

We are God's elect, a special person, an ambassador, priest and king. We need to realize how special we are to Him, and that we are especially important in his Kingdom.

However, we must also know that the devil is a deceiver who wants us to believe that we are unimportant and a victim of our circumstances. The devil tempts us into other things. However, if we walk in the love of God and in the Spirit and not the flesh, and if we love what God has given us and how He has accepted us and loved us, we will have a great life.

Also, we need to see and recognize our worth, our value and our importance. We can stand with our heads held high and our integrity intact, for we were not meant to be insignificant. Instead, God wants us to feel the pride He has when He looks at what He has created in us. He wants us to value our lives as much as He values us, and He wants us to be bold and confident in whom we are. A low self-esteem and lack of confidence will only lead to a life of remorse. We are esteemed because we were created by the Lord God Almighty – the highest esteemed in the heavens and the earth. The last thing we should choose to have is a low self-esteem about who we are and our purpose.

# We Are the Apple of His Eye

*Now He who establishes us with you in Christ and anointed us is God, who also sealed us and gave us the Spirit in our hearts as a pledge.*
– 2 CORINTHIANS 1:21

The first thing we need to do today is stand in front of the mirror and look at what God has created. Look at all the intricate details and see the wonder of his work. We are God's masterpiece. When we look into the mirror today, we can smile and see as well as feel the joy God feels when He looks at us. Even the stars, the beauty of nature and the wonders of the animal and plant kingdom alike could not compare, for He calls us his finest work. We are priceless because God loved us so much that Jesus already paid the price for us on the cross.

He is so proud of what He had created in us that He calls us the apple of his eye. We are prized possessions in his heart and He loves us more than anything else. He has even sacrificed his own Son because He loved us so much. How many of us would do the same? How many of us would sacrifice our children to save a world of sin?

Only God has that kind of love for us. More than anything, that should show us our worth.

CHOOSE GOD'S ACCEPTANCE: 7 AUGUST

# Embrace His Love

*But now thus saith the Lord that created thee, O Jacob, and that formed thee, O Israel, fear not: for I have redeemed thee, I have called thee by thy name; thou art Mine.*
– Isaiah 43:1

We are so valuable to God that He knows each of us by our name, by the number of hair strands on our head, by the wrinkles on our hands and the imprints in our hearts.

In fact, so unique are we that He gave each of us our own fingerprint.

He has ordained us and has such special plans for us. He gave us everything we could possibly need in order to live the lives He wants for us.

And He keeps giving. Every day He reminds us through everything around us how special we are. He made us lords of the world and masters over every living thing; we are only inferior to Him.

He made us rulers over all, and we can take pleasure in knowing that God trusted us so much that He put us in charge. Instead of abusing that trust and walking away from his glory, we need to embrace his love and complete what He has given us in power, talent and grace.

# Put Your Trust in God

*Those who know Your Name will put their trust in You,*
*for You, O Lord, have not forsaken those who seek You.*
– Psalm 9:10

We often hear people say that the most important thing in a relationship is trust, and if a couple has no trust, they have nothing. In the same way, we each have a relationship with God, but if that relationship lacks trust in Him, then we have nothing, for without trust, we can never have faith, confidence, strength, love or grace. If we choose not to trust God, we can never grow into the will of God.

There are many examples in the Bible that shows how trusting God led to victory and fulfilment. God delivered Gideon because he trusted Him; Joshua's trust in God saw the walls of Jericho come tumbling down; Moses saw the people of Israel being led out of Egypt; Abraham and Sarah welcomed their first son even though they were way past the accepted child-bearing age; Joseph trusted God and was led to victory. It goes on and on.

Trust is vital for doing God's will and completing our purpose. It allows us to believe that nothing is in vain, for God will follow through. When we trust God, we can walk confidently through any situation and He will provide all our needs. Through trust we will see God perform many miracles in our lives. But like everything else, trusting God is a choice we have to make. Then God is able and willing to take his rightful place in our hearts.

CHOOSE TO TRUST GOD: 9 AUGUST

# Hear God's Word and Grow

*Then Jesus said, 'He who has ears to hear, let him hear.'*
– MARK 4:9

Jesus' story of the sower – perhaps the best loved of all the parables – is about hearing the Word (Mark 4:1–20).

Jesus told this story for He wanted people to see the importance of placing their trust in God. When people start trusting God as a choice they make for their lives, it pleases Him. He wants his Word to be sowed deeply in our hearts, so that our actions can be based on that trust. There will be no need for Him to forgive us then, because our trust in Him will allow us to make better choices for our lives which are absent of sin.

# Jesus Is Our True Friend

*He put a new song in my mouth, a song of praise to our God; many will see and fear and will trust in the LORD. How blessed is the man who has made the LORD his trust, and has not turned to the proud, nor to those who lapse into falsehood.*
– PSALM 40:3–4

There is an old song or hymn which talks about trusting God. The words are:

Trust in the Lord with all your heart for He is a friend so true.
No matter what your troubles are, Jesus will see them through.
Sing; sing as the day is bright.
Sing, sing the darkest night.
Trust in the Lord with all your heart for He is a friend so true.

Jesus is our true friend and regardless of what we are going through, if we trust Him, He will see us through. And He will put a new song in our hearts because we trust Him. He wants us not to worry, but to sing his praises, for there is nothing He will not help us through.

# Put Your Trust in God

*He thou passes through the waters I will be with thee; and through the rivers, they shall not overflow thee; when thou walks through the fire, thou shalt not be burned; neither shall the flame kindle upon thee.*
– Isaiah 43:2

Remember the story of Shadrach, Meshach and Abednego? They were faithful to God and believed in their heart of hearts that God was real and would always look after them. They placed all of their trust in Him. And when they disobeyed king Nebuchadnezzar by refusing to worship the huge golden statue he wanted them to worship, they were thrown into a fiery furnace as punishment. But they were not afraid. They trusted that God will see them through it, and they loved God too much to disobey Him.

After they were thrown into the furnace, the king proudly went over and looked into the fire, but instead of the three men, he saw four men walking around in the flames, and one looked like an angel. They were all walking around completely untouched by the heat and fire. The king released them. They examined the men carefully. Not one thread of clothing had been singed, and they did not even smell of smoke.

And Nebuchadnezzar said: 'Bless the God of Shadrach, Meshach and Abednego who has sent his angel to protect them from the fire. I command this day that anyone who speaks evil about the God of Shadrach, Meshach and Abednego will be cut to pieces. For there is no other god that will protect his people in this way.'

Nebuchadnezzar promoted the three and gave them great jobs in his empire. And just as God promised, they were prosperous in everything they did because they chose to trust Him. Choose today to trust our Lord God Almighty for He is worthy of all our praise.

# Take Refuge in the Lord

*It is better to take refuge in the Lord than to trust in man.*
*It is better to take refuge in the Lord than to trust in princes.*
– Psalm 118:8–9

After the flood, Noah's people obeyed God for a while. But as they began to increase in number, a large group turned away from God. They did not believe his promise that He would never again send another flood to cover the whole earth. Noah's righteous lifestyle was so different to theirs that they did not want to live near him anymore.

A large number of them moved from the mountains of Ararat to the plain of Shinar. Here they built a large city. They also talked to one another about their disbelief in God's promise not to send another flood, yet they planned what they could do to prepare themselves, should God change his mind. They decided to build a tower. They thought that if God did change his mind, all they would have to do is climb to the top of their tower and they would be saved.

God was watching what these people were doing. He was not pleased. If He let such disobedience go unpunished, what else might these people plan to do? But what could He do?

Everyone at that time spoke the same language, so God said, 'Let us go down and mix up their languages so that they cannot speak to one another.'

Everyone was busy building. Then all of a sudden everything went terribly wrong. The workers could not understand one another. Men became angry with one another. Fights broke out here and there. So they packed up their tools and went back to their houses. Slowly people found others who spoke the same language as themselves and moved away together. So the Lord scattered the people everywhere as He originally intended.

The place in Shinar, where the people built their city and tower, was called 'Babel', because the Lord here mixed up all the languages. The people who stayed here later changed the name to 'Babylon'.

This story shows us that it is always better to trust in God than to trust other human beings, or what we can build for ourselves.

– ADAPTED FROM BIBLICAL STUDIES.NET

# Allow God To Help You through Your Trials

*Blessed is the man who trusts in the Lord, whose trust is the Lord.*
– Jeremiah 17:7

When good things happen in our lives, we are quick to take those blessings, thank God and indulge in them. But when bad things happen, we are quick to blame God for causing these things. We refuse to see or acknowledge that God may have great things in store for us that will come out of that situation.

We lose our trust in Him, his will, and the promises He has made to us.

But God never *causes* bad things to happen in our lives. He may *allow* them to happen so that we can trust Him to see us through the hardships, and ultimately learn the lesson which comes from it.

Sometimes, we need to trust God in his promise, for He may allow certain things to happen to save us from the pain of something much worse. If we take the time to look at past trials, we will see how trusting God has brought us through our trials and led us to better things, which were probably revealed only later.

Rather than blaming God, let us thank Him for the grace He will give us and the promises He will keep by taking us to a higher place through our trials.

Only trust in Him will allow us to see what He will reveal to us, otherwise we will remain blind to his power, mercy and grace.

# Trust with the Innocence of a Child

*Thou wilt keep him in perfect peace, whose mind is stayed on thee: because he trusted in thee.*
– Isaiah 26:3

Take the time to observe an infant and the amount of trust they have in their parents and adults around them. I know one friend who complained that if she did not keep an eye on her child, he would gladly take the hand of any stranger and go with them.

But children are innocent; they trust with their hearts.

They love everyone because they do not yet have the wisdom or experience to see bad in anyone.

They just believe that every person is good.

In the same way, we must learn to trust God with all our heart and with the openness and innocence of a child, for He has the best intentions and wants the best for us. He is the one person or source that can be trusted, for He will never allow us to be harmed.

He loves us completely. All we need to do is choose to trust Him and we will see Him work in our lives.

# Under His Wings You Will Find Refuge

*He who dwells in the shelter of the Most High will rest in the shadow of the Almighty. I will say of the LORD, 'He is my refuge and my fortress, my God, in whom I trust.' Surely He will save you from the fowler's snare and from the deadly pestilence. He will cover you with His feathers, and under His wings you will find refuge; His faithfulness will be your shield and rampart. You will not fear the terror of night, nor the arrow that flies by day, nor the pestilence that stalks in the darkness, nor the plague that destroys at midday. A thousand may fall at your side, ten thousand at your right hand, but it will not come near you. You will only observe with your eyes and see the punishment of the wicked. If you make the Most High your dwelling – even the LORD, who is my refuge – then no harm will befall you, no disaster will come near your tent. For He will command His angels concerning you to guard you in all your ways; they will lift you up in their hands, so that you will not strike your foot against a stone. You will tread upon the lion and the cobra; you will trample the great lion and the serpent. 'Because he loves me,' says the LORD, 'I will rescue him; I will protect him, for he acknowledges My Name. He will call upon me, and I will answer him; I will be with him in trouble, I will deliver him and honor him. With long life will I satisfy him and show him My salvation.'*

– PSALM 91

What better Scripture is there in the Bible that describes God's protection better than this one? The Lord does protect us, but we need to abide in Him and we will see just how much He protects us.

CHOOSE GOD'S PROTECTION: 16 AUGUST

# Are There Weeds Growing in Your Life?

*The Kingdom of heaven is like this. A man sowed good seed in his field. One night, when everyone was asleep, an enemy came and sowed weeds among the wheat and went away. When the plants grew and the heads of grain began to form, the weeds showed up. The man's servants came to him and said, 'Sir it was good seed you sowed in your field; where did the weeds come from?' 'It was some enemy who did this,' he answered. 'Do you want us to go and pull up the weeds?' they asked him. 'No,' he answered. 'Because as you gather the weeds you might pull up some of the wheat along with them. Let the wheat and the weeds both grow together until harvest. Then I will tell the harvest workers to pull up the weeds first, tie them in bundles and burn them, and then gather in the wheat and put it in my barn.'*

– Matthew 13:24–30

There are times when the devil will cause weeds to grow in our lives, but God has the power to destroy them if we choose to allow Him to. We choose to have his protection. We are never safe from the devil and from evil, but we can be sure of one thing, and that is that God is ever-willing to help and protect us. His protection is able to prevail even in the midst of the worst kind of evil. It will stand strong and take us out of the muck and the mire, and lead us to his safe dwelling.

CHOOSE GOD'S PROTECTION: 17 AUGUST

# You Don't Have To Be Macho with God

*The Lord will protect you from all evil; He will keep your soul. The Lord will guard your going out and your coming in from this time forth and forever.*
– Psalm 121:7

There is nothing wrong about calling out to God and needing Him to help and protect us. This is one of his promises to us. As his heirs, it is part of our trust fund in Him. He is there to care for us. As his beneficiaries we are meant to benefit from his power and grace. He is always there to take care of our needs and protect us.

Sometimes we try to be stronger than we actually are based on an ego trip and being macho, but we do not need to be macho with God. He wants us to be able to come to Him with our needs and ask Him for his grace to come into our lives. We will always be faced with evil, whether it is in our surroundings or from the people who come into our lives. We cannot avoid it, for it is the way of the world, but we can speak to God about it and ask Him for his goodness to surround us and for his powerful grace to fall on us.

And He will answer. He will never turn his back on us and not do what we ask Him.

God is always with us and among us. Good always triumphs over evil – for God's protection never leaves us.

CHOOSE GOD'S PROTECTION: 18 AUGUST

# God Watches over Us

*I lift up my eyes to the hills – where does my help come from?*
*My help comes from the LORD,*
*the Maker of heaven and earth.*
*He will not let your foot slip –*
*He who watches over you will not slumber;*
*indeed, He who watches over Israel*
*will neither slumber nor sleep.*
*The LORD watches over you –*
*the LORD is your shade at your right hand;*
*the sun will not harm you by day,*
*nor the moon by night.*
*The LORD will keep you from all harm –*
*He will watch over your life;*
*the LORD will watch over your coming and going*
*both now and forever more.*
– PSALM 121

This psalm is another perfect promise of God's protection. God is always present to watch over us and to make sure we are kept safe.

# God Promises Us Supernatural Protection

*Let the beloved of the LORD rest secure in Him, for He shields him all day long, and the one the LORD loves rests between his shoulders.*
– DEUTERONOMY 33:12

God promises us supernatural protection. He never fails on delivering his promises. But He requires us to obey Him and his Word, as well as follow his teachings in all that we do, despite the trials we face.

If we stay faithful to Him, He will always protect us, even if a solution may seem impossible.

If we are able to trust God and place our faith in Him, He will ensure that his highest protection order is on our lives. Nothing the devil does or tries to do will bring us down, for He will place a shield before us and take on the form of armour to protect us from all the things which could hurt us, harm us and destroy us.

Speaking God's Word out loud is also very powerful in the Kingdom of Heaven. Knowing God's Word and speaking it builds a wall around us that cannot be penetrated. So we must choose to have God's supernatural protection in our lives every day.

# Choose God As Your Refuge

*He who fears the* L*ORD has a secure fortress,*
*and for his children it will be a refuge.*
– Proverbs 14:26

There is nothing small about God. In fact, He is so big that He is able to provide a shelter for all of us and his refuge is able to cover all of humanity. But in order to have that protection, there are certain criteria we have to meet.

Firstly, like the Scripture says, we have to fear the Lord, not be afraid of Him, but acknowledge that He will hold us accountable for our sin.

Then we have to be obedient to his commandments, because we need to be delivered. We need to love, and we need to be bold and never fear. We also need to abide in God's Word and live lives that are favourable to Him – lives which include faith, endurance, righteousness and patience – in order to receive his huge promise of protection and not just a portion thereof. God's protection in our lives transcends all, but unless we give Him control of our lives and access to it, we will never be able to experience our right to his protection.

CHOOSE GOD'S PROTECTION: 21 AUGUST

# Put Your Soul in the Palm of His Hand

*Those who know your name trust in you, for you,*
*Lord, have never forsaken those who seek you.*
– Psalm 9:10

It is funny how we go through life protecting everything we have and yet we still doubt God's ability to protect us.

We protect our cars and homes with alarm systems, food by putting it in the fridge, bodies with suntan lotion, and illness with medication. And yet we fail to protect our souls.

We want the best of everything, and go after the newest trends. We buy state-of-the-art equipment, top cars, and houses in exclusive suburbs. Yet when it comes to our souls, we take it for granted and neglect to give it what it needs.

All it needs is a close relationship with God, and all God needs is for us to have and maintain a close relationship with Him, so He can protect us from all evil and protect our souls from running on empty.

But doing that requires that we make a choice to have Him reign supreme and take charge. We need to put our souls into the palms of his hand and like Jesus did, commit our lives to Him. Then we can be assured of his promise of protection in all things.

CHOOSE GOD'S PRESENCE: 22 AUGUST

# Draw Near to God

*Draw near to God and He will draw near to you. Cleanse your hands, you sinners; and purify your hearts, you double-minded.*
– JAMES 4:8

When we feel like God is not in our lives and as if He has rejected us, we have only ourselves to blame, for God promises never to leave us. It is imperative for us to draw near to Him in all we do.

In order to do this, we need to walk in faith and obedience and reject sin and all the evil that comes from the world.

Only we can decide how close we want God to be. God is a God of invitation. He will not force Himself on us and push his way in, but He will wait for us to invite Him in. When we do that, He will come in and dwell in us. So God's distance from us is based primarily on how far we want Him to be – the choice is ours as to where we want Him.

If we are two-faced, double-minded and have hearts which are not completely set on Him, then He will wait until we are able to fully commit to Him, so that his presence can abide in us and in all we do.

CHOOSE GOD'S PRESENCE: 23 AUGUST

# He Is Eager To Come into Our Lives

*Even though I walk through the valley of the shadow of death, I will fear no evil, for you are with me; your rod and your staff, they comfort me.*
– Psalm 23:4

Life will get difficult – that is something we can always be sure of. In spite of that, the other assurance we have is that God is always with us regardless of how terrible things get in life. He promises to care for us and to be our guide and companion. He is alive in our hearts and in our lives and will never move away from us. He is powerful and mighty over all things. There are times when we will feel powerless, when we feel a loss of hope and joy. But we will feel the presence of God when we seek Him and ask Him to come in.

As the well-known chorus says, 'Alive, alive, alive forever more' – He is working in us and through us. If we choose to draw near to Him, then He will draw near to us, and his presence will surround us. Life in Christ is this personal, this real, and this near when it comes to knowing God. A relationship with God is a personal one – one that requires us to keep our eyes fixed on Him and our hearts strengthened in Him.

He is so eager to come into our lives and make his presence felt.

CHOOSE GOD'S PRESENCE: 24 AUGUST

# Look, He's Right before Your Eyes

*He does not take His eyes off the righteous.*
*He enthrones them with kings and exalts them forever.*
– Job 36:7

In whatever we do in our lives, God's presence is with us. We are never out of his sight or out of his mind. He surrounds us with his unfailing love; He strengthens us and gives us peace.

We can also see the presence of God in our lives and in the things around us – from the rising of the sun to its setting, in the way the waves meet the sand, a butterfly touching a leaf, trees dancing in the wind, frogs croaking near a pond, the burbling of a stream, dew on the leaves, mist in the mornings, raindrops on a tin roof, the giggling of a baby, the majesty of the mountains, the magnificence of the snow gleaming in the sun.

There are so many ways in which we can see God's presence in our lives every day, but we are too busy, so we choose to ignore it. We choose to wait for Him to personify Himself to us, to reveal Himself to us in his real likeness. If He does not, we call Him a coward; we begin to doubt Him and question his might.

But his presence is everywhere. Just choose to look at it and not for it. Look at it – because it is right there in front of us, in everything.

CHOOSE GOD'S PRESENCE: 25 AUGUST

# He Is the Air We Breathe

*[As Paul said, describing the one true God,]*
*'in Him we live and move and exist.'*
– ACTS 17:28

God is alive, active, working, and moving in our hearts. God's presence is in everything we do. And everything we do, we are able to do because of his presence in our lives. He has given us the very breath of air we breathe, the impetus to move, the strength to overcome, the hope to go on, the peace to be comforted, the love to love, the blessings to bless, the joy to share, the ability to do all things. If we choose Him, there's nothing in life we cannot do.

God cannot be confined to the image of stone, wood, plastic, metal or another substance. He is real, and we need to be real for Him. We need to be real, especially when we come into his presence.

# God Has a Positive Answer ...

You say: 'It is impossible.' God says: 'What is impossible with men is possible with God' (Luke 18:27).

You say: 'I'm too tired.' God says: 'I will give you rest' (Matt 11:28–30).

You say: 'Nobody really loves me.' God says: 'I love you' (John 3:16).

You say: 'I cannot go on.' God says: 'I will direct your steps' (Prov 3:5–6).

You say: 'I cannot do it.' God says: 'You can do all things' (Phil 4:13).

You say: 'I'm not able.' God says: 'I am able' (2 Cor 9:8).

You say: 'It is not worth it.' God says: 'It will be worth it' (Rom 8:28).

You say: 'I cannot forgive myself.' God says: 'I forgive you' (1 John 1:9).

You say: 'I cannot manage' God says: 'I will supply all your needs' (Phil 4:19).

You say: 'I'm afraid.' God says: 'I have not given you a spirit of fear' (2 Tim 1:7).

You say: 'I'm always worried and frustrated.' God says: 'Cast all your cares on Me' (1 Pet 5:7).

You say: 'I do not have enough faith.' God says: 'I've given everyone a measure of faith' (Rom 12:3).

You say: 'I'm not smart enough.' God says: 'I give you wisdom' (1 Cor 1:30).

You say: 'I feel all alone.' God says: 'I will never leave you or forsake you' (Heb 13:5).

# All We Have To Do Is Let Him in

*Let us then approach the throne of grace with confidence, so that we may receive mercy and find grace to help us in our time of need.*
– Hebrews 4:16

Many of us deny ourselves the privilege to be close to God because we have the impression that God is far away, up there in the sky, soaring among the eagles or bouncing between the planets. So far away, in fact, that we make ourselves believe that He is untouchable, unreachable and invisible, but nothing is further from the truth.

God is here, not outside us, but inside us – right in the depths of our hearts, lodged in our minds and deep in our souls. So embedded is He in us that nothing will ever be closer to us than the presence of God. The only time we will not feel his presence is when we choose to lock Him out, shut Him out and ignore his voice. But when Jesus died on the cross, it allowed us to be directly in God's grace and to have a close relationship with Him. All we have to do is let Him in through prayer, because we are his dwelling place and in the direct presence of God.

# Lord, I Feel ...

Beaten … yet You have made me more than a conqueror (Rom 8:37).

Bound … yet You are my deliverer (Rom 11:26).

Confused … yet You are my counsellor (Isa 9:6).

A failure … yet You have made me an overcomer (1 John 5:4).

Fearful … yet You did not give me a spirit of fear, but of power, of love, and of a sound mind (2 Tim 1:7).

Friendless … yet You are a friend who sticks closer to me than a brother (Prov 18:24).

In darkness … yet You are a light unto my path and a lamp unto my feet (Ps 119:105).

Lonely … yet You promised never to leave me nor forsake me (Heb 13:5).

# You Are My Peace

Misjudged … yet I am accepted and approved by You (Eph 1:4).

Poor … yet You supply all my need according to Your riches in glory (Phil 4:19).

Sick … yet You are the Lord who heals all my diseases (Ps 103:3).

Troubled … yet You are my peace (John 14:27).

Unclean … yet You are the purifier and refiner of my life (Mal 3:3).

Vulnerable … yet You are my strength and my strong tower (Ps 18:2).

Worthless … yet You see me as a pearl of great price (Matt 13:46).

# Never Lose the Presence of God

*[David committed adultery with Bathsheba,]*
*'... and the thing that David had done displeased the Lord.'*
– 2 Samuel 11:27

If we don't have God's presence in our lives, we can never be happy. We will live lives of regret, remorse and grief. One of the first things that happen if we lose the presence of God is that we become extremely depressed.

And God's presence does depart from our lives when we choose to disobey Him, and when we are not sincere about his Word.

When his presence departs, we also allow a spirit of envy to fall on us because we lose faith in the promise of his wealth. We start to allow wealth and material things of the world to become our first priority, aspiring to the wrong things in life.

We also become fearful because we are not secure in the knowledge of God's protection.

After the fear comes a spirit of hopelessness, emptiness, anger and hate. So we must never lose the presence of the Lord in our lives.

# Have a Passion for God's Presence in Your Life

*Then He inaugurated Joshua the son of Nun, and said, 'Be strong and of good courage; for you shall bring the children of Israel into the land of which I swore to them, and I will be with you.'*
– Deuteronomy 31:23

Joshua became Israel's leader during one of the most difficult times in its history. But it was the Lord's presence in his life and his earnest desire for it which led him to that victory.

He had a deep passion for God to be with him and never allowed himself to lose the presence of God in his life. So great was that passion for God's presence that he remained obedient to God and his commandments.

He also maintained the integrity and character of God, and was faithful to his role under Moses.

Those attributes in Joshua's life allowed him always to have God's presence in his life, and, through that presence, God was able to work in him and lead him to victory.

We need to be like Joshua and have the same passion for the presence of God and stay in the character of God. When God is in us, nothing can come between us and the purpose God has called us to fulfil. He will guide us and lead us and ensure that we are victorious to do and achieve his will for us.

# September

## CHOOSE TO BE IN HIS LIGHT

*Who is more foolish, the child afraid of the dark or the man afraid of the light?*

– Maurice Freehill

## CHOOSE TO WALK IN TRUTH

*Today, I ask that the TRUTH be revealed to me.*
*TRUTH is eternal. TRUTH is the essence of my soul.*
*TRUTH is my connection to the divine source of all life.*

– Iyanla Vanzant

## CHOOSE PERFECTION

*The pursuit of perfection, then, is the pursuit of sweetness and light.*

– Matthew Arnold

## CHOOSE TO PRAY

*Our Father Who Art in Heaven*
*Hallowed Be Thy name …*

– Matthew 6:9

# We Will Grow And Flourish

*'In the same way, let your light shine before men, that they may see your good deeds and praise your Father in heaven.'*
– Matthew 5:16

One of the parables Jesus used when talking about the importance of God's light in our lives is about being rooted in God so that we do not wither in the light of the Gospel.

> 'Behold, a sower went forth to sow … Some fell upon stony places, where they had not much earth: and forthwith they sprung up, because they had no deepness of earth: And when the sun was up, they were scorched; and because they had no root, they withered away. But he that received seed into the good ground is he that heareth the word, and understandeth it; which also beareth fruit, and bringeth forth, some a hundredfold, some sixty, some thirty.'
>
> – Mark 4:3–8

We need to thrive in the light of God's Word in order to grow. If we embrace the lessons in the Scriptures and apply it to our own lives, we will grow and flourish in the will of God.

When the Word is rooted deeply in our hearts, no darkness will be able to enter our lives, for we will live our lives in the light of the Lord.

Through that light we will produce a life that is favourable to God and that will never wither.

CHOOSE TO BE IN HIS LIGHT: 2 SEPTEMBER

# Let Your Light Shine

*If we claim to have fellowship with Him, yet walk in the darkness, we lie and do not live by the truth. But if we walk in the light, as He is in the light, we have fellowship with one another, and the blood of Jesus, His Son, purifies us from all sin.*
– 1 John 1:6–7

So many Christians claim to love the Lord and be committed to Him. Yet they live their lives outside of his light. Since actions speak louder than words, God wants us to not just talk about it. If we say we are walking in God's light but we do not act in the character of God in the lifestyle we have, then we are actually still in the darkness.

We cannot say we love the Lord when we do not love one another. We cannot claim to be in his light if we have hatred, contempt, envy and greed filling our hearts. We cannot be in the light if we are loyal to materialism instead of spiritualism. If that is the kind of life we choose, we will never be out of the darkness. We should not be too consumed with ourselves and our own lives. Instead, we must focus on God and his commandments. He commands that we are to have fellowship with each other and let his light shine through us in the way we treat others.

The Book of Revelation refers to churches as lamp-stands. As we fellowship in them, we too become lamp-stands. If the purpose of a lamp-stand is to provide light in an otherwise dark place, then we need to choose to be lamp-stands for Christ.

CHOOSE TO BE IN HIS LIGHT: 3 SEPTEMBER

# The Meaning of Life

*'You are the light of the world. A city that is set on a hill cannot be hid … Let your light so shine before men, that they may see your good works, and glorify your Father which is in heaven.'*
– Matthew 5:14–16

The following story was told by Robert Fulghum, a Unitarian minister, about a seminar he once attended in Greece. On the last day of the conference, the discussion leader walked over to the bright light of an open window and looked out. Then he asked if there were any questions. Fulghum laughingly asked him what the meaning of life was.

Everyone in attendance laughed and stirred to leave. However, the leader held up his hand to ask for silence and then responded 'I will answer your question.' He took his wallet out of his pocket and removed a small round mirror about the size of a quarter. Then he explained: 'When I was a small child during World War II, we were very poor and lived in a remote village. One day on the road, I found the broken pieces of a mirror. A German motorcycle had been wrecked in that place. I tried to find all the pieces and put them together, but it was not possible, so I kept the largest piece. This one. And by scratching it on a stone, I made it round. I began to play with it as a toy and became fascinated by the fact that I could reflect light into dark places where the sun could never shine. It became a game for me to get light into the most inaccessible places that I could find. As I grew up, I would take it out at idle moments and continue the challenge of the game.'

'As I became a man, I grew to understand that this was a metaphor of what I could do with my life. I am not the light or the source of the light. But light – be it truth or understanding or knowledge – is there, and it will only shine in many dark places if I reflect it. I am a fragment of a mirror whose whole design and shape I do not know. Nevertheless, with what I have, I can reflect light into the dark places of this world – into the dark places of human hearts – and change some things in some people. Perhaps others seeing it happen will do likewise. This is what I am about. This is the meaning of my life.'

# Build Your Child's Value and Moral System

*Once you were in darkness; but now you are light in the Lord, walk as children of light. For the fruit of the light or the spirit consists in every form of kindly goodness, uprightness of heart and trueness of life. And try to learn what is pleasing to the Lord.*
– EPHESIANS 5:8–10

When we chose to receive God into our lives, we choose to receive the Light of the Lord. And because we are his children, we need to adopt the character of our Father. In daily life, we need to build a value and moral system for our children which will be the core of who they are.

I listened to a couple who complained that their children were so different from what they were, and that they could not understand it. They spoke about the number of children who nowadays put their parents into old-age homes and forget about them.

Yes, the world has changed and our children are daily exposed to and influenced by a world that we cannot really relate to, because we grew up in a different time and era altogether. Even so, if we are able to build our children at the core and establish in them the light that reflects God and his character, which includes proper values and morals, nothing will move that child from what is rooted in Him. Yes, he will be influenced, yes, he will have a different mindset from our own because of that influence and, yes, he may lead a life and make decisions or handle situations totally differently to how we would. Still, that core will never change. And we will find that they will come back to that core which their parents strengthened in them.

It is our responsibility to our children to ensure they have that core. God is our Father and has given us the light at the core of who we are – so we need to let his light shine.

# A Lamp on a Stand

*'No one lights a lamp and hides it in a jar or puts it under a bed. Instead, he puts it on a stand, so that those who come in can see the light. For there is nothing hidden that will not be disclosed, and nothing concealed that will not be known or brought out into the open.'*
– Luke 8:16–17

In the times that Jesus walked the earth many of the cities were founded on the summits or sides of mountains, and they were visible from far away.

In the above parable Jesus refers to the disciples and to us as those cities on the hills.

His example of the shining lamps inside those houses is a metaphor for our actions.

Our actions cannot be hidden from anyone. Christians are first to be criticized for their actions and the lives they lead.

It is therefore important for us to live a life that is holy, humble and righteous. We have to have the character of Jesus and let our light shine before men. In so doing we will give God the glory.

# Freedom That Comes from Living in the Light

*Your word is a lamp to my feet and a light for my path.*
– Psalm 119:105

God promises never to let us walk in darkness. He will always guide our steps in whatever we do in life and wherever we go – provided we choose to let Him be the lamp at our feet. Like so many things on earth (e.g. plants, animals and other life forms) depend on the sun for their light to live, so too, we need the light of the Lord to live.

God's light takes away the darkness of sin in our lives by filling it with joy and peace. His light is what sets us free from sin and temptation. There is great freedom for us when we choose to live in the light of God.

We will always be led in truth because of the light of the Lord in our lives. We will never walk blindly again, for the light of the Lord will reveal to us what needs to be revealed, and then we will clearly understand the will of God for our lives. In turn, we will be able to display that light to others by our words and our actions.

CHOOSE TO BE IN HIS LIGHT: 7 SEPTEMBER

# Live in His Light

*For He rescued us from the domain of darkness,*
*and transferred us to the Kingdom of His beloved Son,*
*in whom we have redemption, the forgiveness of sins.*
– COLOSSIANS 1:13–14

When we accept God, we are rescued from Satan's darkness and we are redeemed in God. As soon as we allow God's light to fill our lives, we are forgiven all our sins and transgressions, and then we are no longer children of the devil but children of God.

Furthermore, when we are forgiven and living in his light, obeying his Word, we will know God's will. When we allow the Lord to lead us to his will while being in his light, we will find favour in Him and become heirs in his Kingdom.

We will be sanctified and fit to receive his rewards for us.

CHOOSE TO WALK IN TRUTH: 8 SEPTEMBER

# What Does Your Mirror Reflect?

*As in water face reflects face, so a man's heart reveals the man.*
– PROVERBS 27:19

We are not living in the Snow White story where we can order mirrors to tell us what we want to hear. Instead, when we look into a mirror, regardless of how much we hope the wrinkles, spots and blemishes will vanish, they will remain and just like a mirror shows us who we are, so too do our hearts and actions reveal our character, integrity and humility.

It is a true reflection of who we really are. The only time that image will change is when we choose to change our hearts, first by choosing to make the right choices in life and choices that are in truth.

When our hearts are pure, we will produce lives evident of that purity, but when our hearts are evil, the fruit to come out of it will reflect that evil.

An evil person may have millions in the bank, but will never be able to buy a good life. A good life only comes when we choose to live and walk in the truth of the Lord. When we lead a righteous life, we allow people to see God in it and working through it. Our lives are then filled with goodness and truth and we become confident, because we know we are living lives that are void of evil and wickedness, and that are pleasing to God.

# Raise God's Banner

*Do you not know that your body is a temple of the Holy Spirit, who is in you, whom you have received from God? You are not your own.*
– 1 CORINTHIANS 6:19

God created us and calls us temples of his Holy Spirit, because it is our bodies in which the Spirit resides. We belong to Christ, and as his children we need to walk in Him and reflect his truth.

Everything we are and have belongs to God, and we should not abuse that which God has given us. If we abuse what He has given us, He will hold us responsible, and on the Day of Judgement we will have to explain what we did with the many gifts He has given us: gifts of wisdom, grace, confidence, strength, and life, as we know it.

Therefore, we need to make the most of what God has given us and use it to extend his Kingdom and give Him glory.

We need to live a life that is pleasing to Him – a life that reflects who He is in us – so we can produce the results He wants for us. When we stand before Him, He will commend us for being his good, faithful and trusting servants, who have helped raise his banner on the earth and among his children.

# Watch What You Say

*Speaking the truth in love, we are to grow up in all aspects into Him who is the head, even Christ.*
– Ephesians 4:15

One of the most difficult things to do in life is hold our tongue and refrain from saying nasty things when we are provoked. But Jesus refers to the inability to hold our tongues as a great deception. Words can sometimes bring such hate that we believe we are victors over the victim of our words. However, we will realize that we often end up feeling worse about our own evil thoughts which produced those words than the person at the receiving end. We must never allow people or circumstance to provoke us into letting go with our tongues. There is great power in the tongue – besides from being the strongest muscle in the body, it can also control the entire outcome of an individual's life – for whatever is in our hearts comes out in our speech and can cause our downfall.

It is also important to use the right tone of voice when we speak. We can say 'I love you' in various tones, and each time it could have a different meaning based on the tone we use when we say it. So tone is important, as it tells us how important it is for us to be conscious of not only what we say but how we say it. We must also choose appropriate times to speak – speaking when we are not called or required to can also have detrimental consequences.

So, in life, speech and our ability to control that speech, is vital – especially if we are doing it in the Name of God.

Everything that comes forth from our mouths should be only that which would be glorifying to God.

# Stay Connected to God and His Word

*Be sober, be vigilant; because your adversary the devil, as a roaring lion, walked about, and seeking whom he may devour.*
– 1 PETER 5:8

The best way to walk in truth is to know the Word of God and what it stands for.

We can never stand for something if we do not believe in something. When we are knowledgeable in the Word of God, we will be able to stand for God and walk in his truth – for we will know the truth.

The devil will never be able to destroy that which is in our mind. God has given us the gift of free will. And if our will is to walk in truth, and we obey his Word, know his Word and stay true to his Word, nothing the devil does can destroy it.

Being confident in the world will allow us to resist the attacks of the devil. Satan attacks more often when we are weak, so our best line of defence would be to stay connected to God and his Word. We must choose to allow God to show us his truth.

# Humility Allows Us To Listen

*But whoever lives by the truth comes into the light, so that it may be seen plainly that what he has done has been done through God.*
– John 3:21

Humility is vital to walking in truth. This is one of the most essential characteristics of Christ. If we are able to show humility to anyone, regardless of the power they hold, we will win God's favour.

In order to walk in truth we need to obey God and be respectful of his Word.

We also need to be submissive to certain things that God commands us, and we need to listen to what He wants us to do.

Walking in truth means walking in God. If we choose to ignore what He is telling us, we can never do what He intends for us to do.

Humility therefore allows us to listen. Humility gives us the grace to know that we may not know everything. Sometimes we need to ask the Lord and others to lead us to it.

# He Is Waiting for Us To Walk with Him

*The heavens declare the glory of God;*
*And the firmament shows His handiwork.*
*Day unto day utters speech,*
*And night unto night reveals knowledge.*
*There is no speech nor language*
*Where their voice is not heard.*
*Their line has gone out through all the earth,*
*And their words to the end of the world.*
– Psalm 19:1–4

He who practises the truth comes to the Light. The existence of God is evident from his works, as we see in the verses above. How can we not walk in truth when we serve a God of truth and life? Many of us try to see evidence of whether God is real or not before we make a choice to walk in his light and in his truth. But if we look around us, we will see the evidence of who He is and what his truth is. God is the creator of the earth. He reigns, has spoken, will judge, is love. He sent his Son, his spirit, and He is worthy of our praise. If we choose to walk in his truth, we have to first believe that what we are worshipping and walking in is truth indeed. We need to believe in Him and his truth. We need to rise from where we are into his light. He is waiting for us to walk with Him.

CHOOSE TO WALK IN TRUTH: 14 SEPTEMBER

# Be a Doer of His Word

*My little children let us not love in word or in tongue, but in deed and in truth. And by this we know that we are of the truth, and shall assure our hearts before Him. For if our heart condemns us, God is greater than our heart, and knows all things. Beloved, if our heart does not condemn us, we have confidence toward God.*

– 1 John 3:18–21

An ideal way to walk in truth is through our actions, because it is our deeds which reveal our hearts and ultimately the character of Christ in us. God does not want us to be hearers, to give lip service, and then still claim to be Christians. He wants us to be shining examples of what Christians should be by being doers of his Word. God sees everything we do and knows all things. He knows where our heart lies, and He wants us to do as He would do.

Our hearts reflect who we truly are: If we seek God and his Word, we will find the guidance to walk in his truth, and we will be the true Christians God wants us to be.

# Strive for Perfection

*Not that I have already obtained all this,*
*or have already been made perfect, but I press on to*
*take hold of that for which Christ Jesus took hold of me.*
– Philippians 3:12

It is true that God will accept us, regardless of who we are. We can come into his presence just as we are. However, He wants us to strive for perfection in his presence and aspire to be complete in our lives. As a result of God's presence in our lives, we are already perfect. Abraham's faith was made perfect and complete by what he did. If we obey God's Word, his love is truly made complete and perfect in us.

We can never truly be perfect, but we have to aspire to be perfect in the way we live our lives. We have to do our very best in whatever we do, in order to reach our potential. By living in Christ, we are able to do what He requires from us, because He has a perfect hand over us.

And when we strive for that perfection through Christ, we add value and quality and meaning to our lives, as opposed to shallowness, greed and despair.

# Get Connected to His Will

*Let love be without dissimulation. Abhor that which is evil; cleave to that which is good. Be kind and affectionate one to another with brotherly love; in honour preferring one another; Not slothful in business; fervent in spirit; serving the Lord; rejoicing in hope; patient in tribulation; continuing instant in prayer; Distributing to the necessity of saints; given to hospitality. Bless them which persecute you: bless, and curse not. Rejoice with them that do rejoice, and weep with them that weep. Be of the same mind one toward another. Mind not high things, but condescend to men of low estate. Be not wise in your own conceits. Recompense to no man evil for evil. Provide things honest in the sight of all men. If it be possible, as much as lies in you, live peaceably with all men. Dearly beloved, avenge not yourselves, but rather give place unto wrath: for it is written, Vengeance is mine; I will repay, said the Lord. Therefore, if thine enemy hunger, feed him; if he thirst, give him drink: for in so doing thou shalt heap coals of fire on his head. Be not overcome of evil, but overcome evil with good.*

– ROMANS 12:9–21

Again, the way to perfection is to lead lives which are exemplary for God's purpose.

One of the ways for us to do that is to know the perfect will of God. By accepting and being rooted in his will, we are able to have renewed minds and to crave Christ's perfection.

When we are knowledgeable in the will of God and what He wants us to do with our lives according to the potential which He knows we have, we will ultimately get closer to the Christ-like perfection we are meant to have. By being obedient to God and the commandments in his Word, we will be better connected to his will. The more wisdom we have in his Word, the deeper we get into the will of God. We also become closer to achieving it. We will choose to be transformed through it, and we will choose to have God's perfect guidance in our lives and hearts.

CHOOSE PERFECTION: 17 SEPTEMBER

# The Value of Leading a Good Moral Life

*Be perfect, therefore, as your heavenly Father is perfect.*
– Matthew 5:48

The moral lives we lead are imperative to the perfection we achieve through and in Christ. As Christians, we have moral obligations that we have to fulfil in order for us to portray the Christ-like character God wants us to. God requires us to be completely committed to Him in our hearts, minds and souls, and morally. He will not accept anything less than perfection from us.

Leading good moral lives also adds to our emotional and mental well-being, since there is no guilt, fear or hate attached to leading a life that is morally perfect.

If we choose to follow Christ, then we choose to lead lives according to his standards and not our own. In order to do that, we have to be obedient to his will, his Word and his purpose for us.

Allowing ourselves to conform to the morals of the world means we deny ourselves the opportunity to transform into God's perfect realm. This will prevent us from leading the life He has ordained for us.

CHOOSE PERFECTION: 18 SEPTEMBER

# What Is God's Definition of Perfection?

*This is the account of Noah. Noah was a righteous man, blameless among the people of his time, and he walked with God.*
– Genesis 6:9

Noah was not perfect, but blameless – because he lived a life that God saw as righteous.

In the same way, when God speaks of perfection, He talks about being well-rounded, balanced, healthy, sincere, innocent, whole-hearted and complete.

If we consider the simplicity in these words, then there is no excuse for us not to achieve that kind of perfection.

No one in the Bible was as perfect as we think perfection should be. They were not without fault, flaw or defect, but they led lives which incorporated aspects which are perfect in the eyes of God.

God wants us to be able to walk in his will, be mature in the lives we lead, make responsible decisions and act according to the way Christ would. Remember the bracelets with the letters WWJD – What Would Jesus Do?

Do we ever stop for a moment – before we act on something – to think about what Jesus would do in that situation? If we know the will of God, the answer becomes easy.

If we act like Him, we will achieve his perfection.

# All God Cares about Is the Depth of Our Faith

*For you are all sons of God through faith in Christ Jesus. For as many of you as were baptized into Christ have put on Christ. There is neither Jew nor Greek, there is neither slave nor free, there is neither male nor female; for you are all one in Christ Jesus.*
– Galatians 3:26–28

God does not care about our physical qualities like how we look, how thin or fat we are, whether we walk straight or not, can hear or not, can see or not, have red hair or are blonde, the colour of our skins, or the number of beauty titles we have won. He does not care how rich we are, how famous we are or what ranks we have in the world. He does not favour men over women, or women over men, or people from India over people from Europe.

All God cares about is the depth of our faith and the degree of righteousness in our lives.

He looks at the passion in our hearts to serve Him and the confidence we have to reach the potential He has given us. And the only way we can impress God is by including those aspects in our lives. If we are able to be faithful, confident and passionate about our purpose, He will be faithful in providing what is necessary for us to lead the lives He wants us to lead.

We need to choose to change our mindsets, and start thinking along the lines God did. We need to start acting the way He would.

# Let Your Spiritual Relationship with God Grow

*'Therefore you shall be perfect,*
*just as your Father in heaven is perfect.'*
– Matthew 5:48

God takes great pride in seeing us obey his commandment to strive for perfection. When we strive for perfection, we also allow ourselves to grow spiritually, mentally and emotionally, and we are then closer to understanding God's perfect law and plan for our lives.

We have to grow into a deeper and more mature spiritual relationship with God, and never neglect or stray from it.

We therefore need to pray earnestly to be in the will of God and in his likeness so that we may live lives in keeping with the potential with which we have been blessed. When we do, we will experience the sanctification, holiness, redemption, cleansing, death to sin, and perfection, which come from God.

CHOOSE PERFECTION: 21 SEPTEMBER

# Life Is Not Fair

*For if God did not spare angels when they sinned, but sent them to hell, putting them into gloomy dungeons to be held for judgment; if He did not spare the ancient world when He brought the flood on its ungodly people, but protected Noah, a preacher of righteousness, and seven others; if He condemned the cities of Sodom and Gomorrah by burning them to ashes, and made them an example of what is going to happen to the ungodly; and if He rescued Lot, a righteous man, who was distressed by the filthy lives of lawless men (for that righteous man, living among them day after day, was tormented in his righteous soul by the lawless deeds He saw and heard) – if this is so, then the Lord knows how to rescue godly men from trials and to hold the unrighteous for the day of judgment, while continuing their punishment. This is especially true of those who follow the corrupt desire of the sinful nature and despise authority.*

– 2 Peter 2:4–10

It is a fact of life that life as we know it is not fair, but if we choose to use that as an excuse for not striving to lead the life God wants us to in his perfection, we will experience the wrath of God. God becomes angry when we choose to ignore what He wants from us and if we don't use the potential with which He has blessed us to reach that level of perfection.

Just like He did with angels who sinned, prophets and men of God whom He called and who then chose to be disobedient, so too will He allow us to fall short of his grace. We must never ever take God's mercy and love for granted and convince ourselves that He will still love and accept us regardless of our actions. He commands us to reach perfection. If we remain obedient and righteous in those commandments, He will bless us, but if we choose not to, He will hold us accountable.

# God Wants Us To Talk To Him through Prayer

*Pray continually.*
– 1 THESSALONIANS 5:17

The best way to please God is never to lose our connection with Him. He wants us to pray without ceasing, because prayer is the only way we can communicate with God. When we pray, we will find the answers, strength, grace, mercy and peace that we seek.

But prayer must not be an obligation, or forced. God wants us to come to Him of our own free will and wants us to communicate joyfully and enthusiastically with Him through prayer. When we pray, we can bring anything to God's feet. Prayer allows us to offload our burdens, anxieties, fears and worries onto his shoulders. It gives us the comfort of knowing that we have someone who is listening to our hearts and is willing to help us and take care of us.

When we pray, we must also not make the mistake of telling God what we believe He wants to hear, but we must be completely honest with Him. There is nothing we cannot tell Him. He wants us to be real and honest in our prayer and time with Him. We can pray at any time and all the time if we so choose. The more we pray, the stronger our relationship becomes with God. We also become more spiritually, mentally and emotionally mature in Him. As Christians, we sometimes spend hours doing things of the world, like watching television, reading naughty magazines, working, listening to music and whatever else it is we do. We sometimes find it hard to talk to God. However, we must try to talk to Him anywhere, any time and in everything we do.

# He Is Our Constant Companion

*Praise awaits you, our God, in Zion; to you our vows will be fulfilled. You who answer prayer, to you all people will come.*
– Psalm 65:1–2

We need to pray for the right reasons and not only when we want something from God. We must pray because we love Him and want to be in his presence. We must pray because He is dependable and we are confident that He is listening to our prayer, and that He will answer it faithfully. We must pray in order for God to give us the will and power to resist temptation. We must pray because we want salvation to be ours. We must pray in order for us to give God thanks for what He has done in our lives. We must worship Him for the great things He is about to do.

And finally, we must pray because God commands us to. It is necessary for our faith. It is necessary for us so as not to lose heart. It is essential so we can experience his miracles and grace and see his power in our lives.

He is not there just as an overseer in our lives; He is our constant companion. We need to keep Him close at all times.

# There Is No Right Or Wrong Way To Pray

*The LORD detests the sacrifice of the wicked, but the prayer of the upright pleases him.*
– PROVERBS 15:8

When we pray, God wants us to pray with sincere hearts. He wants us to love being in his presence, talking to Him.

Think about when we are in the courting phase of a relationship with someone. We spend hours talking to each other about absolutely nothing, and then, when the time comes to say goodbye, we each take turns to say goodbye, but it continues with one telling the other to say bye first, and vice versa, and on and on it goes. Finally, we spend another hour just waiting for the other one to be the first to put the phone down. Why? It is the excitement of being in love and the desire to always talk to the person and hear his or her voice.

God wants us to have the same desire for Him, and when we do, it is pleasing in his eyes. There is no right and wrong way to pray. All we need to do is to come to Him, be in his presence and talk to Him, because we love Him as He loves us, and He gets excited when He hears our voice. Just talk to Him. Tell Him what is on your mind. Tell Him what you feel bad about and what you want to change in your life. Thank Him for what He has already done for you, and ask Him for what you need.

He will never judge you based on how good you are at talking to Him. You do not have to be a spokesperson or communications officer. You just need to go to Him, and be in his presence – even if it is to lash out at Him do it so He can give you the answers you are looking for and the grace to know you are never alone.

It's only through prayer that we are able to feel how strong God's presence is in our lives.

# God Wants Us To Be Authentic

*'And when you pray, do not be like the hypocrites, for they love to pray standing in the synagogues and on the street corners to be seen by men. I tell you the truth; they have received their reward in full. But when you pray, go into your room, close the door and pray to your Father, who is unseen. Then your Father, who sees what is done in secret, will reward you. And when you pray, do not keep on babbling like pagans, for they think they will be heard because of their many words. Do not be like them, for your Father knows what you need before you ask Him. This, then, is how you should pray: "Our Father in heaven, hallowed is Your name, your Kingdom come, Your will be done on earth, as it is in heaven. Give us today our daily bread. Forgive us our debts, as we also have forgiven our debtors."'*

– MATTHEW 6:5–12

It is always surprising to see how many of us only pray when we go to church on Sunday. And why? Because everyone is looking and we have to show them we can pray. Other times, we listen to how the pastor or deacons pray and then we copy their prayer and the verses they use. We believe that it is the expert way to pray. But God does not want us to pray like hypocrites. Praying is not about doing God a favour; it is about doing ourselves a favour – for only when we pray will we understand God's will in our lives, reaffirming his Word.

There are no rules for prayer, except to pray sincerely and with true hearts. If we prayed for an hour, believing that is sufficient for God, but our prayer had no basis, then we wasted an hour of God's time and our own. He does not want us to be jabber mouths in his presence; He wants us to be authentic.

A five-minute prayer (conversation) with God can have more meaning than one which takes hours. A short prayer can sometimes reveal more of what is in our hearts.

God is not stupid, and we should never offend Him by thinking He is. He knows our hearts, He sees our lives, our actions and our needs, and that is what He wants to talk to us about.

# When One Door Closes, Another Door Opens

*'Ask and it will be given to you; seek and you will find; knock and the door will be opened to you. For everyone who asks receives; he who seeks finds; and to him who knocks, the door will be opened.'*
– Matthew 7:7–8

They say when one door closes, another opens. God wants to open other doors in our lives. The way to open other doors is through prayer.

In the story of 'Ali Baba and the Forty Thieves', Ali Baba knew that the way to get to the riches inside the tomb was by asking for the door to be opened. He said: 'Open Sesame' and the door was opened.

Likewise, God is waiting for us to come to Him in prayer and ask for the doors we want opened to be opened. He promises that whatever we seek, need and ask for will be given to us. We need to stand in God's presence, knock on his heart with our voices and our hearts, and ask in his Name.

When the door is opened, it will take us closer to the rewards and riches He has promised us in heaven.

# A Sure Heart

*Very well then, with foreign lips and strange tongues*
*God will speak to this people, to whom He said,*
*'This is the resting place, let the weary rest'; and,*
*'This is the place of repose' – but they would not listen.*
– Isaiah 28:11–12

Many times in life we will come across people who seem to have a direct line to God. It seems like everything they want and ask God for, they just receive. And then, instead of allowing it to encourage us, we allow it to discourage us, because we believe that God is partial to some and therefore not listening to us. But we need to take notice of what we are praying for. It is no use asking God for something when we are not sure of what it is that we want. We have to be clear about what we want God to do in our lives and where we want Him to lead us. God can only give us what we need if we are sure about it ourselves.

He can read our minds. He knows our hearts, but He wants us to be sure of what we want Him to do. Many times, when we are unsure and ask God for what we think we want, we blame Him for giving it to us when we realize it is not what we needed. We are quick to blame God, but we never take the time to consider that it may be what we actually asked God for. This is why it is so important to pray with a sincere heart and not with a troubled heart.

We have to choose to pray and be in God's presence with a heart that is sure of itself and a mind that knows exactly what it wants God to do.

# He Wants Us To Have Gratitude in Our Hearts

*It is good to begin your prayer with thanksgiving and praise. 'Enter into His gates with thanksgiving, and into His courts with praise. Be thankful to Him, and bless His name.'*
– Psalm 100:4

We must not only pray with intentions of expecting something from God. Instead, we must first go to God with thanksgiving and praise. Give Him the glory He deserves. It is not that we have to first boost his ego in order for Him to give us what we need. God is not stupid, and certainly not egotistical. He just wants us to have gratitude in our hearts. He wants to know that we recognize what He has done in our lives, and that we feel and see his presence in it. God loves us and wants to give us what we need, but He wants us to give thanks as well for whatever He has already given and done.

He will answer our prayers, but we need to be mature enough to understand that nothing in life comes for nothing, especially if we have no appreciation for it.

As our Father, He has already shown us his power in so many ways and has made the biggest sacrifices for us, so the least we can do is honour Him and give Him praise and glory for never ceasing to work in our lives: He is always opening the doors we want opened and He is always with us, even when the world seems to be against us.

CHOOSE TO PRAY: 29 SEPTEMBER

# The Five-Finger Prayer

*We always thank God, the Father of our*
*Lord Jesus Christ, when we pray for you.*
– Colossians 1:3

One day I was watching a group of Sunday school children being taught the five-finger prayer, and I was deeply humbled.

Many times we believe that praying should only be about what *we* need, but we must also pray for others. We must never forget that if we pray for others, it could make a huge difference to their lives.

The five-finger prayer calls for people to put their hands together, keep their eyes open so they can see their hands, and then take notice of each finger.

If we do this, we will notice that the closest finger to the face is the thumb, and because it is the closest it should be a reminder to pray for those who are closest to us, like family and friends.

The next finger is the index finger, which is used for pointing and should remind us of the people who help point us in the right direction, like our spiritual leaders, teachers and bosses.

The next finger is the tallest finger and reminds us to pray for our leaders. Pray for the president and other leaders in our government and those who are leaders in our town.

The fourth finger is called the ring finger, which in fact is the weakest of all the fingers. It should remind us to pray for those who are sick.

Last but not least is the smallest finger. The Bible says, 'Do not think of yourself more highly than you ought.' The little finger reminds us to pray for ourselves.

What better way is there to be in God's presence than to bring the cares of the world to Him before ourselves?

# Does Prayer Change Things?

*The prayer of a righteous person is powerful and effective.*
– James 5:16

They say that prayer changes things, but does it *really* change anything?
Oh yes! It really does!
Does prayer change your present situation or sudden circumstances?
No, not always, but it does change the way you look at those events.
Does prayer change your financial future?
No, not always, but it does change who you look to for meeting your daily needs.
Does prayer change shattered hearts or broken bodies?
No, not always, but it will change your source of strength and comfort.
Does prayer change your wants and desires?
No, not always, but it will change your wants into what God desires!
Does prayer change how you view the world?
No, not always, but it will change whose eyes you see the world through.
Does prayer change your regrets from the past?
No, not always, but it will change your hopes for the future!
Does prayer change the people around you?
No, not always, but it will change you – the problem is not always in others.
Does prayer change your life in ways you cannot explain?
Oh, yes, always! And it will change you from the inside out!
So does prayer *really* change *anything?*
Yes! It *really* does change *everything!*

– Teressa Vowell

# October

## CHOOSE PATIENCE

*Patience is power; with time and patience*
*the mulberry leaf becomes a silk gown.*

– Chinese Proverb

## CHOOSE PURITY

*If a man's mind becomes pure, his surroundings will also become pure.*

– Siddhartha Gautama Buddha

## CHOOSE KINDNESS

*Never look down on anybody unless you're helping him up.*

– Jesse Jackson

## CHOOSE TO BE MOTIVATED IN GOD

*One of the strongest characteristics of genius*
*is the power of lighting its own fire.*

– John W Foster

CHOOSE PATIENCE: 1 OCTOBER

# Our Patience Reflects Our Determination

*And we desire that each one of you show the same diligence so as to realize the full assurance of hope until the end, so that you will not be sluggish, but imitators of those who through faith and patience inherit the promises.*
– HEBREWS 6:11–12

Patience is the ability to endure while waiting. It reflects how determined we are and how strong our will is, which allows us to victoriously overcome all that we face, according to the will of God. As God is patient in all things, especially in waiting for us, so too does He desire for us to be patient in his faithfulness to do for us what He promised He would do.

If we have patience (a virtue in life), then we will be able to do and achieve all things in our lives.

God is not an instant God or a drive-through. He is God and there are 6 billion of us on earth whom He has to care for. Do not for a moment think we are superior to everyone else, and that our needs should be taken care of first before others. God wants us to be patient so that we are not selfish. He wants us to be patient so that we can learn to endure. He wants us to be patient so that we can grow in faith. He wants us to be patient so that we can learn the lesson before we receive, and He wants us to be patient so that we can seek Him.

# Do You Have a Heart of Patience?

*So, as those who have been chosen of God, holy and beloved, put on a heart of compassion, kindness, humility, gentleness and patience.*
– Colossians 3:12

In the Bible, Paul tells us to have a heart of patience, and to let the peace of Christ rest in our hearts. Only we can choose to have a heart of patience.

Paul describes patience as a deliberate and wilful attitude, resulting in good godly behaviour.

In the Book of Ephesians, he describes patience as walking in a manner worthy of Christ. He talks about patience as the ability to encompass humility and gentleness and in so doing show tolerance towards others – thereby maintaining peace. He talks about the importance of having a heart that is patient, so that characteristics such as these can be added to it.

We need to choose to have patient hearts, because with patience we will also experience other Christ-like aspects of faith, which will allow us to grow in the love of God and earn grace from waiting on Him.

# Patience Ultimately Leads to Joy

*Those who wait upon the Lord, they shall inherit the earth.*
– Psalm 37:9

Patience is one of the fruits of the spirit and therefore assuredly one of the characteristics which is of Christ. With patience comes the endurance that ultimately leads to joy, because we have faith that we will overcome through Christ, and that nothing will come between us, our endurance, patience and the victory.

Patience also brings hope and motivation to believe that we have a purpose as well as the potential to fulfil that purpose. Because of the promises God has made to us, we will never fail at anything and never be alone.

There are great examples of patience in the Bible, which show evidence of victory. Job is a prime example: Though he endured great suffering, he was patient for God to come through for him as he remained faithful to receive the joy at the end of it. Job's perseverance saw God multiply his blessings upon him. Likewise, if we endure patiently, we can be sure that God will multiply our blessings.

CHOOSE PATIENCE: 4 OCTOBER

# Patience Allows Us to Grow

*And you have been given fullness in Christ, who is the head over every power and authority.*
– Colossians 2:10

Patience allows us to grow because through patience we learn about God's role and power in our lives.

As believers, we mature in Him and in the truth of God.

Patience also allows us to experience the strength of God to see us through even the most trying times in our lives. It allows us to change our attitudes, and we begin to look at our situations differently while waiting for the change to happen. Sometimes we will even change our minds about the situation.

Patience also allows us to grow in wisdom, and that wisdom allows us to walk in truth and have a deeper spiritual understanding of God.

But, as with everything else, we must wait on the Lord and give Him thanks for everything.

# Patience in Prayer

*The Lord sustains all who fall and rises up all who are bowed down. The eyes of all look to You, and You give them their food in due time.*
– Psalm 145:14–15

When the idea is not right, God says, 'NO'.

No – when the idea is not the best.

No – when the idea is absolutely wrong.

No – when, though it may help you, it would create problems for someone else.

When the time is not right, God says, 'SLOW'.

What a catastrophe it would be if God answered every prayer at the snap of your fingers.

Do you know what would happen? God would become your servant, not your master.

Suddenly God would be working for you instead of you working for God.

When you are not right, God says, 'GROW'.

The selfish person has to grow in unselfishness. The cautious person must grow in courage. The timid person must grow in confidence. The dominating person must grow in sensitivity. The critical person must grow in tolerance. The negative person must grow in positive attitudes. The pleasure-seeking person must grow in compassion for suffering people.

When everything is alright, God says, 'GO'.

Then miracles happen: A hopeless alcoholic is set free. A drug addict finds release. A doubter becomes a child in his belief. Diseased tissue responds to treatment, and healing begins. The door to your dream suddenly swings open and there stands God saying, 'GO!'

Remember: God's delays are not God's denials. God's timing is perfect.

Patience is what we need in prayer.

– Joe Gatuslao

CHOOSE PATIENCE: 6 OCTOBER

# There Is Light at the End of the Tunnel

*As an example, brethren, of suffering and patience,*
*take the prophets who spoke in the Name of the Lord.*
*We count those blessed who endured. You have heard of*
*the endurance of Job and have seen the outcome of the Lord's*
*dealings that the Lord is full of compassion and is merciful.*
– JAMES 5:10–11

In order to endure suffering, we need to have patience to deal with the situation while we wait for relief. There is a light at the end of every tunnel, and if we adopt this attitude when we face trials, we will have the patience to endure whatever we are going through, until we see the light at the end of the tunnel. The Lord promises to bless us through our suffering, because we had the patience to wait for his grace. Patience is also a way of finding favour with Him, for it shows our faith and perseverance in what we want the outcome to be. So, if we remain patient in the Lord, there is no suffering or trial we will not overcome through his glory.

CHOOSE PATIENCE: 7 OCTOBER

# It Pays To Be Patient

*Therefore, as God's chosen people, holy and dearly loved, clothe yourselves with compassion, kindness, humility, gentleness and* patience.
– COLOSSIANS 3:12 (EMPHASIS ADDED)

Once there was a rich man who fell seriously ill. He sold all his belongings just to cure his illness. After he became healthy, he realized that he had nothing left. He had difficulties feeding himself, but he thought that in no time things would be back to normal again, and that he would be rich again.

He waited for a long, long time, but nothing happened. His life was dreadful, and so he decided that if he took his own life, it would be over. So he did.

While on his way to hell, he met two angels who were carrying a heavy load. He asked them where they were going.

After their long explanations, this man realized that the two angels were coming to him. The heavy load they were carrying was a bag full of money. But since he was no longer alive, he would not have been able to receive it.

– AUTHOR UNKNOWN

Some people go through so many rough times and because of that they wish to take their own lives. I hope this lesson will help them to deal with their problems – you have to be patient with everything.

CHOOSE PURITY: 8 OCTOBER

# God Is Our Only Source of Purity

*Do not you know that you yourselves are*
*God's temple and that God's Spirit lives in you?*
– 1 CORINTHIANS 3:16

Purity simply means something of God, because God is the purest form of pure.

If we are like God, we are pure through Him.

For God, purity is not part of a person's character. Instead, it is an essential element of life. God is the only source of purity.

Without God's purity we are like lepers who have to succumb to being like those with an incurable disease. Instead of growing, we deteriorate into a life of decay – a life far from the pure presence of God, a life void of his mercy.

When God created us, He created us to be pure. That purity was only lost when Adam and Eve chose to disobey God, falling short of his glory.

If we stay true to Him and to his Word, we can lead lives that are pure in his eyes and be secure in the knowledge that we will have eternity.

# Do You Have a Clean and Pure Heart?

*Create in me a clean heart, O God,*
*and renew a steadfast spirit within me.*
– Psalm 51:10

As Christians, we are the first to lose the sense of purity because we become so complacent in the knowledge that we serve a God of grace and mercy. However, as children of God, we are to lead a life that is righteous in the ways of God; we must aspire to be like God.

We have to faithfully pursue holiness and have a clean and pure heart. The way to achieve pureness of heart is to confess our sins first, repent and have faith.

God accepts nothing else but our purity or our attempt at purity through the life we lead. When we try to have pure hearts and characters like Christ, we can aspire to the things God wants us to have. Then we can live the life He wants for us.

CHOOSE PURITY: 10 OCTOBER

# Beware of False Purity

*Be self-controlled and alert. Your enemy the devil prowls around like a roaring lion looking for someone to devour.*
– 1 PETER 5:8

If we choose to have comparative purity, we choose to be false in that we measure our pureness against the backdrop of a false standard, like money, people, or power.

When we do this, we allow ourselves to be part of a fantasy world where we believe that we lead successful lives compared to the next person. But this is not the case.

It is the worst kind of mentality to have, as it is furthest away from the purity that God desires for us.

Another type of false purity is when we allow ourselves to have faith in false teachers and false teachings.

If we are not deeply rooted in the Word of God, we may fall victim to deception and thus lose our purity.

CHOOSE PURITY: 11 OCTOBER

# God Is Waiting for Us to Come Back to Him

*Above all else, guard your heart, for it is the wellspring of life. Put away perversity from your mouth; keep corrupt talk far from your lips. Let your eyes look straight ahead, fix your gaze directly before you. Make level paths for your feet and take only ways that are firm. Do not swerve to the right or the left; keep your foot from evil.*
– Proverbs 4:23–27

When God put us together when He created us, his intention was for us to be examples of Him and lead like Him in purity. Instead, we chose to place our faith in our own understanding and to make choices not of God but of the flesh. By doing this, we choose to walk away from the will of God and from being Christ-like in Him.

Even so, God has not turned his back on us. He is waiting for us to come back to Him and his grace and mercy.

He wants us to walk in a path of righteousness and to attempt daily to be more like Him – leading lives glorifying Him and being examples of his love and light.

Choosing to lead that kind of life in God and walking in his image requires a commitment and dedication, but it is possible through God.

It will not happen overnight, but it is achievable and will take us closer to Him. The closer we get, the more God will restore us and fulfil his purpose in us.

CHOOSE PURITY: 12 OCTOBER

# Do Your Actions Reflect Purity?

*... Treat younger men as brothers, older women as mothers, and younger women as sisters, with absolute purity.*
– 1 Timothy 5:1–2

Our attitudes towards others are vital to display the kind of purity we have in our hearts. If we have hateful actions and thoughts, hold grudges, seek revenge and lose our tempers, we will never even be in close proximity to the Lord or to being pure.

If we are envious and jealous, we will also choose to distance ourselves from God's purity. If we are consumed with pride, we will never be pure. If we choose to have no respect for human life, we will surely place ourselves furthest away from the glory of God and his purity.

The sad thing is that we live in a world today which is filled to the brim (sometimes overflowing) with crime, rape, murder, suicide and rampant violence. We compete with each other, trample on each other, hate each other, and live in contempt. Even so, we still believe we are Christians. How can we be Christians when there is no purity in any of our actions? God wants us to be pure and live lives which are pleasing to Him.

CHOOSE PURITY: 13 OCTOBER

# Are You Doing Your Bit To Make the World a Better Place?

*He who has been stealing must steal no longer, but must work, doing something useful with his own hands, that he may have something to share with those in need.*
– Ephesians 4:28

God wants us to make our lives purposeful and to act according to his commandments and his law. He wants us to lead lives that are in his glory and have elements of the type of purity He expects from us.

He wants us to use our hands to do positive and productive things, as an example to others. He wants us to do things that would be of benefit to others, thereby doing our bit to make the world a better place for everyone.

He wants us to do his will and be of service to the community, society and mankind as a whole. And that comes from respecting one another, loving one another and being in one another's grace.

CHOOSE PURITY: 14 OCTOBER

# Watch What You Say

*Finally, brothers, whatever is true, whatever is noble, whatever is right, whatever is pure, whatever is lovely, whatever is admirable – if anything is excellent or praiseworthy – think about such things.*
– PHILIPPIANS 4:8

When we choose to allow our character to become devoid of God's purity, we choose to lead lives of darkness and grief.

Even the words which come from our mouths reveal our level of purity in Christ.

If we choose to slander and carry tales, then we choose to be false and captivated in that darkness.

When we say things which are false and malicious, then we choose to live our life in darkness.

Even cursing and choosing to use any kind of profanity or obscenity is choosing to live outside of the purity of God.

God wants us to display the best possible example of Christ-like behaviour there is. He wants us to live in his light and not allow simple things like the words we use to remove us from that light.

# Enjoy the Fruits of Your Kindness

*A kind man benefits himself,*
*but a cruel man brings trouble on himself.*
– PROVERBS 11:17

Kindness is about having a helping nature, which means helping others through our generosity, warmth, gentleness, empathy and consideration.

It is about being compassionate and gracious to one another in keeping with God's will and commandments.

When we live a life in Christ, kindness becomes essential to our Christian belief and character. If we cannot demonstrate kindness, then we cannot walk before God in his likeness, for the Bible tells us that kindness is about experiencing the fruits of the Spirit. When we choose to be unkind, we choose to live in the flesh and succumb to the things of the flesh and the temptations which come with it.

The best feeling in the world is to see the fruits of our kindness through the eyes of the recipient. We should not allow bad behaviour to rob us from experiencing that kind of feeling. It is an emotion which will see us transformed and renewed in Him.

The Bible is full of examples of men and women who showed kindness and were blessed for it. The worthy woman of Proverbs had the 'law of kindness' in her mouth, keeping her words in check. The men of Malta showed their kindness to the apostle Paul. The servants of Christ proved themselves 'by kindness'.

Solomon said: 'That which makes a man to be desired is his kindness; and a poor man is better than a liar' (Prov 19:20).

Therefore, we need to choose to show kindness in all things. We will be blessed and transformed by it.

CHOOSE KINDNESS: 16 OCTOBER

# Is Your Kindness Constant?

*'Verily I say unto you, Inasmuch as ye have done it unto one of the least of these my brethren, ye have done it unto Me.'*
– MATTHEW 25:40

The only way we can be kind is to love. Paul, in the Book of 1 Corinthians 13:4, describes love as being kind. This is the expression of God's good will in our lives. And just as God is always kind to us, so too must we be kind in everything we do and to everyone we encounter – not only selected people, and certainly not on the basis of racial, social or ethnic considerations.

We should show kindness in the same way in which the Father has shown his kindness toward us – all of us – even the unthankful and evil, because when we hold back kindness, we become evil.

The Book of Luke describes kindness also as not fickle, so we must never choose to be kind when it suits us and unkind when it does not. When we do that, we behave like hypocrites. We should consider what Jesus would do and measure ourselves against God's standard. Only then will we be able to remain constant in all things, even our display of kindness.

God is the standard; his kindness is constant.

CHOOSE KINDNESS: 17 OCTOBER

# What Exactly Is Kindness?

*But the fruit of the Spirit is love, joy, peace,*
*forbearance,* kindness, *goodness, faithfulness,*
– Galatians 5:22 (emphasis added)

The Bible describes kindness in various Scriptures and verses, and also tells us how to be kind. We are kind when:

- we are honest in our dealings (Gen 21:23)
- we reward good received from another (Gen 40:14)
- we are sympathetic and comforting (Job 6:14)
- we exhibit honourable behaviour (Ruth 3:10)
- we share another's burdens (1 Sam 15:6)
- we show friendship (1 Sam 20:15, 16)
- we honour the dead (2 Sam 2:5)
- we are merciful toward our enemies (2 Sam 9:7)
- we demonstrate loyalty (2 Sam 16:17)
- we show gratitude (1 Kgs 2:7)
- we have compassion (Jonah 4:2)
- we are benevolent (Luke 6:35)
- we are courteous (Acts 27:3)
- we are hospitable (Acts 28:2)
- we are forgiving (Eph 4:32).

So we have constant guidance from the Lord as to what kindness is and how it can be applied. With this knowledge, we have no excuse not to do what the Lord has so graciously taught us to do.

# Make an Effort To Be Kind

*'A new commandment I give unto you,*
*That ye love one another; as I have loved you …'*
– John 13:34

Selflessness, showing love, and being affectionate and compassionate towards one another all contribute to kindness and how God wants us to include it in our lives. Showing this kind of kindness separates us from the rest of the world, especially from selfish people.

We choose to be selfish when we show kindness because we want to get something back that is beneficial to us. So we choose the people we are kind to. But God wants us to lead lives of value and not of selfishness. He wants us to make an effort to be kind in our everyday lives.

He wants our actions to make us rejoice in the world and in what we have produced in it – for through our kindness we create a change and become sensitive to others and what they are going through. It also opens our minds to the great extent of need in the world today.

CHOOSE KINDNESS: 19 OCTOBER

# Love Your Neighbour

*In reply Jesus said: 'A man was going down from Jerusalem to Jericho, when he fell into the hands of robbers. They stripped him of his clothes, beat him and went away, leaving him half dead. A priest happened to be going down the same road, and when he saw the man, he passed by on the other side. So too, a Levite, when he came to the place and saw him, passed by on the other side. But a Samaritan, as he traveled, came where the man was; and when he saw him, he took pity on him. He went to him and bandaged his wounds, pouring on oil and wine. Then he put the man on his own donkey, took him to an inn and took care of him. The next day he took out two silver coins and gave them to the innkeeper. "Look after him," he said, "and when I return, I will reimburse you for any extra expense you may have." Which of these three do you think was a neighbor to the man who fell into the hands of robbers? The expert in the law replied: "The one who had mercy on him." Jesus told him, "Go and do likewise."'*

– LUKE 10:30–37

We are commanded to love our neighbours as ourselves. God wants us all to be good Samaritans. Even though there was such political turmoil between the Samaritans and the Jews, the Samaritan put the revenge aside to help the injured man. If we could practise such kindness in our lives, how wonderful life would be!

CHOOSE KINDNESS: 20 OCTOBER

# Never Lose Heart; God Always Wins

*Beloved, do not avenge yourselves, but rather give place to wrath; for it is written, 'Vengeance is Mine, I will repay,' says the Lord.*
– 1 Thessalonians 5:15

Again, God will take care of correcting wrongs. We should not allow ourselves to be overcome by evil, but instead we should overcome evil with good. God is on our side. Evil cannot overwhelm us. The devil can never have victory over us. We need to start believing that. The only thing God wants us to do is to love as He has loved us, and leave the rest to Him.

We can never get satisfaction from revenge, but we can have comfort in knowing that God will see to it that vengeance is ours. God always does a better job, anyway.

Oh, we will suffer some injuries, that is for sure, but in the end, goodness through God will always triumph. The Christian life is a life of overcoming this sin-cursed world, and of triumphing despite evil and opposition. Never lose heart; God always wins.

– Taken from cbn.com

# What Are the Fruits of the Spirit?

*The Fruit of the Spirit are listed as: love, joy, peace, patience, gentleness, kindness, goodness, faithfulness, meekness and temperance.*
– GALATIANS 5:22–23

The outcomes of our lives depend on how we respond to those circumstances while using the fruit of the Spirit as the basis of our lives.

We will always be surrounded by sin and depravity and therefore life will always be full of difficulties, but if we remain true to the fruits of the Spirit, we will always respond positively.

God is able and willing to assist us if we keep true to his Word and the fruit of his Spirit. He will always, through the fruit of the Spirit, give us the wisdom and understanding to turn the negatives into positives, and the losses into triumphs.

For, when we have these fruits, we will grow in our faith and benefit from it – thereby being a blessing to others.

CHOOSE TO BE MOTIVATED IN GOD: 22 OCTOBER

# Our Motives Must Be Pure

*For consider Him who has endured such hostility by sinners against Himself, so that you will not grow weary and lose heart.*
– Hebrews 12:3

God wants us to be properly motivated to do his work. He motivates us by giving us all the gifts and assurances that we need to do his work. However, we should not only be motivated by external factors, but by what God promises will happen in our hearts if we do his work.

We also need to have the right motives in life for doing the things that we do. It is not only about personal gain, but about making an impact on the lives of others as well. It is not about impressing people but about leaving impressionable gifts in their lives, in that our actions cause a positive change in them.

He wants us to have pure hearts, which are able to repent, and through that be guided by his love and motivated by his glory.

# You Don't Have To Grin and Bear It!

*For if I do this voluntarily, I have a reward; but if against my will, I have a stewardship entrusted to me.*
– 1 CORINTHIANS 9:17

Paul was talking about doing what is right, because our hearts allow us to, and because we are willing, humble and passionate to do the will of God.

God knows when we do things grudgingly. He does not want us to be false in anything we do. He does not want us to grin and bear everything. Instead, He wants us to be filled with joy, eager to obey his commandments and do his work, for He promises us rich rewards in heaven. Choosing to be motivated in life and in God is a daily choice that comes out of a certain mindset. If we change our mindsets to do things selflessly, we will become eager and motivated in all things we do. Like Paul, who chose to be motivated, we will then overcome the obstacles and readily preach the Word of God. We will also get our reward from the Lord. God seeks those who willingly, eagerly, and readily seek his glory in all that they do and say.

The following quote from cbn.com puts it in a nutshell:

> If we find ourselves in a place where we have lost our joy and are going through the motions against our will, we must not stop doing right and good. Even if we find ourselves battling self-righteousness, we must keep serving the Lord. We still have a stewardship that we are responsible for. We aren't to go and sit on the sidelines of the fight of faith until our motives change. We need to keep striving for righteousness and the advancement of the Kingdom of God, praying all the while for the Lord to change our hearts. As we do this, God will show us how and where we need to repent if we humble ourselves before Him and ask Him to lead us into truth. He will show us where we are seeking our own glory rather than his; but let us not stop pressing on toward the prize and the upward call in Christ.

# Doing the Right Thing with the Wrong Motivation

*Therefore, to one who knows the right thing to do and does not do it, to him it is sin.*
– JAMES 4:17

Disobedience and a stubborn heart is the worst case scenario. Neither, however, should we do the right religious things without the God-honouring motivation. The right things get done, but the proper motivation is lacking.

This is not where God wants us to be, for it robs us of eternal rewards and makes us miserable and self-righteous.

Christ has enabled us to have our will controlled by his love, but if our flesh gets in the way, our motivations will go astray. There are no rewards for dutiful but unwilling service to God. This is who Christ wants us to be: people whose motivations are pure, who are not self-seeking, and who desire to serve God in all that they do.

Only a heart ruled by Christ and fully surrendered to his will can truly delight in the Lord and serve Him whole-heartedly.

When it comes to living the Christian life, it is not acceptable to say that our hearts are not in it. May God enable us to serve because we want to, may we serve faithfully, may we serve Him in all things, may we earn many heavenly rewards, and may we want God to get the glory, always, only, and for ever.

# We Can Choose To Be Righteous

*Therefore I run in such a way, as not without aim;*
*I box in such a way, as not beating the air; but I discipline*
*my body and make it my slave, so that, after I have*
*preached to others, I myself will not be disqualified.*
– 1 CORINTHIANS 9:26–27

We are born again of Christ and we are new creatures in his Name. Therefore, we are no longer enslaved by sin or captives of the devil.

We are saved and we are Christ-like in his Name.

The curse of sin is broken and death is no longer victorious over us.

We can now choose to be righteous and live lives that reflect his life, because we will always be made whole again.

We have the grace of the Lord and we are free from corruption, which comes with the devil.

We are restored in his Name and in his Word.

We are conquerors in Christ and victorious over all things.

We can walk in the light of the Lord and in his holiness.

The curse over our lives has been broken and we are redeemed. We experience regeneration as well as freedom to walk in truth.

What motivation do we need other than the many promises from God, and his power?

# God Has a Plan for Your Life

*'Do not seek what you will eat and what you will drink, and do not keep worrying. For all these things the nations of the world eagerly seek; but your Father knows that you need these things. Seek His Kingdom, and these things will be added to you.'*
– Luke 12:29–31

God knows everything, especially his will for each of us. Yet He is waiting for us to seek Him first.

But we must always remember that we cannot blame God for bad things that happen in our lives, because He has given us the gift of free will. He cannot control our thoughts and actions, but He can provide us with the opportunities to change them if we choose to.

But we must also understand that in all things God knows what He is doing, and He will do it. He does not doubt the future. Whatever He wants to be done will be done because He does not work in the time frame that we do, and He does not depend on us to do his will. If we continue to make the wrong choices, He will use someone else to fulfil his will.

Indeed, God has a plan for our lives that has existed even before we were born. If we choose to believe that God has ordained our every step, then we can rest easy, knowing that all we have to do is choose to seek Him and He will lead us to it. But we have to choose to work according to his plan and his will for us.

# Joy, Passion and Enthusiasm Is What We Need

*Whatever you do, do your work heartily,*
*as for the Lord rather than for men.*
– Colossians 3:23

God wants us to be filled with joy, passion and enthusiasm when we are called to do his work, just like we are when we have to do things in the world that we know will lead to a higher purpose and a great achievement.

God does not want us to come into his presence with heavy hearts and sullen faces, dragging our feet behind us and grudgingly taking on the tasks He has set for us. When we do that, we show God how ungrateful we are for what He has done in our lives, and that we place more value on the things of the world than on his promises for us.

Just as He enthusiastically works in our lives because He loves us so much, so too does He want us to have the same pleasure when we do his work. He wants us to be filled with his joy and his will for us. But we need to choose to have joy in his Word and seek Him earnestly, desiring his presence, and standing tall to do his will. He wants us to have the mind of Christ and delight in his works and in our future in Him – devoid of anxiety and dread.

# God Will Guide You

*'But when He, the Spirit of truth, comes,
He will guide you into all the truth.'*
– John 16:13

We have no reason to tread carefully in the presence of God, for his truth and his Word will always guide us to achieve the purpose in our lives.

We need to be patient and seek his will, counsel and wisdom. We can do this by praying.

We need to give our ambitions and desires to the Lord so that He can work with us and through us to achieve what He wants for his children.

When we are able to commit to the Lord, He will redirect us according to our hearts and give us the very things we lack. In this way we may be made whole.

He will lead us to where we want to go and position us in the place we need to be, in order to be conquerors in his Name.

He will open the doors that need opening, and close the doors behind us that are reminders of our lives in sin. He will harness the desires He has put in our hearts and take us to the best life He wants for us.

Therefore, it is imperative for us to obey Him and seek Him so that we can walk with Him in his glory.

# Learn To Listen

*See to it that you do not refuse Him who speaks. If they did not escape when they refused Him who warned them on earth, how much less will us, if we turn away from him who warns us from heaven.*
– Hebrews 12:25

God is always speaking to us, but we have to choose to listen. When we listen we will have the motivation to soar above all things to the place of glory where God wants us to be. He speaks to our hearts, and we find direction through his Word.

And when we have faith in Him, look to his Word, pray and then wait upon Him, as well as honour Him in all areas and aspects of our lives, the Spirit will speak to us, lead us and give us the wisdom, understanding and power we need to do what we were called to do.

If we are truly children of God, delighting in Him, having a humble heart, feeding on his Word, and having no outstanding sin, we will enjoy God's guidance as He speaks to our hearts. All we have to do is choose to listen.

CHOOSE TO BE MOTIVATED IN GOD: 30 OCTOBER

# Who Is God?

*'His master replied, "Well done, good and faithful servant! You have been faithful with a few things; I will put you in charge of many things. Come and share your master's happiness!"'*
– Matthew 25:21

We need to understand who God is and the power He has in our lives.

He is the one we need to put up on a pedestal, and in his glorious magnificence, we should revel.

He is perfect and awesome; He is gracious, merciful and in control. He is everything and everything is in Him.

He is on the throne, and He is majestic and holy, a god of perfection and a God of authority. It is with this wisdom and understanding of who He is that we can go forth in his Name.

All He wants us to do is to praise Him, worship Him, thank Him and commit to Him, so that He can do the rest for us.

He is beautiful beyond description, too marvellous for words, too wonderful for comprehension, like nothing ever seen or heard.

He has infinite wisdom; and He has a depth of love that we will never understand.

He can do all things in us and through us if we submit to Him.

We need to be faithful to Him by keeping his commandments close to our hearts, for He knows what is best and will hold us accountable if we choose not to.

For only He can give us the satisfaction, honour and glory we crave.

# There Is No Limit to What God Can Do

*Would not God search this out?*
*For He knows the secrets of the heart.*
– PSALM 44:21

God knows us – in fact, He knows every little thing about us and yet He still loves us.

And because his grace abounds in us, He gives us many gifts that are beneficial to us – one of them is freedom.

We can be free from our past and the mistakes we have made.

Free from pretence and free from trying to be something we are not.

He also makes us accountable for our sins. When we believe that there is someone who sees everything, we make choices which will not be sinful and disapproving of God. Because of our need to please Him and find his favour, we will lead more honest lives and see things for what they really are.

But most importantly, God allows us to be forgiven, and we have comfort in knowing that despite our sin, He forgives us. We can therefore depend on Him to rescue us, love us, accept us, teach us, restore us and give us the power to have victory.

God is infinite. God is all-powerful, all-knowing, and all-capable. There are no limits to Him.

# November

## CHOOSE TO KNOW WE ARE AVENGED

*The best manner of avenging ourselves is by not resembling him who has injured us.*

– Jane Porter

## CHOOSE TO KNOW WE ARE SANCTIFIED

*The best things in life are nearest: Breath in your nostrils, light in your eyes, flowers at your feet, duties at your hand, the path of right just before you. Then do not grasp at the stars, but do life's plain, common work as it comes, certain that daily duties and daily bread are the sweetest things in life.*

– Robert Louis Stevenson

## CHOOSE TO KNOW HIS POWER

*Nearly all men can stand adversity, but if you want to test a man's character, give him power.*

– Abraham Lincoln

## CHOOSE TO OVERCOME

*If you want to shrink something, you must first allow it to expand.*
*If you want to get rid of something, you must first allow it to flourish.*
*If you want to take something, you must first allow it to be given.*
*This is called the subtle perception of the way things are.*
*The soft overcomes the hard. The slow overcomes the fast.*
*Let your workings remain a mystery. Just show people the results.*

– Stephen Mitchell

# Don't Be Fooled: Revenge Does Not Bring Relief

*The LORD helps them and delivers them; He delivers them from the wicked and saves them, because they take refuge in Him.*
– PSALM 37:40

At some point or another we all want to get revenge on someone who has hurt, rejected or persecuted us. Even so, if we look at the basis from which the desire for revenge comes, we will see that revenge comes from our own insecurities and hatred and our need to feel powerful and superior to others. Research shows that many criminals find joy in crime and violence because that is the way they let out their anger and take revenge on something that had happened to them earlier in their lives. There is also the story of the woman with Aids, who slept around and infected many men as a form of revenge. So let us look at what revenge does – it adds to our pain – it does not give us any relief but it causes more pain, despair and hopelessness.

But as sweet as revenge may sound or seem, God wants us to know that He will and can deliver us from the wicked negativity. He will avenge us from the situation which has caused us pain.

Taking revenge is a choice, and we must never choose to expend our energy on something that the Lord promises to take care of on our behalf. Instead, we must choose to do his work and live according to his will. Then He will give us peace.

Dear friends, never avenge. Leave that to God. For it is written, 'I will take vengeance; I will repay those who deserve it,' says the Lord (Rom 12:19).

# Leave the Punishment To God

*'You have heard the law that says the punishment must match the injury: "An eye for an eye, and a tooth for a tooth." But I say, do not resist an evil person! If someone slaps you on the right cheek, offer the other cheek also. If you are sued in court and your shirt is taken from you, give your coat, too. If a soldier demands that you carry his gear for a mile, carry it two miles. Give to those who ask, and do not turn away from those who want to borrow.'*

– MATTHEW 5:38–42

It is hard not to hate someone who has hurt us, in fact, God commands us to love them. There are places in the world, where people use drastic measures to punish those who hurt others. I got an email recently about a little boy who had his hand run over by a car, because he had stolen something! Sometimes people do things to us because of a need in their own life which we may not understand. Still, it is not our place to measure out judgement or punishment. That is the Lord's job.

God promises to take care of those who persecute us. He will take vengeance for us. He will come with his mighty angels and avenge us with his two-edged sword, and we will see judgement done. All we have to do is wait on Him, and not change our Christ-like character.

# Don't Waste Your Time Judging Others

*'Do not judge others, so that God will not judge you,*
*for God will judge you in the same way as you judge others,*
*and He will apply to you the same rules you apply to others.*
*Why, then, do you look at the speck in your brother's eye, and pay no attention to the log in your own eye? How dare you say to your brother, "Please, let me take that speck out of your eye," when you have a log in your own eye? You hypocrite! First take the log out of your own eye, and then you will be able to see clearly to take the speck out of your brother's eye. "Do not give what is holy to dogs – they will only turn and attack you. Do not throw your pearls in front of pigs – they will only trample them underfoot."'*
– Matthew 7:1–6

Judging others is futile and completely against the will and character of God. It robs us of our humility and makes us assume that we are superior to others. Like God accepts us, we need to accept and love one another, not waste time looking for faults in other people. No one but God has the power to judge man, so we cannot self-appoint ourselves to that power.

God will take care of the judgement and vengeance we seek. All we need to do is focus on ourselves and our hearts. We should not waste so much time judging others, and neglect what we need to be nurturing in ourselves.

CHOOSE TO KNOW WE ARE AVENGED: 4 NOVEMBER

# Do Not Seek Revenge

*When He was insulted, He returned no insult;*
*when He suffered, He did not threaten; instead*
*He handed Himself over to one who judges justly.*
– 1 PETER 2:23

Jesus teaches us that equating one evil act with another is unacceptable to God. The first example is in the Gospel of Matthew, when Jesus specifically speaks about retaliation against others. Jesus leaves no uncertainty in his explanation and guidelines for seeking revenge. He says, 'Offer no resistance to one who is evil. When someone strikes you on your right cheek, turn the other one to him as well' (Matt 5:39)

In the writings of Peter, the anti-revenge message is again present. Once again, passive action is advocated, as it clearly states that Jesus never returned an evil deed of another, but sought the power of God. The message of this passage is that we must not get caught up in unjust and harmful acts against others. For the Lord will always judge you justly.

In Romans, the author makes perhaps the strongest argument in the New Testament against seeking revenge. Here it says, 'Do not repay anyone evil for evil; be concerned for what is noble in sight of all' (Rom 12:17). This verse calls for Christians to act as role models to others when he urges 'be concerned for what is noble in sight of all'. One verse later, the author pleads, 'Do not look for revenge but leave room for the wrath' (v 19).

This helps to remind Christians that in the end God will act against those who sin. God calls for us to be idle (live in peace) so He can punish those who sin against us.

The theme of God punishing those who seek revenge is explained in Ezekiel, as he talks about the Philistines.

Ezekiel says: 'Because the Philistines have acted revengefully, therefore, thus says the Lord God: "See! I am stretching out my hand against the Philistines"' (Ezek 25:15–16).

This verse gives the ultimate reason why we should not seek revenge – because God will punish you if you do.

– TAKEN FROM gsbBiblecommenter.com

# When You Feel Like God Has Abandoned You ...

*Then Samson prayed to the LORD, 'Sovereign LORD, remember me ...'*
– JUDGES 16:28

In Judges 13–16 we read the story of Samson who demonstrated God's majesty, power and strength. He was betrayed by Delilah after giving away the secret to his strength. He was captured by the Philistines, who grabbed him, gouged out his eyes and took him to Gaza, where they shackled and taunted him. They ridiculed him after chaining him to two pillars, and it was here that God avenged him. Samson reached out to the two central pillars that held up the building and pushed against them, one with his right arm, and the other with his left, saying: 'Let me die with the Philistines.' Samson pushed hard, with all his might, and the building crashed down onto the tyrants and all the people in it. He killed more people in his death than he had killed in his life.

Even at our weakest point, when we feel like God has abandoned us, He has not. He will ensure that we have vengeance, and will avenge us against those who persecute us.

# God Will Avenge

*'Now, will not God bring about justice for His elect, who cry to Him day and night, and will He delay long over them?'*
– Luke 18:7

Let us have a look at the following story that Jesus told in Luke 18: 'In a city there was a judge who did not fear God or respect people. 'And there was a widow in that city; and she came unto him, saying, "Avenge me of mine adversary." And he would not for a while: but afterward he said within himself, "Though I fear not God, nor regard man; yet because this widow troubled me, I will avenge her, lest by her continual coming she weary me, literally, beat me down with her blows."

It is a metaphor taken of wrestlers who beat their adversaries with their fists or clubs: in the same way those that are persistent beat the judge's ears with their crying out, even as it was with blows. And the Lord said: 'Hear what the unjust judge saith. And shall not God avenge His own elect, which cry day and night unto him, though He bears long with them?'

Though He seems slow in avenging the harm done to his own, God will avenge us through his various roles. He is the prince of peace and will never fail until his children receive that peace.

# When God Gets Angry ...

*For God's anger is being revealed from Heaven against all impiety and against the iniquity of men who through iniquity suppress the truth. God is angry.*
– Romans 1:18

God hates sin, but He especially hates those who are wicked. When He gets angry, his wrath is beyond comprehension. He commands us to live in his likeness. If we disobey Him, He will take action against us. Yet He will also take action especially against the wicked, who cause his children pain. We can be guaranteed of God's wrath in their lives. He has promised that we will be avenged.

The great writer, CS Lewis, once said: 'God is the only comfort, He is also the supreme terror: the thing we most need and the thing we most want to hide from. He is our only possible ally, and we have made ourselves his enemies. Some talk as if meeting the gaze of absolute goodness would be fun. They need to think again. They are still only playing with religion. Goodness is either the great safety or the great danger – according the way you react to it. And we have reacted the wrong way.'

And when we react in the wrong way, we no longer have the comfort of the Lord but the wrath of God to contend with. But when we are faithful to Him, He is our best possible ally and will make sure the wicked realize the error in their ways and stand accountable for it.

We have to choose to be the character God wants us to be – for then we will see his wrath fall on those who hurt us, hurt Him, and are disobedient to his will.

CHOOSE TO KNOW WE ARE SANCTIFIED: 8 NOVEMBER

# God Has Set Us Apart for a Purpose

*'As you sent me into the world, I have sent them into the world. For them I sanctify myself, that they too may be truly sanctified.'*
– JOHN 17:18–19

The word 'sanctify' means 'to set apart'. God has set us part from the rest to do a certain job.

Like He set apart the firstborn of Israel, the Levites, the priests, the altar, the Sabbath, Israel as a nation, Noah and his family, Joseph, Samson, John the Baptist, Paul, and many more, so too has God set us apart to do a job for which He has sanctified us through the love of the Lord, who died for us.

We are not God's elect only, but God's select. We were set apart from sinners and the things that are unholy. We are special in his eyes, because He believes in us and in the abilities that He has given us. We need therefore to recognize that we are sanctified and worthy in his presence to do what we were called to do.

# Strive for Perfect Sanctification

*Dear friends, now we are children of God, and what we will be has not yet been made known. But we know that when He appears, we shall be like Him, for we shall see Him as He is.*
– 1 John 3:2

Although we are already sanctified, our present actions will determine our sanctification for eternity in God.

If we choose to live sanctified lives, we choose to be holy and live life like Christ. We know that we are already forgiven, but that does not mean we can continue sinning and expect to be rewarded based on past sanctification.

When we are sanctified the moment we accept God into our lives, we become perfect, like He is, and through his power and his Word, we continue to be sanctified. Therefore, the way we choose to lead our lives will determine the strength of our daily sanctification through Him.

So, based on our daily actions, our sanctification becomes a progressive sanctification, which is not perfect, but which we should strive to make perfect. Again, it completely depends on us and the choices we make.

# Seek Him before You Attempt Anything

*But we ought always to thank God for you, brothers loved by the Lord, because from the beginning God chose you to be saved through the sanctifying work of the Spirit and through belief in the truth. He called you to this through our gospel that you might share in the glory of our Lord Jesus Christ.*
– 2 Thessalonians 2:13–14

The way to achieve daily progressive sanctification is to stand firm in our beliefs. And the way to reaffirm our beliefs is to be one with the Word of God.

If we understand what we are taught through reading the Bible and being rooted in the Word, it becomes easier to obey God's commandments from our hearts, and to see Him drawing us closer to Him and working in us.

We need to pray for the wisdom, patience and understanding when we start our journey of yielding to the Word of God. We need to choose to seek Him before we attempt anything.

# We Need To Change Our Mindset

*Do not conform any longer to the pattern of this world,*
*but be transformed by the renewing of your mind.*
*Then you will be able to test and approve what*
*God's will is – his good, pleasing and perfect will.*
– Romans 12:2

As much as our actions have to be right in the Lord to triumph in progressive sanctification, it is also important to possess the mind of Christ. We need to change our mindset and the attitudes we have regarding all things.

We have to stop living in the past, and embrace change. The value systems of our societies have changed, as well as their priorities and patterns, which are very different to the ones from the past. In no way must we conform, but we must change from our past way of thinking to embrace a new mindset, in order to stand firm in our faith and be sanctified.

Yet, in order to have a Christ-like mindset, we need to completely submit to Him and allow the Holy Spirit to work in our lives. We also have to choose to heal emotionally, by letting go of fears, anxieties and despair. We have to commit our lives to the Lord, who is able to deliver us.

Furthermore, we need to guard against having an attitude of bitterness, resentment, rebellion and selfishness. This will only lead to an unsanctified life and heart.

So, we need to change all aspects of our mental well-being in order to completely experience the sanctification in our lives.

# Live in the Truth and Be Sanctified

*'Sanctify them by the truth; Your Word is truth.'*
– John 17:17

We are sanctified in so many ways through Christ. The most important of all is being sanctified by the truth of the Lord. That truth comes in the Word. It will allow us to make the right choices for our lives, because they will be choices based on truth and the conscious wisdom of being able to differentiate between right and wrong.

If we stay truthful in all the things we do, we will always lead lives worthy of sanctification in his Name.

We were also sanctified through obedience and by the blood of the Lord, and we have been made pure in Him. Therefore, if we choose to continue to be obedient and live in truth, we will continue to be sanctified in Him.

We must defy the devil and resist temptation. We must pray and allow God to work in us so we may receive his sanctity.

# God Can Keep You from Stumbling

*Now to Him who is able to keep you from stumbling, and to present you faultless before the presence of His glory with exceeding joy, to God our Savior, who alone is wise, be glory and majesty, dominion and power, both now and forever.*
– Jude 24–25

It's human nature to be tempted and at times stumble and fall, but Jude tells us that not only is God able to keep us from stumbling, but He is able to pick us up and put us back on our feet.

God knows the many things we have to face, and He is realistic about the fact that as humans, we may yield to temptation.

It is God's hope that if we live in Him, we will be able to resist temptation, but if that is not the case and we ask Him to help us from the pit we're in, He will faithfully guide us to safety.

He may lead us along our path, but if we choose to put a step wrong, we can ask Him to put our feet back on solid ground again, so we may continue to be progressively sanctified.

We shall then be fully sanctified, or fully set apart, and possessed by Him. We are in the process of that practice. We shall ultimately be concerned with a maturing Christian life, something which is accomplished with the help of various people in our lives and in many ways. Our past and future sanctification are all of God. As to our present, progressive sanctification, the Lord expects us to do our part as well, and to use all the aids to godliness that He has so graciously provided.

# The Phases of Sanctification

*Discipline yourself for the purposes of godliness.*
– 1 Timothy 4:7

There is an excellent, though simple story which illustrates the phases of sanctification. It concerns the little girl who had just come out of the candy store having spent her allowance on a lollipop, when she spied her best friend coming down the street toward her. Being a properly brought-up child, she knew that unless she could think of something quickly, she would be obliged to offer the lollipop to her friend. Her dilemma between courtesy and hunger was solved by an action which quickly, certainly, and for ever sanctified the lollipop for her own use alone. And that action was simply to lick it all over on both sides before her friend joined her. By licking the lollipop, she set it apart for herself; it was not something the friend would want. This is like positional sanctification. The moment we receive the Lord as Saviour, God sets us apart for Himself, instantaneously, certainly and for ever.

But, to get back to the story, that first lick did not mean much assimilation of the lollipop for our shrewd little girl. Nevertheless, she took care of that problem post-haste. She proceeded to keep on licking the lollipop to make it practically what it already was positionally – her very own. This is progressive sanctification, and it is a process that continues throughout life. But finally there came that moment when she had the whole lollipop in her mouth – when it was totally possessed by her.

God's grace sanctifies us and He does do good work in us, but we have to be all consumed by Him and live lives filled with his presence, and aimed at giving Him glory.

# The Power of God's Creation

*God that made the world … giveth to all life, and breath, and all things … in Him we live, and move, and have our being.*
– Acts 17:24–28

If there is ever any place we will see the power of God, it is by looking around us at his creation. He took a barren planet and engineered it into the wonders of today. It was his power that created the heavens and the earth, his power that created every living thing, and his power that put life into every one of us.

He fills us all with his Spirit and undying love, and his glorious power flows from Him and radiates over the earth and everything it touches.

We are fortunate enough to be God's select, and therefore we are never without that power.

Take time to look at a newborn baby and marvel at this tiny life. Everything is perfect and to a mother, there can never be any imperfections. This little life is nothing short of a miracle. Miracles are possible through God's incomprehensible power. He is involved in everything He created every minute of our lives.

# God's Power Abides in Us

*Through mighty signs and wonders,*
*by the power of the Spirit of God.*
– ROMANS 15:19

Jesus' life on earth was filled with miraculous signs and wonders. From stilling the storm in Galilee, to causing miraculous catches of fish, feeding thousands with only a handful, raising the dead, healing the sick, bringing the lame to their feet, opening the eyes of the blind and the ears of the deaf, healing diseases, delivering possessions, turning water into wine. Everything Jesus did, He did with the power of God behind Him and in Him.

Just like God worked in his Son, He works in us, and his power abides in us. There is wonder-working power in his blood.

Through the acts of Jesus, He made his power evident on earth, and this should give us the peace we need to know that nothing will bring us down or move us, for we have his power in our lives.

We need to choose to recognize that power and allow it to resonate from us.

# God Empowers Us Every Day

*By His power God raised the Lord from the dead.*
– 1 CORINTHIANS 6:14

In life, there is one thing that we can be certain of and that is death. Nothing has more finality than death itself.

Just ask someone who is grieving for a loved one. They wish they could bring that person back, but no power on earth can. Nothing, except a power such as God's, can bring a person back from the dead, like when Jesus called back Lazarus, and God raised Jesus from the tomb.

Can we imagine the strength and depth of that power to bring someone back to life? God can. This should give us great joy, for it is through the same kind of power that God empowers us every day.

We may not be able to call the dead back, it is not our place, but we can certainly go forth in all we do, confident that we have that kind of power behind us and in us.

CHOOSE TO KNOW HIS POWER: 18 NOVEMBER

# We're All Blessed with Many Gifts

*For to one is given by the Spirit the word of wisdom; to another the word of knowledge by the same Spirit: to another the gifts of healing by the same Spirit; to another the working of miracles; to another prophecy; to another discerning of spirits; to another divers kinds of tongues; to another the interpretation of tongues.*

– 1 Corinthians 12:8–10

Through his power and grace God has blessed us with many gifts. As long as we depend on Him, remain faithful to Him, and obey Him, his power will move those gifts to work through us.

He believes in us as much as He does, because unlike us, He knows the extent of his power and of the power He has given us.

And if we have hope coupled with faith and an eagerness to do the will of God, nothing will hold us back, for his power will see us through and result in the fulfilment of his purpose for us, to reach the potential He has set for us.

We must never be dismayed because we feel God has overlooked us and chosen other people to bless with gifts. Neither must we wonder why we do not have gifts of healing, ministry and song; for, whatever our gifts, and regardless of how big or small, God's power will manifest them in us.

# Make the Right Choice

*God that made the world … giveth to all life, and breath, and all things … in Him we live, and move, and have our being.*
– ACTS 17:24–28

In order for us to experience God's power, we need to choose who we want to serve and what kind of lives we want to lead.

Choice is vital to a Christ-like life and a life of discipline. We have to make choices in everything we do on a daily basis. God hopes that we will make choices based on his Word, and not based on the world. If we are able to make spiritual choices for our lives, we will receive spiritual answers through the power of God.

The Bible tells us repeatedly how important it is to make the right choices, based on what the Bible asks us to do. God wants us to choose life over death, and to live righteous lives, filled with humility and the fruit of his Spirit.

CHOOSE TO KNOW HIS POWER: 20 NOVEMBER

# With God All Things Are Possible

*Jesus looked at them and said, 'With man this is impossible, but with God all things are possible.'*
– Matthew 19:26

There is such power in this verse because it reveals to us how great God is. There is nothing He cannot do, and nothing we cannot do in Him.

Look at how many people God came over in the Bible. It was his power that brought the Israelites out of Egypt, and his power that brought them through the Red Sea when He opened the waters.

With his power He is able to do anything for us: He is especially able to strengthen and avenge us, keep us safe, and restore our hope, faith and vision for our lives.

# The Holy Spirit Fills Us with Power

*But you will receive power when the Holy Spirit comes on you …*
*All of them were filled with the Holy Spirit and began to speak*
*in other tongues as the Spirit enabled them.*
– Acts 1:8, 2:4

When we allow the Holy Spirit to dwell in us, we receive power through the Spirit which allows us to receive and be in the grace of God.

When the Spirit is within us, it will take us closer to Christ by reminding us of his presence. It will give us the confidence we need to do the work of the Lord effectively.

The Spirit will fill us with the power to fulfil our mission on earth, and will allow us to see the many great miracles, signs and wonders which come from that power. We need to live lives which are a testimony to the world and especially to the Lord.

CHOOSE TO OVERCOME: 22 NOVEMBER

# God Wants Us To Be 'Overcomers'

*[Jesus was] 'tempted in all things, yet without sin.'*
– Hebrews 4:15

We often misunderstand temptation and perceive it to be sin. But temptation is not sin; falling for it is.

We are tempted in many ways every day, which could cause us to abandon our Christ-filled life – just like Jesus was tempted on the earth.

But God wants us to be 'overcomers', and the most important thing to overcome is temptation, which could lead to sin. It is sometimes hard to overcome sin, because the devil knows when to attack, and it usually occurs when we are at the lowest points in our lives. Yet, if we recognize the devil's deceit and temptation, we will be able to overcome the temptation to sin.

We must never allow ourselves to become victims of temptation. Instead, we should stand firm in God's covenant with us and resist it. We should look at the outcome of temptation and recognize how negatively it would impact on our lives if we were to fall for sin.

We can overcome temptation and sin by being honest with God, by recognizing and resisting the enemy, and by praying and asking God for help.

# Let Go of Your Guilt

*All have sinned and fall short of the glory of God.*
– Romans 3:23

If we don't let go of our guilt about our past sins, we will never be free to worship God. In fact, we will drive ourselves away from his presence.

But if we choose to let go of the guilt, we can have a more fulfilling and meaningful relationship with God.

The best way to do this is to accept that we have all sinned, and that we are not black sheep in God's family.

We have all fallen short of his glory.

We need to work through the guilt and realize that we were made new creatures in Christ when He died on the cross, for He died to free us of all our past sins and transgressions.

Another way to overcome guilt is to draw near to God through our faith and trust in Him. We need to repent and receive his mercy, and ask Him to continue to work in our lives. When we are able to overcome the guilt, we are able to lead guilt-free lives, with a clear conscience.

CHOOSE TO OVERCOME: 24 NOVEMBER

# Why Do We Feel the Need To Judge?

*'Do not judge, lest you be judged.'*
– MATTHEW 7:1

In addition to overcoming our guilt, we also need to overcome the tendency to judge others. Having a critical attitude will never allow us to walk in God's grace the way we should.

We develop a critical attitude when we have selfish interests. Being selfish is not of God and not what He commands us to be.

Sometimes, if life is not turning out the way we want it to, we hide our own frustrations by finding fault in others. It is because we allow ourselves to believe that their success came at our expense.

But we have to overcome our need to judge.

We can, by understanding the nature of God's judgement. God is a righteous judge and only He has the right to judge.

Although we can never make up for our past mistakes, we can learn from them and strive to lead our lives differently, making new choices and changing our hearts.

We need to take responsibility for the outcomes of our lives. By asking ourselves why things did not work out the way it was supposed to have, we will realize that there is no one else to blame but ourselves. So, if there is anyone we should judge, it is ourselves. Remember the story of the woman who was almost stoned. Jesus said: 'Whoever is without sin, cast the first stone' (John 8:7). And no one did, because they were all sinners.

Also remember that for every finger we point, there are four pointing back at us, so we need to choose to overcome our need to judge and rather leave that task to the Father.

# Why We Need To Overcome Our Worries

*Blessed are those who fear the LORD,*
*who find great delight in his commands.*
*... Wealth and riches are in their houses,*
*and their righteousness endures forever. Even in*
*darkness light dawns for the upright, for those*
*who are gracious and compassionate and righteous.*
*Good will come to those who are generous and lend*
*freely, who conduct their affairs with justice.*
*Surely the righteous will never be shaken;*
*they will be remembered forever.*
*They will have no fear of bad news;*
*their hearts are steadfast, trusting in the LORD.*
*Their hearts are secure, they will have no fear;*
*in the end they will look in triumph on their foes.*
– PSALM 112:1–8

God hates it when we worry. To us, worry may seem a normal emotional reaction, but to God it is sinful, because through our worry we are really telling Him that we have no faith in his power or ability to do great things in our lives.

This is why we need to choose to overcome worry, anxiety and stress. We can do this by giving our burdens over to the Lord and trusting Him to take care of them. God says we should not worry about anything but pray about everything. If we bring anything to his feet, He is faithful to take care of the rest.

We need to overcome by letting go and letting God. When we do this, his peace will guard our hearts and his grace will fall on us, for He is a God of power, the Almighty and the One who is ever willing to do what He must do, in order to see that we have the desires of our hearts.

Give your burdens to the Lord, and He will take care of you. He will not permit the godly to slip and fall.

CHOOSE TO OVERCOME: 26 NOVEMBER

# The Only Thing We Have To Fear Is Fear Itself

*The LORD is my light and my salvation – so why should I be afraid?*
*The LORD protects me from danger – so why should I tremble?*
*When evil people come to destroy me, when my enemies and foes attack me, they will stumble and fall. Though a mighty army surrounds me, my heart will know no fear.*
*Even if they attack me, I remain confident.*
– PSALM 24:1–3

Fear is another human emotion that is offensive to God, for He tells us over and over again that He has not given us a spirit of fear. Again, having fear dishonours the power of God and what He promised to do for us. Fear makes us tremble at the knees and so we become weak in our relationship with God.

Franklin Roosevelt assured people that, 'The only thing we have to fear is fear itself.' The Bible makes an even bolder promise: We have nothing to fear, period.

We must never allow fear to overwhelm us. Instead, we need to overcome fear. One of the most powerful messages in the Bible can be found in Psalm 23, where it says that even when we walk through the valley of the shadow of death, we must not be afraid, for God is with us and will protect and comfort us. He prepares feasts for us in the presence of our enemies and anoints us so much so that our cup overflows in his presence.

God is also our refuge and our strength – so how can we fear? We need to overcome it, and the way to do that is by remaining faithful to God's Word and his promise.

# Are You Lonely?

*'I will ask the Father, and He will give you another Helper, who will stay with you forever.'*
– John 14:16

Even in the beginning of time, when God created Adam, He never meant for loneliness to be part of our lives. That is why He created Eve. He knew that Adam would get lonely and would need someone with whom he could share his life. God wanted someone that Adam could love, and someone who could love Adam in return.

Therefore, by the way the Lord created the earth, we will always have a need to be loved and to belong. We can find affection and a sense of belonging from many sources, including our family, friends and co-workers.

But sometimes, many of us are still lonely due to our personal circumstances and various other factors which influence our lives. Yet, God has no intention for us to be alone, and if we choose to walk with Him, we will always have his presence, as well as that of Jesus and the Holy Spirit with us.

We can also overcome loneliness through fellowship with others at church. But, we first have to admit to ourselves that we are lonely and then consider what the cause of our loneliness is. We have to accept that there are certain things that cannot be changed – like the death of a partner or spouse. However, God will use these losses in our lives to give us new experiences and allow others to come into our lives if we are able to let go and move on.

Then we have to change what we can in our lives, and learn to see our worth through the eyes of God. And even though we do not feel like it, we have to try to go out and meet people or get involved in something outside our home. We must also develop our self-esteem and take steps to improve the things about our lives that need improving or enhancing.

And most importantly, we need to pray and get into fellowship with God, because, with his help, we will overcome our loneliness so we may never feel alone again.

# With God's Help, We Can Overcome the World

*Whoever believes that Jesus is the Christ is born of God, and everyone who loves Him who begot also loves him who is begotten of Him. By this we know that we love the children of God, when we love God and keep His commandments. For this is the love of God, that we keep His commandments. And His commandments are not burdensome. For whatever is born of God overcomes the world. And this is the victory that has overcome the world – our faith. Who is he who overcomes the world, but he who believes that Jesus is the Son of God?*

– 1 JOHN 5:1–5

Sometimes the very thing that we need to overcome in our lives is the world itself. The world has a way of sometimes overwhelming us and taking us away from the will of God and his love for us. We forget that which is important in life. We start to take things for granted. But again, if we remain obedient to God and his Word, if we resist temptation and lust, show humility in all we do and to everyone, have a godly conduct, and keep a strong mind and clean heart, then we will overcome the world.

We must never allow anyone to steal our thunder, so to speak, and snatch away our joy and sense of purpose in life. We must listen to God and understand his will. We must keep walking with Him. Then the world will be overcome.

# Putting Things in Perspective

*I can do all this through him who gives me strength.*
– PHILIPPIANS 4:13

The following is a motivational story by Jason M Gracia of a young boy who overcame his adversity and was led to victory: 'Sometimes in life, we make too many excuses for why we cannot do things but fail to see those who use every opportunity they get even with the little they have to make their life purposeful.

'Often, it takes a light tap on the shoulder – or a slap in the face – to put things in perspective and bring a brighter note to our seemingly difficult times. One such tap is the story of Ben Underwood, a young boy, who, due to the onset of cancer, has been blind since the age of three.

'While this could limit – and certainly has limited – the goals, dreams, and daily activities of many, this particular case was different. Not only did Ben decide at age six that he was through using a cane, but three years before that he began using a technique called echolocation, the same method used by bats and dolphins to perceive their environments.

'It soon became apparent that Ben's skills were off the charts, even called "extraordinary" and "pushing the limits of human perception" by medical doctors. Simply by using a series of clicks and gauging the time it takes for the sound to return and in exactly what fashion, he can operate in the world like any other child.

'He skateboards, plays kickball and even chases down his brother to return a sneak-attack tackle. Ben can even tell the difference between a parked car and a truck, all through the use of clicks with his mouth.

'The point of this story, as far as we are concerned, is not that Ben Underwood has an amazing ability, but that he took a weakness and turned it into a source of creativity, skill, and strength. He did not dwell in, nor did he accept, a state of life below his desires. Instead, he accepted the facts and moved forward with his life.

'It is the example of overcoming adversity that I want you to take to heart. If a young boy can function and manoeuvre without the use of his eyes, can't we not find a way to overcome our challenges?'

# Free Will and Self-control

*Do not you know that when you offer yourselves to someone to obey him as slaves, you are slaves to the one whom you obey – whether you are slaves to sin, which leads to death, or to obedience, which leads to righteousness? But thanks be to God that, though you used to be slaves to sin, you wholeheartedly obeyed the form of teaching to which you were entrusted. You have been set free from sin and have become slaves to righteousness.*

– Romans 6:16–18

God's greatest honour that He gave us was free will. There are times when we choose to take on habits and addictions in our lives which are not pleasing to God. And only we have the power to control those choices and habits.

To overcome these, it is imperative for us to have self-control. We have to take control of our minds and bodies, just like we control our minds and bodies when we choose to become addicted and have bad habits. If we can tell ourselves to do something, so too can we tell ourselves not to do it.

Paul expresses these thoughts with an athletic metaphor, saying: 'Everyone who competes in the games exercises self-control in all things. They then do it to receive a perishable wreath, but we are imperishable' (1 Cor 9:25).

Like an athlete, we must exercise self-control in all things. If we do, we will be able to control our minds, which control our bodies, to overcome bad habits and addictions.

We must also walk in the Spirit. For if we abide by the fruits of the Spirit, which are love, joy, peace, patience, kindness, goodness, faithfulness, gentleness, and self-control, we will be able to overcome all things in life that is of the flesh, because God will empower us. And to be empowered we have to bring it to Him in prayer and keep ourselves connected to the Word of God.

If we abide in Him, we will be 'overcomers' over all things.

# December

## CHOOSE TO KNOW YOUR IDENTITY

*In most of our human relationships, we spend much of our time reassuring one another that our costumes of identity are on straight.*

– Ram Dass

## CHOOSE TO EMBRACE LIFE

*When I stand before God at the end of my life, I would hope that I would not have a single bit of talent left, and could say, 'I used everything you gave me.'*

– Erma Bombeck

## CHOOSE HIS WORD

*I delight in your decrees; I will not neglect your word.*

– Psalm 119:16

## CHOOSE THIS DAY

*Remember, if you're headed in the wrong direction, God allows U-turns!*

– Allison Gappa Bottke

CHOOSE TO KNOW YOUR IDENTITY: 1 DECEMBER

# We Should Never Feel Worthless

*'I am your Creator. You were in my care even before you were born.'*
– ISAIAH 44:2

Sometimes it is easy to fall into the trap of thinking that we are worthless, but it is vital for us to know our identity and claim the freedom which comes with it. Not one of us is an accident, for we were created by a supernatural power who knew us. He had plans for us, even before we were born.

Long before we were even a thought in our parents' minds, we were already conceived in God's mind, and He delighted in creating us to live a purposeful life.

He planned every detail of our lives, and He knows us inside out. He made us for a reason. Therefore, we must never think that we were unplanned. God wants us to know how much He loves and values us.

So we should never feel worthless, because we have a standing with God, we are his creation, his children and his masterpieces, and He knows his will for us. We just have to choose to accept it and live it.

# We Need To Stand Firm in Our Identity

*Your eyes saw my unformed body. All the days ordained for me were written in your book before one of them came to be.*
– Psalm 139:16

Because God made us for a reason, He also decided when we would be born and how long we would live.

He planned the days of our lives in advance, choosing the exact time of our birth and death.

The Bible says: 'You saw me before I was born and scheduled each day of my life before I began to breathe. Every day was recorded in your Book!'

How then can we doubt who we are in Him? Like a parent plans for their child's future, so too did the Lord God Almighty plan ours.

He knows exactly who we are in Him, what we are capable of, what our gifts are, and where He wants us to go.

All we have to do is to stand firm in the identity that we have been blessed with, and live life according to his will for us and in accordance with his purpose.

# God Is Painting the Canvas of Your Life

*And we know that all things work together for good to those who love God, to those who are then called according to His purpose.*
– Romans 8:28

When God looks at us, He sees the many blessing and gifts we have. The following testimony reflects our identity in the eyes of God:

> I dreamed one night after I had prayed about so many things in life that were troubling me; I asked the Lord the question most of us ask during those horrid times … 'Why?' I dreamed I was sitting beside the painting of my life as God spoke these words:
>
> 'My Child, I have heard your question of why. I would like to show you what I have been painting on the canvas of your life. I know you thought I did not hear your prayers, but I assure you I heard each word, for I was there with you. You see, I was painting on the canvas of your life. I saw each tear, and in each of those times I painted on the canvas of your life. I took the times in your life when you hurt so much and painted a sapphire blue. I took the times in your life when you felt all alone and painted a crimson red. I took the times in your life when you knew such joy, and painted a golden hue. I took the times in your life when you ran into My arms, spending much time with Me and I painted a vivid violet.'
>
> He held up the portrait and I caught my breath – He had painted a rainbow of such splendour I have never seen. And it was then that I realized He had been there all the while in my life, through all the times, using each of them to make the portrait of my life into a rainbow of promises fulfilled. Then I awoke from the dream. Never again would I doubt such a love. And somehow I knew that in all the times to come I would remember the rainbow, and God's love, always …
>
> – Marsha Brickhouse Smith, cbn.com (adapted)

# Hold Your Head Up High

*It is in Christ that you, once you heard the truth and believed it, found yourselves home free – signed, sealed, and delivered by the Holy Spirit. This signet from God is the first instalment on what's coming, a reminder that we'll get everything God has planned for us, a praising and glorious life.*

– Ephesians 1:1–13

We are all part of God's heritage. We are kings, priests and heirs, for He has created us and ordained us to be. We are not mistakes, but part of his wonderful plan for our lives.

Jesus has already paid the great price for us on the cross, and through that purchase, we were made children of the Most High God.

We are free, and we can thus walk in his light, love, vision, purpose and destiny for us. We should never allow anyone to exercise their authority or power over us, for we have a Father in heaven who is greater than any power on earth. Therefore, we can hold our heads up high and walk in confidence – for we are more than victors in his Kingdom.

# He Calls Us Saints and Holy Ones

*Beloved, now we are children of God … And everyone who has this hope fixed on Him purifies himself, just as He is pure.*
– 1 JOHN 3:1–3

In the King James version of the Bible, believers are called 'saints', 'holy ones', or 'righteous ones' more than 240 times. In contrast, unbelievers are called 'sinners' over 330 times. Clearly, the term 'saint' is used in Scripture to refer to a believer and 'sinner' is used for an unbeliever.

The Bible never ever refers to God's children as sinners. Yet, as Christians, we are more than capable of sinning.

However, because we are born again through Christ, we have been sanctified. Like a mother can never see the flaws in her children (or she might see them but still love her children unconditionally), so too is God's love for us.

It is so wonderful that He refers to us as holy and as saints, for that is who He is. He expects us as his children to be the same.

# Do You Have a Clear Sense of Identity?

*So I will always remind you of these things, even though you know them and are firmly established in the truth you now have.*
– 2 Peter 1:12

Do we really know who we are? We should all have a sense of identity, but we seem to lose it along the way. However, if we go back into our lives – our childhood and upbringing – we will notice how they have left an imprint of who we are, and thereby giving us our identity.

As we grow older, it forms the basis of the identity we choose to have as adults, in terms of the professions we choose. In the same way, we also have an identity in Christ, which has already been established in us and will change and grow with us.

Our identity is connected with our actions, and our spiritual identity also depends on our walk with God.

So we need to choose to recognize the identity we have in Him, and then establish how we want our actions to compliment that identity.

# Do You Have an Identity Crisis?

*... and do not go on presenting the members of your body to sin as instruments of unrighteousness; but present yourselves to God as those alive from the dead, and your members as instruments of righteousness to God.*
– Romans 6:13

The Bible places a huge emphasis on our new identity in Christ and gives us a broader understanding of what that identity is.

Because identity precedes and affects behaviour, the Word of God reminds us of the fact that we are new creatures in Christ because our old selves were crucified with Him, and therefore no longer exists. Our sin and our past sinful nature have also been washed away.

Our old selves have been destroyed, and we are now new creatures who are in the grace of God and in his mercy. Our new life needs to reflect his character, love and purpose.

And we can do this through knowledge, consideration for our actions, and by choosing to affirm what God says about your identity. We must do it in spite of all the contrary feelings, thoughts, and past behavioural evidence, and in spite of what other people say about our identity. We have to also present a life that is favourable to God. And this means we have to choose to step out in faith and act in ways that are consistent with our new identity. In doing so, we will walk in victory.

# Have You Chosen Life?

*'He who believes and is baptized will be saved.'*
– Mark 16:16

Choose this day to embrace your potential in life and to mould that potential into action. Baptism is the affirmation of our belief in Christ. It provides us with our Christian identity.

With our Christian identity, there is nothing in life that we cannot accomplish. We are the same as Christ, as we have the same Spirit.

God has blessed us each with unique gifts so that we may fulfil his unique plan in each of our lives.

His plan unfolds when we trust in Him completely and live our lives to please Him.

When we choose Christ, we choose life.

CHOOSE TO EMBRACE LIFE: 9 DECEMBER

# Surrender Your Life to God

*'This day I call heaven and earth as witnesses against you that I have set before you life and death, blessings and curses. Now choose life, so that you and your children may live and that you may love the Lord your God ...'*
– Deuteronomy 30:19–20

Make your choice today. Christ has laid upon us all the choices in life there could possibly be. He blessed us with free will so we could take responsibility for our actions. Each of our actions start with a simple choice – right or wrong, life or death (spiritual), moral or immoral, right or left, stay or go, worship or blaspheme, pray or curse. Every moment in our lives is a choice that is made by our own free will. We must make the decision to choose life by choosing to serve the Lord. The Bible gives us many stories of hope for those who chose to follow the Lord – from Noah and the Ark, to Sodom and Gomorrha ... God saved those who chose to obey Him, who chose to have his will completed in their lives as opposed to their own will. Choose to surrender your life to God.

CHOOSE TO EMBRACE LIFE: 10 DECEMBER

# With God, We Can Weather Any Storm

*'My sheep listen to my voice; I know them, and they follow me. I give them eternal life, and they shall never perish; no one can snatch them out of My hand. My Father, who has given them to me, is greater than all; no one can snatch them out of My Father's hand.'*
– JOHN 10:27–29

Today, choose to embrace life by becoming an overcomer in Christ. There is nothing that you cannot overcome. God keeps you safe in the hollow of his hand, and as long as you listen to his voice, no evil can seize you from Him.

We are now children of God, and with Him we must have nothing but optimism. While strife may come, and the storms around you build up fiercely, know that He keeps you in the eye of the storm where it is calm and where no harm can come to you. The energy of the storm shall be spent, and you shall have nothing but blue sky around you.

We are victorious in Christ. God will protect us from all evil. He has given us the authority to overcome any harm.

# Embrace Your Life Gifts

*And God is able to make all grace abound to you, so that in all things at all times, having all that you need, you will abound in every good work.*
– 2 CORINTHIANS 9:8

We must choose today to embrace the gifts in our lives. God has blessed us with talents. All we have to do is pursue them with passion and a willing heart. Let everything we do please God and everything that we would like to do be done for the glory of God. Then He will pour out his richest blessings on us.

We each have a purpose in life that God has ordained. We need to look to Him to show us our purpose and trust that He will lead us beyond heights unimaginable.

He promoted David from shepherd to a king, Joseph from a labourer to a ruler. He promoted a carpenter to the risen Lord. When we embrace our life gifts, we can only move forward.

# Let's Renew Our Minds

*Do not conform any longer to the pattern of this world,*
*but be transformed by the renewing of your mind.*
*Then you will be able to test and approve what God's*
*will is – his good, pleasing and perfect will.*
– Romans 12:2

Choose today to be transformed and to renew your mind. Know that your God is willing to be tested.

If we believe in Him and his perfect will for our lives, then there is nothing that He will not do for us.

We have to renew our mind by delving into the Scriptures. God's Word and purpose for your life will reveal itself.

When we delight ourselves in Him and his Word, He has promised to give us the desires of our hearts.

# Serve Him and Only Him

*'Now fear the LORD and serve Him with all faithfulness. Throw away the gods your forefathers worshiped beyond the river and in Egypt, and serve the LORD. But if serving the LORD seems undesirable to you, then choose for yourselves this day whom you will serve, whether the gods your forefathers served beyond the river, or the gods of the Amorites, in whose land you are living. But as for me and my household, we will serve the LORD.'*

– JOSHUA 24:14–15

Choose today to accept the power that we have been given, which is the power to choose. When we choose what is right, it will not be taken away from us. When we choose life, we choose blessings. Every good choice results in a blessing.

When we choose exercise over stagnation, we will be blessed with good health, when we choose God over riches, we will be blessed with abundance … this is the power of the choices we have, the power that God has given us that will determine our eternal rewards.

But we have to choose to serve Him and no one else. God is a jealous God and wants us for Himself. If we disobey Him, and mock Him by worshipping false gods, He will become angry, especially because we allow ourselves then to fall outside of his plan for us. But if we choose to serve Him and only Him, we can rest assured that we will lead the best possible life we can.

# Embrace Life in Him

*Praise the* L*ORD, O my soul; all my inmost being, praise His holy Name. Praise the* L*ORD, O my soul, and forget not all His benefits …*
– PSALM 103:1

Choose today to understand and accept the benefits of your new identity in Christ, for when we accept the Lord we are able to embrace a more than beneficial life through Him.

He will fill us with all the gifts He has promised us, and He will also give us the power to embrace these gifts.

If we choose to embrace life through Him, by following his commandments and living a life that is pleasing to Him – a life in righteousness, then He is willing to bestow us with his richest and most prized reward, which is the gift of eternal life in Him.

We can do this by being true to the fruits of the Spirit and by allowing our actions to follow suit. We need to love everyone, have patience and show kindness, as well as be involved in his work. We need to be of service to Him.

And when we do this, we will earn our rightful inheritance through Jesus Christ.

CHOOSE HIS WORD: 15 DECEMBER

# Become Christians with Honours

*The way of man is not in himself; it is not in man who walks to direct his own steps.*
– Jeremiah 10:23

In everything we do in life, we need guidance and direction. We need to be taught or gain the wisdom and understanding first, before we can go out into the world to practise.

And the more professional the status of the job, like medicine or law, the more we have to study. It is all about principles. No doctor would graduate into medicine right out of matric. Then they would have no patients, because no one would trust them to take care of them.

In the same way, God trusts us to take care of his children. The world expects Christians to have all the answers for them as well as for their own lives. The way to do that is by becoming engrossed in the Word of God and making it a rule of thumb in our lives.

The Bible is God's book of wisdom and power, and it has all the answers. Whatever it is we are searching for in our lives, God provides the solution to us and the answers through the Word.

His Word will direct our steps and show us how to lead the most prosperous and satisfying life we can.

It is, however, not a get-rich-quick scheme, or a seminar on better living. It is real, because it reflects God and his will for us.

Choose to be firmly knowledgeable in life through the Word of God. Become Christians with honours.

# The Best Therapy Is the Word of God

*Never will I leave you; never will I forsake you.*
– Hebrews 13:5

God will not fail nor forsake us. Men may fail, mistreat, or disappoint us. Not God. He always remains faithful to us, provided that we remain faithful to Him.

When we seek his Word, we are reminded of his presence in our lives and that we are never alone. We are reassured of how much the Lord cares for us and how much He loves us.

We learn of the many acts and sacrifices He has made as a result of that love. So we may understand the intimacy and affection with which He cares.

The Bible reminds us of how valuable we are, and reinforces our belief in ourselves and our Father in heaven.

And it also shows us the many ways in which God is able to assist and deliver us in all the areas of our lives.

In essence, there is no need to pay hundreds of rands to a psychiatrist when we have the best possible therapy in our hands, through the Word of God.

# Don't Throw Life's Instruction Manual Away

*Every good and perfect gift is from the Father.*
*Every blessing we receive shows that God cares about us.*
– James 1:17

We all have been blessed with a special talent in order to fulfil God's purpose for us. These talents show us how much He cares, and they allow us to reach the potential God wants us to reach.

But we dishonour Him when we use our gifts in the pursuit of materialism, instead of spirituality, humanitarianism and love.

God's gifts are not meant to be used to climb up the rungs on life's ladder of success, but to change things for the better.

The best way to see our higher purpose and God's intentions for our gifts is to go back to the Word of God. With the gifts, God also gave us an instruction manual on how to use our talents – the Bible. We should never waste our talents, for a wasted talent is wicked in the eyes of the Lord. Instead, we should eagerly go forth and produce with it, thereby glorifying the Name of the Lord.

Many of us, when we buy new things, throw away the instruction manual and attempt to make it work on our own. When we fail, we run back to the trash can to retrieve the manual.

Do not throw life's instruction manual aside. Rather read it first, get rooted in it, and allow it to work optimally in your life.

CHOOSE HIS WORD: 18 DECEMBER

# God-Breathed

*All Scripture is God-breathed and is useful for teaching, rebuking, correcting and training in righteousness.*
– 2 Timothy 3:16

The Bible was inspired by God himself and is his direct words and commandments written through chosen men and women of God. It also helps us find the answers to frequently asked questions, such as: What is the purpose of life? Where did we come from? Is there life after death? What happens after death? How do we get to heaven? Why is the world full of evil? Why do we struggle to do good?

In addition to these 'big' questions, it gives a ton of practical advice on subjects such as: What to look for in a mate; how to have a successful marriage; how to be a good friend; how to be a good parent; what is success and how to achieve it; how to change; what really matters in life; how to live so that we do not look back with regret; how to please God; how to gain forgiveness; how to handle the unfair circumstances and bad events of life victoriously.

Thus, there is actually no aspect of our lives that the Bible has no answer to. When God created us, He created us in his image and likeness, and He knew exactly what we would need.

CHOOSE HIS WORD: 19 DECEMBER

# The Bible Is Our Guiding Light

*'Man does not live by bread alone, but by every word that proceeds from the mouth of God.'*
– Matthew 4:4

It is true that nothing and no one on earth is as reliable as the Word of God. The Bible is without error. It is the only holy book which allows us to test its various teachings and prophesies, by checking the historical accounts and scientific facts it records and relates.

The Bible also gives us numerous assurances and promises of God's intentions for us, and this never changes. Through the Scriptures God gives us a lasting joy and the ability to live the fullest possible life if we take heed of its teachings.

The Bible also equips us to serve God. It shows us how to be saved from sin. On meditating and obeying its teachings, it brings unimaginable success, and it also helps us see through the eyes of God. Through its wisdom and guidance, it reveals to us how to further enhance or improve our lives.

# When in Doubt, Consult the Bible

*For everything that was written in the past was written to teach us, so that through endurance and the encouragement of the Scriptures we might have hope.*
– Romans 15:4

There are times in life when it will seem like the world is falling apart. The best way to deal with this is to go back to the Bible.

Through it, we can learn from other people's experiences and mistakes and apply it to our own lives.

There are many (both good and bad) Bible characters to learn from. For example, David's defeat of Goliath shows us that God is greater than anything. And when David committed adultery, the Bible shows us how terrible the consequences of sin can be.

The Bible also gives us peace and hope when we need it the most. It is the work of God and meant for our own benefit – to live the best life we can.

CHOOSE HIS WORD: 21 DECEMBER

# Did You know?

*Your word is a lamp for my feet, a light on my path.*
– PSALM 119:105

Let's look at some of the many interesting facts which appear in the Bible:

- The word *Bible* comes for the Greek word *Biblia*, which literally means 'books'. So, reading the Bible is like reading 66 books. Think about it … the Bible was written by over 40 different authors.
- The Bible contains about 773 692 words! It would take you approximately 70 hours to read the whole Bible out loud.
- The Old Testament was written in Hebrew. The New Testament was written in Greek. Now the Bible has been written in over 6 000 different languages around the world!
- The Star of Bethlehem was reported by Matthew, but at the same time Chinese astronomers recorded it, too. To the Chinese it was a bright, unknown star.
- A shepherd boy discovered old clay jars in a cave by the Dead Sea. The old jars contained dusty scrolls, which turned out to be ancient copies of the Old Testament.
- The shortest Old Testament book is Obadiah. It has one chapter with 21 verses.
- The shortest verse in the Old Testament is 1 Chronicles 1:25.
- The oldest parable in the Bible is in Judges 9:8–15.
- The Old Testament has more than 60 references to Jesus.
- The New Testament contains over 260 Old Testament quotations.
- The shortest book in the New Testament is 2 John, with 13 verses.
- The longest book in the New Testament is Acts, with 28 chapters. Matthew also has 28 chapters, but it is shorter.
- The New Testament has 7 959 verses.

How then can we choose not to abide in the Word of God when it is so fact-based?

# If I Could Live My Life Over Again ...

*I know that there is nothing better for people than to be happy and to do good while they live.*
– ECCLESIASTES 3:12

Often I hear people regret things in life, wishing they could live their lives over again and do things differently. A poem I once read spoke about regrets, and I wondered how many of us would want to do things differently.

> I would have talked less and listened more. I would have invited friends over to dinner even if the carpet was stained and the sofa faded. I would have eaten the popcorn in the 'good' living room and worried much less about the dirt when someone wanted to light a fire in the fireplace. I would have taken the time to listen to my grandfather ramble on about his youth. I would never have insisted the car windows be rolled up on a summer day because my hair had just been teased and sprayed. I would have burned the pink candle sculpted like a rose before it melted in storage. I would have sat on the lawn with my children and not worried about grass stains. I would have cried and laughed less while watching television and more while watching life … I would have gone to bed when I was sick instead of pretending the earth would go into a holding pattern if I weren't there for the day.
>
> Instead of wishing away nine months of pregnancy, I'd have cherished every moment and realized that the wonderment growing inside me was the only chance in life to assist God in a miracle. When my kids kissed me impetuously, I would never have said, 'Later. Now go get washed up for dinner.'
>
> There would have been more 'I love you's' … more 'I'm sorry's'.
>
> But mostly, given another shot at life, I would seize every minute … look at it and really see it … live it … Therefore, choose today, choose this hour, this minute, this second to live life and live it to the fullest potential and highest purpose.
>
> – ERMA BOMBECK

CHOOSE THIS DAY: 23 DECEMBER

# Make Every Minute Count

*Teach us to number our days, that we may gain a heart of wisdom.*
– Psalm 90:12

If we stop for a moment to ponder life, we will realize how precious it is, because unlike other things where we can have another chance or try and try again until we get it right, life is a once-only opportunity. A very young acquaintance of mine passed away tragically at the age of 30.

His death brought a re-awakening in everyone around him as we realized the uncertainty of death, as well as the certainty of knowing that we will all die one day. And while we all stood around, regretting all the things he would not experience in the future, someone reminded us of the life he led.

He lived a lifetime in 30 years, laughing, experiencing and achieving every one of his dreams, and never wasting an opportunity.

In fact, up until that point there was no one I knew who died having achieved every one of their dreams. I smiled instantly. For while we waste time wondering how much time we have left, he made the most of the time he had left.

In the same way, God wants us to live in his presence, which is now. He wants us to leave the past behind and not worry about the future, because by his grace, the future will be taken care of. He wants us to live for today and choose today to make our lives count.

# The Lord Is the Only Constant in Our Lives

*God is the same yesterday, today, and forever.*
– Hebrews 13:8

While life changes and time never allows anything to remain constant, we can be sure of one thing – the Lord remains the same. Because of his consistency and his never-ending presence, we are always in his grace. It is his grace, through his consistency, that will guide us through all the inconsistencies in life.

God oversees the events of our lives every day. He has a specific plan for our lives that provides the opportunities for us to harvest the gifts, abilities and opportunities that He has given us.

Because He never changes, his plans for us stay the same and grow with us as our spiritual connection with Him deepens.

We are ordained by Him, and we need to choose today to do what God has ordained us to do. Today is the God-appointed time to rise up from wherever we are and start to serve Him.

CHOOSE THIS DAY: 25 DECEMBER

# He Gave Us Life in Abundance

*The thief comes only to steal and kill and destroy;*
*I have come that they may have life, and have it to the full.*
– John 10:10

This is the day the Lord has made to send his beloved Son to earth to die for us and save us from our sins.

This is the day He gave us our salvation. This is the day on which we were sanctified.

This is the day Jesus came into the world to pay the price for our sins.

This is the day the devil trembled at the birth of the King; this is the day the world and mankind alike was given their Saviour; and this is the day on which we need to rejoice, sing praises to the Most High and give thanks for the great gift God had given us in his Son, Jesus Christ.

God so loved the world. Likewise, we need to choose today to love. As Jesus came to give us life, we too need to choose today to give, and as his birth caused joyous celebrations in the heavens, we need to choose today to celebrate life, for He gave us life and we have it in abundance.

CHOOSE THIS DAY: 26 DECEMBER

# Live in the Present

*And what does the* LORD *require of you? To act justly and to love mercy and to walk humbly with your God.*
– MICAH 6:8

If, at the end of today, we find that our whole day has been preoccupied with thoughts of things to come, we will find that we have lost something valuable that will be gone for ever: Today!

By hoping to be happy about something in the future, instead of being happy right now, we are missing out. We often want more time, more money for that new purchase, a better job, better health. The list goes on.

This is such a waste because there are probably many things to feel really good about each day. Unfortunately, we are encouraged to dwell on things that we have yet to acquire. Imagine, if we were to be bombarded with daily reminders of how lucky we are and how much we have to be happy about, we would retire at night with wonderful days behind us.

Henry Ward Beecher once said, 'No matter what looms ahead, if you can eat today, enjoy the sunlight today, mix good cheer with friends today, then enjoy it and bless God for it. Do not look back on happiness or dream of it in the future. You are only sure of today; do not let yourself be cheated of it.'

Choose today to stop worrying, to stop being overwhelmed and stressed, to stop living in anxiety for what could happen, will happen and must happen. Stop the What ifs, Buts, Maybe I shoulds and I don't knows.

Choose today to know what you want from life and what you want to achieve according to God's will.

Choose today to not be in doubt, but to live in certainty. Choose today to stop wondering about the coulds, and start thinking about what you should do and what should happen.

God has only given us today, and it is up to us to live it. The outcomes should be free of anxiety about tomorrow.

CHOOSE THIS DAY: 27 DECEMBER

# Listen to God

*When I think of the wisdom and scope of God's plan,*
*I fall to my knees and pray to the Father, the Creator of*
*everything in heaven and on earth. I pray that from his glorious,*
*unlimited resources He will give you mighty inner strength through*
*his Holy Spirit. And I pray that Christ will be more and more at*
*home in your hearts as you trust in Him. May your roots go down*
*deep into the soil of God's marvelous love. And may you have the*
*power to understand, as all God's people should, how wide,*
*how long, how high, and how deep his love really is. May you*
*experience the love of Christ, though it is so great you will never*
*fully understand it. Then you will be filled with the fullness of*
*life and power that comes from God. Now glory is to God! By*
*his mighty power at work within us, He is able to accomplish*
*infinitely more than we would ever dare to ask or hope.*
– EPHESIANS 3:14–20

We need to choose today to listen to God and his voice of reasoning and purpose for us. Dr Charles Stanley in his book, *How to Listen to God*, says we need to listen to God's voice because He loves us, can give us direction, comfort and assurance, and because He wants us to know Him.

We need to choose today to listen to what God wants us to do for Him and to live the life He wants for us. God speaks through various ways, including dreams, direct revelation, circumstances and through the Holy Spirit, among others. Most importantly, He speaks to us through our prayer and He always comes through for us. If we choose to listen He will take control of our lives and meet all our needs. He will direct us to where we have to go if we listen and obey, for He is speaking and He wants us to choose today.

CHOOSE THIS DAY: 28 DECEMBER

# The Way to a Better Life

*This day I call the heavens and the earth as witnesses against you that I have set before you life and death, blessings and curses. Now choose life, so that you and your children may live.*
– Deutoronomy 30:9

The way to a better life is to choose today to make little adjustments to the way you think and do things.

Firstly, choose today to count all your blessings. You may not have the material things which are generally associated with success, but in God you are blessed with the fruits of the Spirit. You have grace, strength, courage and confidence in Him.

Therefore, choose today to love what you do, and to deliver more than you are getting paid to do. Choose today to have a positive mindset when you encounter trials, get knocked down, or make mistakes. Look at the lessons learned and use them to reach your goals.

Choose today to reward yourself for hard work. The best way to do this is by giving thanks and praise for grace in completing the work, and then surrounding yourself with the people you love the most.

Another thing to do today is to choose to build your foundation on happy and positive thoughts. You should never allow anything to make you negative, for there is nothing you cannot do in Christ. You have his power within you.

Choose today to allow your actions to speak for you. Let those actions be ones that leave lasting impressions on people, because your actions should be based on love.

Finally, choose today to get rid of clutter and insignificant things in your life and mind, and get ready to accept any of life's challenges.

# Live Today As If It's Your Last

*The LORD has done it this very day; let us rejoice today and be glad.*
– PSALM 118:24

Live life today as if it is your last. Ensure that it is a life that is pleasing to God, one that has service to God, and one that earns God's favour. Forget yesterday's defeats and the problems of tomorrow. Today is the day: So let us make it our day.

Choose today to treat everyone as though they were going to die at midnight. Give them all the love, care and kindness you can and then you will live with no regrets.

Choose today to laugh at yourself and at life with its many idiosyncrasies. Never allow life to become too serious.

Choose today never to take anything for granted and never to put anything off for later. Do it now, do it today.

Choose today to smile more and endeavour to start all your days with a smile, for today will never happen again. Do not start the day with a false start. Start it with your heart.

Choose today to set goals and allow God to guide you to that goal and purpose, so you may live a life of meaning.

Choose today to realize that true happiness can only come from within and from the peace of God's presence in your life. Choose today to let that happiness shine through.

CHOOSE THIS DAY: 30 DECEMBER

# Freedom of Choice

*So, as the Holy Spirit says: 'Today, if you hear his voice, do not harden your hearts …'*
– Hebrews 3:7–8

God has given us free will and freedom of choice, because He trusts us to do the right things and make the right decisions for our lives. The decisions we make today will have a serious and definite impact on our future. So we need to choose today to live our lives in God.

We need to strive to fulfil God's purpose, starting today. The first way to do that is to start developing our potential today. We must do whatever we can to tap into our potential and live it to its fullest. We also need to come out of our comfort zones and stop making excuses. Sometimes we spend so much time shifting blame for our failures that we do not shift ourselves from the rut we're in.

We need to choose today to take control of our lives and submit to God so He can work in us. Finally, we need to choose today to start building the life God has always wanted for us. Nothing should stand in the way.

CHOOSE THIS DAY: 31 DECEMBER

# The Quote of the Year

*What I do today is important because I am exchanging a day of my life for it.*
– Catherine Pulsifer

Start every day with the above quote, and for the next year, understand that we can use each day wisely, or we can waste it. The amazing thing is that we all have one thing in common: God has given all of us the next 366 days, but the difference between us is how we use those 366 days. Successful people understand this quote and therefore make the most of each day, knowing they will never have it again.

They do what needs to be done, whether they like it or not. They focus and know what it is they want to accomplish. And most importantly, they take action and do it.

So many people make wishes, and that is all they do – wish. They never take action; they never think and talk about it. They start a few things but do not finish anything. A noteworthy saying is: 'Never confuse motion with action.'

We should not waste our days by focusing on yesterday's failures – it will only be a failure if you stop trying. Do not waste today with worrying about today's problems. If we can fix the problems, we should do so, if not, we should move on. We must not waste the day on things over which we have no control.

Remember, it is today that we are living, and not tomorrow. And if we do the things that need to be done today, then tomorrow will take care of itself.

Do not procrastinate, for procrastination is the thief of time. And do not give up, because persistence always prevails when all else fails. So choose to make today worthy of a day in your life, because whatever you do today, you are exchanging a day of your life for it.

Henry Ford said, 'When everything seems to be going against you, remember that the airplane takes off against the wind and not with it.'

# Sources

Believer.com
Biblefacts.com
Biblegateway.com
Bibleteachings.net
Bibletools.org
Brentbarnett.com
Btww.net
Capcess.com
Cbn.com
Christianfaith.com
Christianstoriesonline.com
Faithalone.org
Feelmotivated.com
Gatewaytojesus.com
Glorytojesus.com
Godisgroovy.com
Gospelway.com
gsbBiblecommenter.com
Heartnsouls.com
Igreetyou.com
Intouch.org
Motivational-inspirational-corner.com
Onespiritproject.com
Seriousfaith.com
Wesleymission.com